The Biology of Business

John Henry Clippinger III, Editor

Foreword by Esther Dyson
Preface by Paul Saffo

The Biology of Business

Decoding the Natural Laws of Enterprise

Jossey-Bass Publishers
San Francisco

Jossey-Bass books and products are available through most bookstores. To contact Jossey-Bass directly, call (888) 378-2537, fax to (800) 605-2665, or visit our website at www.josseybass.com.

Substantial discounts on bulk quantities of Jossey-Bass books are available to corporations, professional associations, and other organizations. For details and discount information, contact the special sales department at Jossey-Bass.

 Manufactured in the United States of America on Lyons Falls Turin Book. This paper is acid-free and 100 percent totally chlorine-free.

Library of Congress Cataloging-in-Publication Data

The biology of business: decoding the natural laws of enterprise/
John Henry Clippinger III, ed.—1st ed.
    p. cm.—(The Jossey-Bass business & management series)
Includes bibliographical references and index.
ISBN 0-7879-4324-X (hardcover: alk. paper)
1. Organizational change. 2. Complex organizations. 3. Complex adaptive systems.
4. Evolutionary economics. I. Clippinger, John Henry III, date. II. Series
HD58.8 .B525   1999
302.3'5—dc21   99–6510

HB Printing   10 9 8 7 6 5 4 3 2 1   FIRST EDITION

The Jossey-Bass
Business & Management Series

Contents

Foreword

This book assembles an important selection of papers describing how the new ambient metaphors of biology—self-organizing systems, emergence, and the like—apply to today's organizations.

A "cheap" version of this approach is the current fascination with the so-called digital nervous system. But with all due respect, that's getting it only half-right. Even though the brain itself is more of a web than a hierarchy, the digital nervous system concept embodies the same old hierarchical notions of yore, with a brain at the top sending out instructions to the nerve endings in response to stimuli.

The Biology of Business goes further, exploring the details of complex adaptive systems (CAS) and how they apply to organizations and businesses. The underlying principles comprise the seven basic elements outlined by John Holland for any self-organizing enterprise: aggregation, tagging, nonlinearity, flows, diversity, internal models, and building blocks. Master these basics and you will be better equipped to build an organization that can respond rapidly to complex and diverse challenges, in a distributed and self-coordinating way.

How do these ideas translate into real-world practice? Each essayist explores a different angle. Indeed, this book won't tell you how to run your organization, but it will give you important tools for thinking about how you do it—and how you could or *should* do it. In a business context, CAS is not just a question of selection and evolution, but of complex interactions among the people and structures of a business and its marketplace.

In order for these people and the units they constitute to interact, they need discrete identities rather than a guiding "nervous system." In other words, what companies really need to think about is an "immune" system—a distributed system that gives you a sense of identity and lets you know what—not just who—you are. The immune system is a powerful example of how identity and survival depend on a highly distributed, bottom-up process of tagging, interaction, and recombination. Immune systems have evolved repertoires of tactics and strategies for flourishing under any circumstances that could prove to be highly instructive for any executive competing in the Net economy.

Let's go beyond abstract metaphor to see what this means. The companies of the past were black boxes that produced products and had a small surface area, composed mostly of PR and investor-relations people, and perhaps a couple of outspoken top executives. Consumer companies had ads, but they rarely involved anyone from inside the company—with notable exceptions such as Frank Perdue and his chickens, Lee Iacocca and Chrysler, and Richard Branson with his Virgin product du jour. Exceptions were service companies such as airlines, competing on the friendliness of their stewardesses, and at least some retailers competing on the helpfulness of their personnel. Still, most employees were focused internally, designing and building products or perhaps writing ads or documentation. The products and the advertising spoke for the companies.

But now, as companies get onto the Web, they start interacting with the outside world through more than just corporate spokespersons and advertising messages carefully controlled by the digital nervous system and a corporate process. Customers interact one-on-one with employees—or they should. The Net requires companies to communicate individually with outsiders, and to answer their specific questions and needs.

That means that a company has to have its identity well-established globally but not centrally—in other words, within each employee. No time to send a note back to the digital nervous system asking for an approved corporate response; besides, the brain couldn't handle all the variety employees encounter out in the field.

How does an immune system work? It recognizes foreign objects and produces effective responses. The biggest problem many companies will face in the future goes well beyond "knowledge management," which translates roughly—yes, I know some people will consider this insulting—into making sure everyone knows the corporate policy manual or corporate procedures. An immune system does pattern-matching, whereas a digital nervous system processes explicit information.

The challenge is to understand corporate identity at a visceral level: What are we about? That means that each employee should know how to respond to customer requests—not with a canned response, but with an attitude. Let me use a few true stories to illustrate. They come from the airline industry, not from computer companies. Until more companies become truly Net-based, airline companies are one of the best examples of how organizations will operate in the future, with employees with only tenuous connections back to the corporate digital nervous system interacting directly with customers.

The first example shows the disadvantages of a strong digital nervous system. It comes from an airline whose name you could figure out, but why pick on them? Some years ago I was flying back from a meeting in Moscow, where I had the pleasure of meeting Bill Bradley, now running for president of the United States but at the time a U.S. senator and basketball star and already very well-known. The meeting organizers assumed someone had taken care of getting Mr. Bradley—just shy of seven feet tall—upgraded, but no one had (failure of their nervous system?). Two of us who had been at the meeting went to the stewardesses, mentioned that Mr. Bradley was aboard, and wondered if he shouldn't be upgraded to first class (which had several empty seats). "We can't do that," was the response. "It has to come from the local ground station. We'd like to, but we'd lose our jobs."

It was not that they didn't know who Bill Bradley was. Several of the staff went back to pay him their respects. They brought him champagne and found him a relatively comfortable exit-row seat. But they would not move him up.

Now Bradley is a classy enough guy that he didn't particularly want to move up, and this U.S. airline does not stand to gain or lose a lot even if he becomes president. It's simply that the company had turned its people into nerve endings who take central direction and are scared to show any character of their own. And that hurts the airline with the public, not just with a particular politician.

By contrast, take the behavior of a quick-thinking Southwest Airlines stewardess, back in the days when flight attendants were still called stewardesses. The doors of the aircraft had closed, most of us had found our seats, and she took up the microphone. "Hey y'all!" she drawled. "We got a little problem up here—we don't have the peanuts. Now we can set right here for about fifteen minutes, and catering promises we'll have those peanuts right away . . . but I can't guarantee it. Or, folks, we could leave right away without those peanuts. Now I'm just gonna take a little vote . . ." Before she could finish, she was drowned out with shouts and cries: "Let's just go!" "Fergit the pea-nuts!" "As long as we got beer, who needs peanuts!?" We left on schedule and no one complained about the missing peanuts. Without central direction, this woman had perfectly embodied not Texas-based Southwest's rules but its identity— flexibility and humor.

Finally, a recent disaster shows what happens when the nervous system breaks down and there's no immune system to govern local behavior. Last winter, a bad snowstorm created chaos at the Detroit airport, and a number of planes landed and sat on the tarmac for up to eight hours without allowing the passengers to disembark. The airline in question is now facing numerous lawsuits, and the U.S. Congress—a government nervous system, so to speak—is considering legislation to change general airline rules. However, the problem wasn't this company's rules; it was its inability to react locally. To anyone observing—and to all those involved—it sounds ridiculous, but the company's nervous system wasn't operating. Top management didn't know how bad the situation was, and no one took charge. With an immune system, the local people might have reacted properly, instead of feeling helpless without instructions from headquarters.

In the future, of course, we'll have better and better corporate networks. In theory they won't break down. But we all know that in reality they will. That's why companies need distributed immune systems, so that they can react locally. Each individual should have the identity of the corporation, so that he or she can act appropriately even when cut off from the information flow of the digital nervous system. An example is employee Dan Rosen of Microsoft, quoted from one of the numerous Microsoft depositions now open to the public: "That's a difficult question [about authority to make a deal with Netscape] . . . that's . . . not the way the company explicitly operates. My responsibilities were to some great degree formed by myself and then later, you know, verified with others that that was okay to be doing, more than [being] instructed to do something."

Of course no metaphor works perfectly. The purpose of a company's identity isn't just to repel outside objects, but to interact with them. Transform them. Incorporate them. For businesses and organizations, this is a symbolic, not physical, task. It's something like the creation of language, whereby new terms, meanings, and even new jargons are created and incorporated. Here again, the CAS perspective has something to say. Language is a self-organizing process of tagging, forever altering, inventing, and adding new terms and meanings. Companies can (and should) think of CAS as a language through which they can efficiently communicate with their customers in this fast-paced and rapidly changing world.

September 1999   Esther Dyson
                                          Chairman, EDventure Holdings
                                                          New York, NY

Preface
The Business World Turned Upside Down

A funny thing happened to business in the last two decades—it turned upside down. Suddenly, the old rules no longer applied—stability became a liability, size an inconvenience, and command-and-control hierarchies an albatross. Business as usual became business as unusual: unpredictable, unplannable, and above all, unmanageable. Old giants tottered and new players burst into new markets, only to become roadkill for the next wave of upstarts. The stately equilibrium of Keynes yielded with a vengeance to the unnerving creative destruction of Schumpeter.

Buffeted by these changes, management theory was cut loose from its theoretical moorings and cast adrift in a chaotic sea of change. In the cascading uncertainty that followed, the only individuals with job security were the consultants and pundits who, like medieval doctors, pressed one dubious remedy after another into the hands of their anxious patients. We upsized, downsized, right-sized, and reengineered. We searched for excellence, empowered our organizations, jumped chasms, and discovered the power of one. But we failed to find safe harbor from the waves of creative destruction.

Meanwhile, happier storms were brewing in other worlds. A revolution in the new sciences of complex adaptive systems (CAS) was quietly sweeping through one scientific discipline after another. "Complexity," as it came to be called, offered scientists a new intellectual geometry with which to tease previously hidden order from previously incomprehensible phenomena. Meteorologists suddenly began to see into the complex heart of thunderstorms, physicists peered into matter and out into the universe with new eyes, geneticists glimpsed new order in the DNA helix, and biologists discovered new dynamics in ecosystems.

Revolutions beget revolutions, especially when the revolution has chaos at its core. Wall Street noticed what was afoot and quickly demonstrated that the new sciences of complexity were more than mere boffin's tools. There was money to be made at the ragged edge of chaos; newfound understandings of complex adaptive systems were pressed into the service of "rocket scientists" navigating computers through choppy financial waters.

Of course this all did not pass unnoticed in the management world. Biology became the new place to look for organizational inspiration, and, like sailors clutching at wreckage in a storm-tossed sea, management consultants thrashed blindly toward a new paradigm in which organization mutated into organism, markets to ecologies, and mechanical metaphors to biological analogues. Though still in their infancy, these and subtler metaphors such as "hives" and swarming have been extremely helpful to beleaguered managers trying to guide ever-less-manageable organizations.

But now a second wave is following. The management community is looking beyond the obvious analogies to the deeper organizational understandings that complex adaptive systems hold. And better yet, the complexity community is meeting them more than halfway in this exploration. This book is one of the first fruits of this new collaboration. It is an early and substantive glimpse into a new, barely explored terrain filled with breath-taking promise.

The essays in this book argue that biology is not just a source of metaphors. Rather, it is the basis for a set of subtle and profound principles. What some refer to as "universal Darwinism" offers us nothing less than the codes that direct organizational behavior. Complex adaptive systems thus provide concrete methods and tools; as the authors explicate in these pages, armed with these tools, one can move beyond metaphors and models and look toward policies, practices, and procedures based on CAS.

Nearly a hundred years after Frederick Taylor wrote "The Principles of Scientific Management," management and organizational theory seem at long last poised on the edge of becoming scientific. In this spirit, *The Biology of Business* does not advocate the application of CAS to business. Rather it assumes some prior knowledge of complex adaptive systems and an inclination toward seeking their application in the organizational world.

And the authors offer ample practical lessons and applications of CAS even as they map this new space. Manville, Johnson, Stark, Anderson, and Sviokla argue persuasively that what the best managers have done instinctively can be codified around notions such as tagging, recombination, diversity, and self-organizing market-like processes. And Clippinger and Clark remind us that the "sweet spot" on the ragged edge of chaos between too much control and too much disorder has very distinct criteria of success. Survival in this space lies not in optimizing or engineering, but in tolerating error, productive waste, and loose coupling.

Above all, this book argues that organizations make the most sense when examined from the bottom up, rather than from the top down. Viewed thus, it becomes obvious that what defines organizations is what defines all complex systems—change. Heraclitus's epithet—"Panta Rei"—expressed this most modern of ideas very well several millennia ago. Everything is change. One cannot step in the same river—or organization—twice. But if one watches the patterns in the waves, the river will make sense. As the essays in this book suggest, the same is true for organizations.

September 1999   Paul Saffo
Director, Institute for the Future
Palo Alto, California

Introduction

*Most of the grounds of the world's troubles are
matters of grammar.*

Montaigne

*The miracle of the Universe is that we can
understand it.*

Albert Einstein

Change is the one constant in business. The sheer complexity of
the global business environment has rendered traditional economic,
organizational, and management practices obsolete. With the Internet undermining accepted business practices and transforming virtually every significant business process, managers are challenged
not only to make sense of these changes but to devise methods and
practices to cope with them. Yet as dramatic and pervasive as the
impact of the Net is, it is only symptomatic of a deeper change in
the primary scientific and technological ideas that define our culture and commerce. We are rapidly shedding the ideas of the
Enlightenment that have long underscored our scientific, cultural,
political, and economic institutions. Fundamental advances in
physics, with a credible promise of a Theory of Everything (T.O.E.),
and genetic engineering, with the real prospect of evolving new
super-species, coupled with significant advances in computer

science and artificial life have irrevocably changed how we think of ourselves and our futures.

Fortunately, accompanying these changes is a new framework, known variously as Complex Adaptive Systems (CAS) or Self-Organizing Systems, that has abstracted the fundamental principles governing complex physical, biological, symbolic, and digital systems. Unlike the mechanistic or engineering-based principles of the Enlightenment, CAS explanations draw upon the traditions of ecology and evolutionary biology. It is part of a broader trend to regard virtually all forms of organization—genetic, biological, cognitive, ecological, cultural, and economic—as subject to universal Darwinian principles of natural selection.

This book is itself an experiment in self-organization. Could ten different authors from different backgrounds, disciplines, and professions, scattered across the country, come together to write a book that embodied a shared perspective and vocabulary by agreeing to work within a simple set of rules (John Holland's seven basics of self-organization)? We think we have. But not without struggle, including meetings at the Santa Fe Institute, The Aspen Institute, and the Ernst and Young Center for Business Innovation, and numerous conference calls, e-mails, and revisions. Given the schedules of all involved, it was remarkably self-organized.

This book, as one contributor put it, is a 201 not a 101 book, meaning that it is not intended as a general introduction to complex adaptive systems, but rather assumes some prior knowledge. The motivation for all the authors was to move beyond broad themes and analogies to a discussion of how to apply CAS to real-world business problems and issues. The focus is on the application where possible of concepts, principles, and technologies. We show where CAS can make a difference and how this difference matters for today's organizations. We really do believe that this is a new mindset that harbors enormous promise. And we all realize that we are at the very early stages of something that will grow in time as the new sciences come to define and shape our new millennium.

The chapters of the book embody and reference the vocabulary and seven basics of the work of John Holland, the father of genetic algorithms and one of the early pioneers in the study of artificial life. That said, the writings of Stuart Kauffman and Brian Arthur also feature prominently in the chapter discussions, as does the less well-known, but no less impressive work of Andy Clark.

It is strongly recommended that readers begin with Chapter One, John Clippinger's "Order from the Bottom Up: Complex Adaptive Systems and Their Management," as it provides a framework and definitions that are used throughout most of the chapters in the book. Brian Arthur's chapter, "The End of Economic Certainty," provides a concise and provocative critique of classic economic theory that makes the argument for biological models for understanding economic behavior. Andy Clark's chapter, "Leadership and Influence: The Manager as Coach, Nanny, and Artificial DNA," is a thoughtful investigation into how complex genetic and biological processes are "managed," providing insights into how complex organizations can be led.

In Chapter Four, "Tags: The Power of Labels in Shaping Markets and Organizations," John Clippinger shows how one of the mechanisms of self-organizing behavior, tagging, is a critical tool for managers to achieve self-organizing behaviors in organizations and markets. Chapters Five and Six provide case studies and examples of how self-organizing principles can be applied to knowledge management and organizational change. In his chapter, "Complex Adaptive Knowledge Management: A Case from McKinsey & Company," Brook Manville argues for market-like mechanisms for providing self-organizing approaches to achieving knowledge management; Philip Anderson provides a compelling case study in "Seven Levers for Guiding the Evolving Enterprise" on how Capital One successfully applied self-organizing principles. David Stark's chapter, "Heterarchy: Distributing Authority and Organizing Diversity," provides an example of the inventiveness of emergent economies in post-socialist Hungary, and shows how a new kind of organizational form, heterarchy, can accommodate competing social and economic criteria. In Chapter Eight, "Adaptive Operations: Creating Business Processes That Evolve," William Macready and Christopher Meyer explain how operations that have typically been engineered and optimized can, in many cases, be more effectively treated as organic processes that evolve and adapt. The authors provide discussions of a variety of techniques as well as illustrative examples. In Chapter Nine, "Buying and Selling in the Digital Age: An Ever-Increasing Bandwidth of Desire," John Sviokla offers a case study of Optimark to show how rich, multidimensional tags of user preferences can increase market liquidity. He predicts that through the Net such fine-grained expressions of user preferences will increase the power of consumers.

The final chapter, David Johnson's "Emergent Law and Order: Lessons in Regulation, Dispute Resolution, and Lawmaking for Electronic Commerce and Community," offers a thoughtful and provocative analysis of how self-organizing principles can be applied to problems of governance and regulation that have confounded more traditional approaches. Nowhere is the application of the new principles of self-organization more needed and applicable than in the area of global e-commerce, and Johnson offers a convincing argument for how the principles can be of real assistance.

Taken together these authors illustrate the power and the richness of the CAS perspective for a wide variety of issues confronting the managers of complex organizations. These chapters should provide the reader with concrete examples for analyzing and addressing management and organizational issues from a fresh, organic perspective. We are indeed at the cusp of a "paradigm shift" of the most profound and pervasive extent, in not only Western culture but global culture. We are seeing ourselves anew, and neither our economies, cultures, institutions, or even biological compositions will be the same. Buckle up.

Cambridge, Massachusetts   John Henry Clippinger III
August 1999

Acknowledgments

This book would not have been possible without the help and generosity of many fine people at the Santa Fe Institute (SFI). The ideas and principles that constitute the core of this book owe their origin to the fellows and faculty of the SFI: John Henry Holland, Brian Arthur, Andy Clark, David Stark, and Stewart Kauffman. It is fair to say that without the SFI, the entire field of Complex Adaptive Systems and the entire self-organizing perspective would not have the influence or credibility it enjoys today. Special thanks are due to Ellen Goldberg, president of the Santa Fe Institute, and Susan Ballati, vice president of development for the SFI and the Business Network, who helped us organize our meetings and draw upon the intellectual resources of the SFI.

I am especially grateful to my fellow authors, who under the duress of impossible schedules made original and thoughtful contributions. I will miss the genuine enthusiasm of embarking on this intellectual journey and the camaraderie that comes from sharing, critiquing, and creating new ideas. Special thanks to Chris Meyer for making Ernst & Young's Center for Business Innovation available to us for our meeting, and to David Johnson, who during his tenure at the Aspen Institute made its facilities and resources available to us as well. Books such as this, that have new material in an emerging field, have longer than normal gestation periods. I am appreciative of my editor Cedric Crocker, whose patience and thoughtful support helped me pull this book together. A special debt of thanks is due Teresa Lawson, my developmental editor. Her rapid assimilation of the material, as well as her efficiency, professionalism, and extraordinary powers of organization, significantly contributed to the overall quality and coherence of the manuscript. I also want to thank Joel Kurtzman, who encouraged me to undertake this project, and the many friends and colleagues who have had an opportunity to discuss the ideas in this book: Charles Jonscher, Esther Dyson, Mel Horwitch, Paul Saffo, Jonathan Hare, James Pustejovsky, Michael Kleeman, and Charlie Firestone.

The Authors

John Henry Clippinger III is CEO and cofounder of Lexeme, Incorporated, an Internet software company. Previously, Clippinger was CEO of Context Media LLC, a knowledge management software and services company, whose clients included Coca Cola, Motorola, AT&T, and Coopers & Lybrand. Prior to founding Context Media, Clippinger was director of intellectual capital at Coopers & Lybrand, where he launched one of the very first corporate Intranets. Before Coopers & Lybrand, Clippinger was CEO for seven years of Brattle Research Corporation, which developed artificial intelligence and language processing software for financial services, publishing, and intelligence applications. He was a research Fellow at Harvard University; has over fifteen years of strategy, technology, and consulting experience in the public and private sector; and is the author of a book and many papers on technology strategy, artificial intelligence, and computational linguistics.

Clippinger is a graduate of Yale University and holds a Ph.D. degree from the University of Pennsylvania.

Philip Anderson is an associate professor of business administration at the Amos Tuck School of Business, Dartmouth College. His undergraduate degree in agricultural economics is from the

University of California at Davis, and he received his Ph.D. degree in management of organizations from Columbia University.

He currently teaches courses in the strategic management of innovation, Internet strategy, Internet content creation, and venture capital, and he is the founding director of Critical Insight, Tuck's first commercial Internet venture. He is also the research director of Tuck's new Foster Center for Private Equity.

Anderson is coauthor of *Managing Strategic Innovation and Change: A Collection of Readings* (1996, with Michael Tushman), and *Inside the Kaisha: De-mystifying Japanese Business Behavior* (1997, with Noboru Yoshimura). *Inside the Kaisha* was named 1997 Booz Allen & Hamilton/*Financial Times* Global Business Book of the Year for Industry Analysis/Business Context. Anderson's articles have appeared in such journals as the *Harvard Business Review, Research • Technology Management, CIO, Datamation,* the *Academy of Management Executive, Administrative Science Quarterly,* and the *Academy of Management Journal.*

W. Brian Arthur is a Citibank Professor, and PriceWaterhouse-Coopers Fellow at the Santa Fe Institute. His research interests include the economics of increasing returns, specifically the dynamics of technology lock-ins and the role of human cognition in shaping economic behavior. His recent books are *The Economy as an Evolving Complex System II,* edited with Steven Durlauf and David Lane (1997), and *Increasing Returns and Path Dependence in the Economy* (1994). He is the recipient of the Schumpeter Prize in Economics (1990), a Guggenheim Fellow (1987–1988), and a Fellow of the Econometric Society. He was the dean and Virginia Morrison Professor of Population Studies and Economics at Stanford from 1983 through 1986, and is currently a member of the board of trustees at Santa Fe Institute. He received an M.A. degree in mathematics from the University of Michigan, Ann Arbor in 1969 and a Ph.D. degree in operations research from the University of California, Berkeley in 1973.

Andy Clark is professor of philosophy and director of the Philosophy/Neuroscience/Psychology Program at Washington University, St. Louis. He is the author of *Being There: Putting Brain, Body and World Again* (1997), *Micro-cognition: Philosophy, Cognitive Science and Parallel Distributed Processing,* and *Associative Processing: Connectionism, Concepts, and Representational Change* (1993). He has published over sixty articles and edited five books in the fields of biology, philosophy, and cognition. He was a Fellow at the Santa Fe Institute and has lectured widely on cognition, artificial life, and the philosophy of science.

David R. Johnson is a partner in the Washington, D.C., law firm of Wilmer, Cutler & Pickering. His practice focuses primarily on the emerging area of electronic commerce, including counseling on issues relating to privacy, domain names and Internet governance issues, jurisdiction, copyright, taxation, electronic contracting, encryption, defamation, ISP and OSP liability, regulation, and other intellectual property matters.

Johnson returned to WC&P in August 1998 after serving as founding director of the Aspen Institute Internet Policy Project and as founding president, CEO, and chairman of Counsel Connect, an online meeting place for the legal profession. He is also a founder and has served as codirector of the Cyberspace Law Institute. He helped to write the Electronic Communications Privacy Act, was involved in discussions leading to the Framework for Global Electronic Commerce, and has been active in the introduction of personal computers in law practice.

Mr. Johnson is a graduate of Yale College (B.A. 1967, summa cum laude) and Yale Law School (J.D. 1972). In addition, he completed a year of postgraduate study at University College, Oxford (1968).

William G. Macready is a vice president with Bios Group7, a Santa Fe company applying techniques from optimization, machine learning, and complex adaptive systems science to business problems.

Brook Manville is a partner at McKinsey & Company working with the Organization Practice based in Washington, D.C. His work involves research and client service in areas related to knowledge management, organizational structure, and technology, and he is a frequent consultant to McKinsey clients wrestling with those issues. Previously, he was based in McKinsey's New York office as the director of knowledge management at and codirector of McKinsey's Information and Technology function, responsible for information technology support, services, and infrastructure on a worldwide basis.

From 1988 through 1991, Manville led the implementation of McKinsey's Knowledge Management Project, developing knowledge capture and distribution processes and tools in support of client service. In 1995 he co-led a two-year research effort into how companies can improve performance by leveraging knowledge more effectively. His work in knowledge management has been profiled in various publications examining the role of knowledge and learning in organizations. Manville joined McKinsey in 1987, originally working in communications planning and support for several industry practices.

Christopher Meyer is a partner at and the director of the Ernst & Young Center for Business Innovation (CBI) in Boston, and coauthor of the book BLUR: *The Speed of Change in the Connected Economy.*

The CBI is charged with identifying the issues that will be challenging business in the future, and defining responses to them; as director, Meyer is responsible for establishing the CBI's research agenda. His own current research interests include the development of a "New Theory of the Firm," the implications for management of new discoveries in complexity and self-organizing systems and the development of the "connected economy." Meyer is an authority on the evolution of the information economy, the innovative use of information and its impact on strategy, shareholder value, and "informationalization" of the firm. He is also president of BIOS GP, Inc., Ernst & Young's initiative to develop complexity-based solutions for management. He has over twenty years of general management and economic consulting experience.

David Stark is the Arnold A. Saltzman Professor of Sociology and International Affairs and chair of the Department of Sociology at Columbia University. A member of the external faculty of the Santa Fe Institute, he studies organizational innovation. Stark is currently researching new organizational forms among firms in Manhattan's Silicon Alley. In postsocialist Eastern Europe, he studied how interfirm networks facilitated and impeded economic restructuring.

Stark's recent publications include *Postsocialist Pathways: Transforming Politics and Property in Eastern Europe*, with Laszlo Bruszt (1998), a comparative study of the opportunities and dilemmas posed by the simultaneous extension of property rights and citizenship rights. With Gernot Grabher, he coedited *Restructuring Networks in Postsocialism: Legacies, Linkages, and Localities* (1997).

Stark has been a visiting Fellow at the Santa Fe Institute, the Center for Advanced Study in the Behavioral Sciences in Palo Alto, the Institute for Advanced Study/Collegium Budapest, the Ecole des Hautes Etudes en Sciences Sociales in Paris, the Center for the Social Sciences in Berlin, and the Institute for Human Sciences in Vienna. He currently serves as Chair of the Section on Comparative-Historical Sociology of the American Sociological Association.

John Julius Sviokla (svioklaj@diamtech.com) recently joined as a partner at Diamond Technology Partners, headquartered in Chicago, Illinois (www.diamtech.com). At Diamond, he focuses on the core offering of the firm: digital strategy. For twelve years before that, Sviokla was on the faculty of the Harvard Business School where his work focused on the use of advanced information technology. In particular, he addressed how managers can effectively use the power of technology to create more value for customers and extract value through superior financial performance. His latest publication is "Virtual Value and the Birth of Virtual Markets," Chapter Ten in *Sense and Respond: Capturing Value in the Network Era* (1998), coedited by Stephen P. Bradley and Richard L. Nolan. Sviokla's two most recent *Harvard Business Review* articles, "Exploiting the Virtual Value Chain" (November/December 1995) and "Managing in the Marketspace" (November/December 1994) (coauthored with J. F. Rayport), detail some of the findings of his research in this domain. Sviokla's other publications include "Staple Yourself to an Order" with Benson Shapiro and V. Kasturi Rangan in the *Harvard Business Review*, "Expert Systems and Their Impact on the Firm: A New View of XCON" in the *Management Information Systems Quarterly*, and "The Effect of Expert Systems Use on the Information Processing of the Firm" in the *Journal of Management Information Systems*. He has also published two edited books, *Seeking Customers* and *Keeping Customers*, with colleague Ben Shapiro.

1

Order from the Bottom Up

Complex Adaptive Systems and Their Management

John Henry Clippinger III

This book is for those who are responsible for organizations that have become so interconnected, so volatile, and so complex that they have become unmanageable by conventional means. Traditional tools have failed these managers. They have iterated through multiple planning cycles, they have reengineered, and they have reorganized; yet somehow the problems remain the same. How can you manage when you cannot control the particulars or the resources? How can you manage when the future is too uncertain and too unstable to plan for? How can you manage when simple changes have enormous and unanticipated consequences? The truth is that you cannot—not by any classical definitions of management. If we are to manage in this age of hyperchange and hypercompetition, then we are going to have to fundamentally redefine what we mean by management.

This book is intended to help provide a new definition of what it means to manage, based on the application of principles and insights taken from the science of complex adaptive systems (CAS). This "science of sciences" contains a collection of principles and methods that apply across a broad range of sciences—physics, biology, economics, genetics, computer science—and that provide powerful insights into how complex systems can evolve from relatively simple principles to become well-ordered, adaptive systems. This enormous cross-fertilization of the sciences is yielding new knowledge about how the most complex processes function, ranging from the formation of the universe to genetic differentiation, from the evolution of a species to the development of "artificial life." This new science is providing insights into how complex businesses and organizations can be managed and controlled. The goal of this book is to move from theoretical discussions to offering managers new methods, concepts, tools, and examples to help them keep their enterprises balanced between order and chaos—in that "sweet spot" where creativity and resilience are at their maximum. The act of management thus becomes a matter of influencing the forces of self-organization from below, rather than controlling them from above.

The notion that a complex process can be self-organizing or self-regulating is not new. Adam Smith's *An Inquiry into the Nature and Causes of the Wealth of Nations* (1981) introduced the notion of the "invisible hand" of market capitalism. Markets are governed by the laws of supply and demand, not by any central authority, yet they are highly efficient at allocating resources to the material well-being of all.

What *is* new is the application of this concept to management. The traditional view of management was expressed by its leading historian, Alfred Chandler (1977), who defined classical management theory and practice by contrasting the visible hand of management with Adam Smith's invisible hand of the market. Whereas markets were governed by invisible laws and principles, Chandler argued, organizations were different and required the deliberate, visible, reasoned decisions and actions of managers. Management decisions had to be informed by data and controlled by decisions made on rational principles: decision theory, financial analysis, operations research, and planning. For Chandler and his contemporaries, organizational resources were allocated not by invisible laws but by the very visible efforts and interventions of management. Complexity was to be conquered by rational analysis, the mastery of details, the breaking down of complex problems into simple, *manageable* problems. This view of management was the received wisdom of its day and claimed a special legitimacy derived from the scientific legacies of Enlightenment rationalism.

This view of complexity is received wisdom no more. The application of complex adaptive systems theory to organizational and economic behavior by scholars such as David Stark, Brian Arthur, Kenneth Arrow, and others reveals that there is no fundamental divide between market behavior and organizational behavior. The correctness of Chandler's contrast between the visible hand of management and the invisible hand of the market is now in dispute. As complex adaptive systems principles become accepted and applied, it is becoming clear that the same principles that account for the bottom-up miracle of market efficiencies can be applied to organizations and enterprises as well.

The Biology of Business builds on that premise. It shows what is required to create self-organizing processes and explores the application of these ideas and principles to a variety of specific business situations, including organization on the factory floor, knowledge management, improving organizational performance and risk management, new types of legal and regulatory policies, and financial mechanisms for achieving market liquidity.

This book proposes a radical departure from traditional management thinking and practice. It argues that control cannot be imposed—that, instead, control emerges if managers create the right conditions and incentives for it to do so. Management cannot, and need not, have perfect information; the challenge of management is to create the conditions and contexts that select for a range of desired outcomes as in the processes of natural selection. Rather than designing for and enacting a specific outcome, managers should create those conditions that select for a range of desired solutions. Nature does not "design" an outcome and yet is capable of creating the most complex, magnificent, and adaptive forms of organization. The enormous progress in genetics and especially in gene therapies is based on mimicking and harnessing the principles of natural selection to evolve new proteins, genes, and potentially even organs that address human needs. The development of adaptive human organizations and institutions is no less complex a task and hence requires no less powerful approaches and mechanisms.

Examples of Bottom-Up Control

How can simple mechanisms such as making a purchase or expressing a preference account for the ordering and organization of highly complex processes? Consider some examples of the kind of bottom-up control examined in this book.

Developing an operating system is one of the most complex, time-consuming, frustrating, and costly endeavors that a company can undertake. IBM poured billions of dollars into the development of OS2 only to receive marginal market acceptance. Microsoft has also invested billions of dollars in not only the development of its operating systems, Windows 95 and NT, but in establishing them as industry standards. How is it, then, that professional and nonprofessional software developers scattered throughout the world could evolve the "open source" Linux operating system that threatens to challenge the primacy of Microsoft? Who or what manages this process? How does it achieve a quality and performance standard that is in many cases superior to commercially developed software?

For another example, imagine the largest computer network in the world being assembled on the same principles: there is no central command, and no one is in overall control. Its operations are totally distributed. "Impossible," said the traditional managers. "It will crash because it was not designed to handle the capacity demanded of it." And yet this description fits the Internet, the fastest growing network in the world. How can that be?

How can bacteria and viruses "figure out" how to defeat the ingenious attacks of antibiotics and other manmade threats, thereby defeating the efforts of the best scientific minds in the world? How is it that such relatively simple life forms can quickly "invent" such a wide range of ingenious countermeasures?

How are the diverse nutritional, shelter, and recreational needs of millions and billions of people met day in and day out, without anyone managing or overseeing the process? Yet it happens all the time; we take for granted the power of markets to create and allocate resources efficiently, even though "blindly."

All of these are real-world examples of the invisible hand of self-organization. It is fundamental to all living things and to all of the most complex forms of organization. We cannot escape it, be above it, or even apart from it; but we can hope to understand it and to direct it thoughtfully. Perhaps the most powerful form of selective pressure being exerted on our species today is the pressure to understand and embody these principles. Our ability to build adaptive, global organizations and institutions will depend on our understanding and applying the principles of self-organization.

A Framework for CAS Management

Universal principles of organization, replication, and selection govern all complex things, including human artifacts and institutions, such as economies, technologies, organizations, and cultures. The behavior of such complex things is typically neither deterministic nor linear; rather, living systems continuously reorganize themselves in unexpected ways. Universal principles of self-organization are expressed locally and embody the unique history, contingencies, and circumstances of the locality. Unlike mechanistic or linear systems, complex systems cannot be extricated from their settings or easily disassembled into subunits. Their form of organization and complexity is the consequence and the embodiment of how they have interacted with and adapted to their ever changing circumstances. The overall behavior of complex adaptive systems emerges from the manner in which different subunits interact rather than from the behavior or organization of any individual unit. No one unit has any plan or even goal concerning how the overall system should act, and yet the system evolves into a complex structure adapted to its circumstances.

At first glance, an executive, manager, or policymaker might find the implications of complex adaptive systems discouraging. Because complex systems adapt from the bottom up, there is no way of planning for change, and the goals and policies of organizations are emergent and indeterminate. If so, then what role is there for the traditional executive or manager? Managers are expected to exercise their judgment, intervene, and exert visible influence over an enterprise. They are rewarded and held accountable for how well their companies do. Yet how much control does management really have in some cases? Wall Street presumes that management does exert control over outcomes and that the market is efficient and rational. Wall Street is the embodiment of Darwinian selection, the definer and labeler of success and failure; through the allocation of rewards and punishments, it is the ultimate determinant of market fitness. By defining and enforcing the rules of the game, Wall Street shapes business behavior, even if that behavior does not result in the best economic value and even if Wall Street prematurely culls out some promising enterprises.

The CAS approach to management embraces a market perspective and introduces a broad, rich set of concepts, methods, and measures. The CAS perspective is significantly less reductive than the classical view because it does not maintain that events are decomposable and predictable, that complex outcomes are derived from cause and effect, or that disengaged, rational agents can know or direct complex outcomes. Hence, CAS theory offers a very different view as to what can reasonably be expected of managers. By providing a new way of looking at organizational structure and function, and by drawing on new methods of modeling and measuring organizational performance and fitness, a CAS perspective provides new criteria for governing the enterprises of the second millennium.

New Performance Criteria

Darwinian notions of natural selection and fitness conjure up a tooth-and-claw world where survival of the fittest reigns, legitimating a winner-takes-all mentality. The CAS perspective on adaptation and fitness, on the other hand, is more nuanced and does not assert the *necessity* of relentless competition. Even though it might be tempting to appropriate the term "adaptation" into the business lexicon as a key organizing principle, to do so would be misleading. "Adaptation" implies a retrospective view and has nothing to say about the future prospects of an enterprise. A company can be highly adapted to its past business environment yet quite ill equipped to cope with its current and future business environment. Indeed, many previously successful companies end up failing because they are so well adapted to their past that they fail to see their future. A more appropriate term is "fitness"; it is a prospective term that characterizes the capabilities and the state of a company at a given point in time. Unlike the notions of winning and competing, which imply an endpoint and resolution, the term "fitness" implies a state of being, a condition that is contingent on a variety of internal and external factors. Fitness is a measure of the "health" of an organization. Elliott Sober (1984, p. 211), a philosopher of science who has written extensively on the philosophical underpinnings of evolutionary thought, makes the point as follows: "Adaptation and fitness (adaptedness) are complementary concepts. The former looks to the past, reflecting the kind of history that a trait has had. The latter looks to the future, indicating the chances for survival and reproductive success. These retrospective and prospective concepts are mutually interdependent. An adaptation may cause problems for the organisms that have it;

a changed environment may mean that an adaptation is no longer advantageous. Similarly, an adaptive trait may arise by chance; mutation may 'at random' produce a novel character that enhances fitness."

Species are considered fit if they are able to reproduce themselves successfully over many generations, especially if they are able to do so under conditions of intense competition. To the evolutionary biologist, the fitness of a species is its ability to have its unique genetic code persist over time, through many generations. From an organizational perspective, fitness is related to a company's definition of itself and how that definition enables the company to replicate itself over time under adverse conditions. It may have nothing to do with size, earnings, revenues, market share, or even rate of growth, for these are more measures of retrospective adaptation than fitness for the future.

Finding the Sweet Spot

The notion of fitness has been central to evolutionary biology, and it continues to play a pivotal role in the recent CAS work of Stuart Kauffman (1993), John Holland (1992, 1995), and others who study artificial life (Langton, 1992). The challenge to all forms of complex organization, from the simplest proteins to the most complex societies, is how to survive in the particular "fitness landscape" in which they find themselves. In the starkest terms, the challenge of survival is that of searching an enormous landscape, or space of options, in sufficient time to avoid extinction. From a management perspective, this can be rendered as the need to have as many options as possible but not so many that they cannot be identified or enacted.

From a CAS perspective, all self-organizing systems are poised between two poles: too much order and too much chaos. CAS research into this problem has shown that every complex system has its "sweet spot" (Kauffman, 1993)—the place between excessive disorder and excessive order, at the "edge of chaos," where the system is

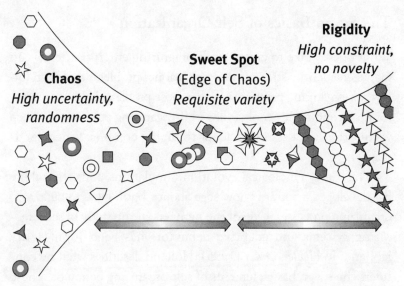

Figure 1.1. The Sweet Spot Between Excessive Disorder and Excessive Order.

maximally responsive to the variety of its environment but sufficiently structured that it can act and perpetuate itself (see Figure 1.1).

A goal of this book is to show managers how an understanding and application of the principles and mechanisms of complex adaptive systems can be used to direct organizations so that they stay within the sweet spot. The goal is to demonstrate in specific terms how managers can use CAS techniques to manage complexity and enact new forms of governance that will enable the emergence of self-organizing interactions within the sweet spot. Meaningful and independent measures of order and disorder that could be applied to businesses have yet to be developed. We can, however, look for reliable indicators of order and disorder to help managers make their groups, divisions, and enterprises more fit. Throughout this book, we suggest such indicators and explore how managers might map out the fitness landscape of their organizations and develop CAS-based strategies for competing and surviving under highly complex and volatile conditions.

The Seven Basics of Self-Organization

What does it take to create a self-organizing enterprise? How can managers identify strategic and operational problems and then follow self-organizing practices to solve these problems? How can organizations and their people follow self-organizing principles to keep within the sweet spot and adapt to highly complex fitness landscapes?

The study of biological evolution, simulations, and artificial life has developed a body of knowledge about what it takes to build self-organizing processes. One of the pioneers in the study of self-organizing systems and adaptive behaviors has been John Henry Holland. In *Hidden Order* (1995), Holland describes what he considers the seven basic elements of self-organizing behavior. These "basics," together with the work of Kauffman (1993), Clark (1997), and Arthur and Arrow (1994), provide the framework that *The Biology of Business* uses to organize a broader discussion of what is involved in adopting a self-organizing mindset for management.

The seven basics include four properties—aggregation, nonlinearity, flows, and diversity—and three mechanisms—tagging, internal models, and building blocks. The properties identify the key formative characteristics of any self-organizing system. They represent those things that managers should look for, work on, and influence. *Aggregation* refers to the fact that collections or groupings display properties that are more than the sum of their parts. The property of *nonlinearity* is displayed when small increments of change can cause enormous and unexpected threshold changes. *Flows* are webs or networks of interactions, such as resources, orders, goods, capital, or people. *Diversity* is a measure of variety; in general, the more diverse an organization, the more fit and adaptable it is, up to the edge of chaos, beyond which too much diversity precludes the formation of order or organization.

The techniques that managers can use to effect changes in the properties are the three mechanisms. Through these mechanisms, managers can initiate sustainable self-organizing processes to achieve specific organizational and strategic goals. *Tagging* is a crucial concept that runs throughout *The Biology of Business*; it refers to the naming, or labeling, of a thing or quality so as to give it certain significance or link it to action. Prices, job titles, reputations, and definitions of all kinds are tags. *Internal models* are simplified representations of the environment that anticipate future actions or events. Stereotypes are types of internal models that simplify the complexity of the environment to anticipate specific behaviors. *Building blocks* are components that can be endlessly recombined to make new components or actions; think of the four proteins that make up all DNA, the words that make up the English language, or a library of code objects that can be used in programming new software.

These four properties and three mechanisms are the core concepts needed to understand and foster self-organization.

Aggregation

Aggregations are collections of self-organizing entities whose behavior in conjunction differs from their behavior individually. As each individual entity acts on its own, a group behavior emerges that is distinct from the behavior of any one entity. This is a fundamental property of complex adaptive systems. In contrast to the notion of hierarchy, behavior is not directed from the top down; rather, it is the emergent consequence of ever changing interactions.

One of the principal roles of management is to aggregate workers and resources into groups to perform tasks. The classical approach has been to create hierarchical structures in which a higher level of "authority" explicitly directs a lower level. In acknowledging the importance of aggregation to organizational fitness, Clark (1997) discusses the notion of "soft assembly," which entails the joining of different components into a loose mixture of robustness and variability. He notes that "adaptive behaviors are soft-assembled in ways that respond to local contexts and exploit intrinsic dynamics. Mind, body, and world thus emerge as equal partners in the construction of robust, flexible behaviors. . . . In situations where a more classical, inner-model-driven solution would break down as the result of the model's incapacity to reflect some novel environmental change, 'equal partners' solutions often are able to cope because the environment itself helps to orchestrate behavior." Clark also introduces the concept of "scaffolding," which describes how environmental factors are used to solve complex problems—for example, as catalysts for biological processes (which are not wholly controlled and are contingent or unpredictable) or as cues to a person's memory that facilitate the correct execution of a complex procedure. As he explains, "Organizations, factories, offices, institutions, and such are the large scale scaffolds of our distinctive cognitive processes. But as surely as these larger wholes inform and scaffold individual thought, they themselves are structured and informed by the communicative acts of individuals and by episodes of solitary problem solving" (p. 187). In the world of robotics, this insight is summarized by the aphorism "The world is its own best representation"; the world, as Clark notes, is also "a natural partner to ideas of soft assembly and decentralized problem solving."

A manager acting to reengineer a business process, for instance, might "hard-assemble" a solution, perhaps by building a factory or buying a machine, but thus lock the business into a particular solution that might become obsolete. In contrast, a solution that is soft-assembled and that uses the external environment (consultants, outsourcing, partners, regulators, customers) as part of the scaffolding with which a solution is constructed is more likely to be able to adapt to continual changes in the demands of the market. In significant contrast to traditional software development and distribution approaches, the open source movement in software development provides multiple examples of soft assembly and scaffolding being used with great success. Perhaps the best-known examples are the development of the Linux operating system and the Java programming language.

Aggregation is neither a mechanism in the classical sense nor a "business process" but, rather, an emergent property and consequence of unique sustained types of interactions and conditions. Therefore how things are aggregated in an organization reflects what is important to an organization. The overall fitness of an organization depends on the appropriateness of that aggregation for its fitness landscapes.

Nonlinearity

By far the most common methods for analyzing markets, economies, and enterprises are based on assumptions of linearity: the whole is the sum of the parts; the future is a linear projection of the past. The principles are crisp and clear and the mathematics simple to grasp. The problem is that very few things in nature or commerce behave linearly. It is the rare exception rather than the rule. In nonlinear systems small, incremental changes can invoke sudden, unexpected threshold changes. CAS theory does not try to avoid the complexity and unpredictability of nonlinearity through simplifying assumptions. Rather, it recognizes that nonlinearity is the more prevalent case and develops methods to cope with it. The property of nonlinearity is closely related to aggregation because the aggregation of disparate events typically results in nonlinear behaviors. The implications of nonlinearity for managing for fitness are enormous. The most difficult fitness landscapes are nonlinear; they are the quintessential "rugged landscapes" (Kauffman, 1993) characterized by vertical peaks, gaping valleys, and abrupt discontinuities. From a manager's perspective, such fitness landscapes are worlds fraught with the danger of unintended consequences.

Flows

Flows are webs or networks of interactions. The nodes of a flow can process and transform the nature and direction of a flow. Flows of people, natural resources, orders, goods, capital, and products characterize an enterprise. The direction, rate, persistence, and typing of flows essentially define the structure and character of an organization. As Holland (1995) describes this process, "In CAS the flows through these networks vary over time; moreover, nodes and connections can appear and disappear as the agents adapt or fail to adapt. These are patterns that reflect changing adaptations as time elapses and experience accumulates." Instead of looking at organizations as functional units that are causally related, the CAS perspective treats organizations as "state spaces," or networks of potentially nonlinear relationships that can reorganize and reconfigure themselves. These relationships and patterns may also include actors and partners outside the immediate enterprise but within its extended environment—the "scaffoldings" that extend the cognitive capacities of a complex adaptive system (Clark, 1997).

In a business enterprise, the management of flows is a major source of value creation. For example, value is created through a redirection of flows when a failing company is acquired and reorganized, then becomes profitable. The new owner may have kept the same people and assets but adjusted the work flows, unlocked bottlenecks, and engendered new forms of self-organization and selection. When a company has become too rigid—too fixed in its ways to recognize new markets or new opportunities—new value can be created when an outside actor comes in, sees what those in the company have failed to see, and is able to unlock value. Another company may be too chaotic and disorganized to realize its value potential. Again, an outside party who has not been blinded by the internal tags of the company can make changes.

Tags provide one of the major management "hooks" by which flow networks can be reconfigured to create new forms of value and fitness. To quote Holland (1995), "Tags almost always define the network by delimiting the critical interactions, the major connections. Tags acquire this role because the adaptive processes that modify CAS select for tags that mediate useful interactions and against tags that cause malfunction." Note that change in flows is not achieved by reengineering a process but through selective tagging, setting in motion forces that select for the more fit flows and relationships. The management challenge in these cases is to manage toward the sweet spot by modifying the degree of order and chaos within a network.

Brian Arthur (Arthur, Derlauf, and Lane, 1997) has documented the impact of flows on markets, arguing that "path dependencies" that result in "technology lock-ins" can evolve within networks. While advantageous for a particular enterprise, such lock-ins tend to be disadvantageous for the social and economic systems in which the enterprise is embedded. Arthur advocates a "cognitive economics" that recognizes the beliefs and counterbeliefs of economic agents as major organizing principles of markets. He points out the importance of tags in the form of branding, "jaw-boning," recommending, rating, predicting, and the like, as a principal mechanism in shaping what Clark (1997) calls the "mind of the market."

Diversity

Diversity is a measure of a system's variety: the greater the variety, the greater the diversity. Typically, the greater the diversity of a complex adaptive system, the more fit it is. In an ecological context, diversity refers to the number of different species that inhabit an ecosystem. Niches are created by the interactions of multiple agents; the greater the number of agents and interactions, the greater and richer the diversity of environment and agents. In the words of Holland (1995), "The persistence of any individual agent, whether organism, neuron, or firm, depends on the context provided by the other agents. Roughly, each kind of agent fills a niche that is defined by the interactions centering on that agent." Diversity can be regarded as a form of economic and social wealth because the greater the diversity, the greater the economic activity and, therefore, the greater the opportunity for new forms of economic growth through the emergence of new niches or markets. Note that from this perspective a market is not a "thing" but a condition of interaction that can support a category of agents or firms.

In those cases where a particular agent or firm fails and a "hole" is created in the system, through a "cascade of adaptations . . . a new agent fills the hole" (Holland, 1995). It appears that commerce, like nature, abhors a vacuum. Given that the niche defines the agent, it should not be surprising that the new agent tends to be very similar to the old even though the two agents may be of different genetic or historical backgrounds. This process, called *convergence* in evolutionary biology, seems to be active in commerce as well.

Whereas fitness can be regarded as a performance measure or indicator for the individual firm, the notion of diversity is akin to the notion of market or economic potential. The greater the diversity, the greater the opportunity for new markets, new niches, and hence for new firms. From a public policy perspective, the nurturing of diversity is fundamental to societal and economic fitness. From a strategic perspective, diversity is a key antidote to the nonlinearity and the volatility of rugged landscapes. The diversity of the organization should be commensurate with the current and potential diversity of the environment with which it is linked and in which it is embedded. If a firm becomes too adapted to a particular niche, and that niche disappears and the repertoire of adaptive responses is limited, prospects for the firm's survival are bleak. For example, newspapers in the digital era might risk that scenario if they equate their identity and survival with printed paper. On the other hand, if they expand their boundary of self-definition (redefine their tags) to include digital media and stress core flows such as editorial content, local knowledge, and a strong and credible reputation or brand (tag), then they may survive, provided the environment in which they are embedded is sufficiently diverse to allow new forms of interaction. If, however, they are precluded from redefining their flows, perhaps because a dominant competitor has effectively locked them out of niches into which they must grow to survive, then a public policy in favor of diversity might lead to intervention.

Tagging

Tags are a way of labeling and giving significance to something, linking it to action. How something is tagged defines what it is and thereby gives it an identity and role in a process of selection. This is one of the most critical and least appreciated components of self-organization; without it natural selection and self-organization are impossible. So critical is the tagging, or recognition, mechanism in the human immune system, for example, that it effectively determines the identity and survivability of an individual by deciding which of the more than a trillion possible proteins are foreign and which are the "self."

Markets are not possible without tagging, as prices are types of tags. Changes in prices drive market behavior. Fashions are also tags; brands are tags; job titles are tags. Politics can depend on getting the right labels, or tags, to stick. Corporate politics and positioning are all enhanced or thwarted by tagging. Tags launch self-organizing behaviors. Although the notion of tagging by itself may not be a startling insight, when seen in terms of how it can be used to affect aggregation, flows, diversity, and the fitness of an organization, tagging becomes a critical management tool. For example, the survival of an enterprise, especially one involved in rapidly changing technologies and markets, depends on senior management's ability to define the core identity of the company. What business are we in? What are our core competencies? These perpetual questions are examples of tagging behavior. Tags are used by management to define the boundaries or membership conditions of an enterprise. A definition that is too narrow can result in an overidentification with a dated generation of technology (for example, Sears as a catalog retailer); a definition that is too broad can result in a failure to focus, adversely affecting near-term market survival. The failure of many technology-based start-up companies to focus on vertical market applications is indicative of too broad a market definition. Some executives of Nets Inc. felt that its failure was due to a definition of its business that was too broad and ambitious: "business-to-business electronic commerce." By contrast, Motorola is an example of a company that has mastered the process of identity boundary management over many decades. Like the human immune system, this company has successfully discriminated between hostile and benign opportunities, transforming itself from a consumer electronics company to a telecommunications and mobile communications company. The fitness of a tagging policy for identity management can usefully be understood in terms of how effectively it either reduces or engenders disorder to keep an enterprise within the sweet spot.

The CAS approach provides a rationale and methods for relating seemingly disparate management activities, such as branding and public relations, to a wide variety of aggregation activities, such as organizational development, change management, and strategy. In this respect, there is a very interesting relationship between tags and the embodied knowledge of mutually evolving languages or sublanguages. It is not difficult to imagine how language competencies grew out the collective attempts of groups of agents to direct and coordinate their behaviors. Fitness selection would favor those groups of individuals that could quickly distribute, share, and coordinate the searching of broad and complex fitness landscapes. Hence, languages, traditions, and cultures have evolved to achieve this end. Languages are always changing and evolving new meanings and sublanguages (Pustejovsky, 1995) and therefore are themselves a form of complex adaptive systems. From a manager's viewpoint, directing change entails the need to create and manage new meanings to achieve coherent, coordinated action. Motorola, for example, has a very explicit six-step policy on how to introduce new terms into the company. According to some executives of Motorola University, the time it takes the organization to absorb new terms and meanings is the single greatest impediment to growth. Thus, the language of an industry or enterprise can be viewed in terms of a fitness scale. That language can range from one in which meanings are chaotic, variable, and not understood to one in which there are stable, shared meanings—the latter indicating a powerful corporate culture.

The personality or persona of an enterprise often reflects its founders and key leaders, and is expressed through its internal models and languages. The notions of internal models, scaffolding, and emergent languages offer tools for understanding how these personae evolve and come to define the culture of an enterprise. The classical approach to trying to instill a culture or manage an enterprise from above has been to have a headquarters, which in effect acts as the head of the organization and prescribes from above what should be. From a CAS perspective, it is not surprising that such endeavors should fail. By being removed from the essential flows and interactions of the enterprise and by interacting mainly with itself, a headquarters often evolves into its own niche with its own culture and languages, independent of the overall enterprise. The better model for a corporate headquarters may not be the head of the corporate body but, rather, its immune system—highly distributed, in the thick of things, playing the defining role in survival.

In high-technology industries, innovations and market consolidation require a company to quickly retag its core business, to acquire new capabilities adroitly, and to move with agility into new markets. Senior managers need a deep appreciation of the membership tags that define the boundaries of their businesses: What are their markets and product lines? Who are their competitors and partners?

When the business landscape is constantly changing and new technologies and forces are coming into play, traditional wisdom and seasoned insight can prove to be a disadvantage. Complex organizations behave differently than simple ones. The past is often not a predictor of the future because technologies can redefine the rules of the game. Therefore, managers of complex organizations are continually challenged to recognize the new in the familiar. They must learn to differentiate between familiar tags and those that signal a discontinuity, that is, new sets of ordering principles and tags. To do this managers must question their assumptions about the complexity of their organizations and environments, and critically evaluate, update, and test their internal models of their organizations and their business environments.

Managers of complex organizations must first correctly characterize the fitness landscape, then find the right set of tags to define their companies' value flows so that the appropriate internal principles of self-organization can be initiated to change, and in some cases completely transform, their organizations. This is often characterized as a communication or marketing skill: the ability to instill a vision of a future that attracts and retains the loyalty of all the key stakeholders. Yet it is more than the "selling" of a product or idea. It entails a deep understanding of the external conditions that are exerting selective pressure *and* the ability to tag things in a way that reflects how the enterprise has culturally and historically responded to change. As leaders of large enterprises know, change cannot be dictated from above; instead, the "virus" of the vision needs to be spread in such a way that thousands of stakeholders, acting independently, self-organize together to achieve a common goal. The leader provides the fitness rules, gives the right feedback, and culls the results until the enterprise is aligned with its markets and its industry.

Internal Models

There is considerable debate over the extent to which self-organizing systems have explicit internal models. The strict emergence school has argued that there is no need for explicit internal representations and that all representations are implicit. Such a view holds that knowledge is embedded and embodied in a variety of actions and activities. The contrary, and more classical, view of older artificial intelligence methods contends that knowledge is explicit, disembodied, and abstract. This latter view is fast receding in popularity and has yet to live up to its earlier claims. However, as Clark (1997) argues, even though knowledge is likely to be derived from actions and even though action-based representations are an essential component of CAS behavior, there is growing evidence to suggest that explicit representations and models are critical to complex adaptive systems.

Holland (1995) recognizes the importance of these two types of knowledge, or models: "A tacit internal model simply prescribes a current action, under the *implicit* prediction of some desired future state, as in the case of the bacterium. An overt internal model is used as a basis for explicit, but internal, exploration of alternatives, a process called *lookahead*." Clark stresses a more extended and distributed notion of models than Holland, seeing embedded knowledge in the scaffoldings of the environment. In his analysis of language as "the ultimate artifact," he argues that the embedded knowledge of language is the consequence of generations of public interactions and that grammar is not so much innate as it is socially emergent.

Building Blocks

Related to the mechanism of models is the mechanism of building blocks, of which models are typically composed. Fitness and the ability to stay within the sweet spot entail being able to recognize regularities and constraints in an environment and to evolve an effective repertoire of reusable responses. These regularities and associated repertoires of actions are the building blocks without which complex forms of self-organization and emergence are impossible. Environments that are relentlessly novel are not survivable; hence, survival and fitness depend upon being able to recognize and exploit environmental constraints. Reusability implies repetition, but novel adaptive responses can be created from reuse of known building blocks.

Holland (1995) speaks of building blocks with respect to models, but building blocks are also used in creating bodies of knowledge and new sublanguages. The notion of reusable units is fundamental to the new practice of software technologies in which "object libraries" are created. MIT's Sloan School of Management has made efforts to identify libraries of reusable business process objects, and virtually all the major accounting and consulting firms are developing libraries of reusable business processes.

Again, as is typical of Holland, seemingly simple notions have deep roots and manifestations: "If model making, broadly interpreted, encompasses most of scientific activity, then the search for building blocks becomes *the* technique for advancing that activity: The use of building blocks to generate internal models is a pervasive feature of complex adaptive systems. When the model is tacit, the process of discovering and combining the building blocks usually proceeds on an evolutionary time scale; when the model is overt, the time scale may be orders of magnitude shorter" (Holland, 1995).

The CAS Manager's Role

The message to managers competing in the age of the Internet should be clear: survival and relative competitive fitness depend on the speed with which tacit knowledge embodied in the flows and interactions of the enterprise is made explicit, tagged, aggregated, and recombined into emergent models that keep the enterprise within the ever changing sweet spot between chaos and rigidity. These are the manager's tasks.

The word "manager," like other words, has changed over time. Derived from the medieval French word for "schooling by hand," the term was initially used in the sense of teaching a horse. In its current usage, the term connotes a rational actor, an individual who collects information, weighs alternatives, makes decisions, and then acts. Management is the act of rational control. In this classical view of management, an artifact of the Enlightenment, the manager is the clock maker, the fixer, the mechanic, the one who diagnoses the flaw, repairs the failed mechanism, and restores the machine to humming efficiency. The manager is the rational agent who guides the visible hand. The manager is not a part of the invisible forces but separate, rational, and in control.

By argument and example, this book seeks to go beyond the classical view of management. Managers, like others, are part of the process; their role cannot be extricated from, or elevated above, the fray of selection and emergence. There is no Archimedean vantage point of pure rationality. There is no simple "objective" reality, as Arthur points out in Chapter Two. The invisible, unpredictable, and diverse forces of selection make the feasibility of rational decision making the exception rather than the rule. In short, reason is not the sovereign we were once taught it was. There are neither simple answers nor certitudes. Far more subtle and mercurial forces are at play. As Clark suggests in Chapter Three, in the new meaning of management, the manager will be more like a coach or a steward than a figure who issues orders and commands. A manager will be someone who can facilitate the spontaneous generation of effective teams, rather than the figure of authority for the team. In the end, however, it is the manager who is responsible for the overall outcome and has the responsibility of selecting for and against certain traits and behaviors; the manager will, therefore, continue to wield significant power.

In the CAS perspective on management, a critical role of the manager will be as the tagger, the labeler, the marker and keeper of boundaries. Marketlike mechanisms will increasingly be used to create and allocate resources within organizations. If this is the case, the manager's role will be like that of a market maker, someone who recognizes a need, mobilizes the appropriate resources, and puts in place the appropriate rules and incentives to evolve specific types of self-organizing behavior. Managers will be masters of the seven principles of self-organization. They might have specific functional competencies in which to apply these principles, such as human resources, manufacturing, product development, or marketing, but their primary role will be to initiate and referee the appropriate processes. They will set the terms for Darwinian selection, but they will not try to control the process.

Mapping the Fitness Landscapes of a Business

With the continued compression of time and distance in global markets, management practices that presume an omniscient, detailed, and up-to-date knowledge of all the factors that can affect development of a product are impractical. Neither complexity nor fitness can arise from such practices, which will be selected against. Bureaucratic and monolithic organizations are ill suited to creating global teams or responding to a myriad of complex technological challenges on short notice. Yet many global companies still attempt to sustain a bureaucratic or monolithic form of organization, imposing management policies and practices that present the ritualized facade of control at the expense of real productivity.

A company's fitness is a function of how well it is able to respond to and anticipate the changes in its business environment. Increasingly, the environments in which companies find themselves today are highly interconnected, volatile, and unpredictable. Gone are the days of predictable earnings, competition, and technology. The regulated monopoly and fixed-course business model are things of the past. Even staid old electric companies are becoming deregulated and rapidly mutating into distribution, power, and even telecommunications companies.

The challenge to contemporary business is to match business strategy and investments to the fitness landscape. Different strategies are appropriate for different types of landscapes. It is management's task to align the structure and function of the organization to the current and anticipated changes in the business environment. Knowing where you are in the fitness landscape and knowing how that landscape is changing are prerequisites for implementing an effective strategy.

Figure 1.2 illustrates "pure" types of organizations for four different fitness landscapes. The horizontal axis displays the degree of interconnectedness of the business environment—the external ruggedness. The business environment includes a variety of factors, such as natural resources, suppliers, competitors, technology, regulators, customers, and socioeconomic trends. The more dominant and interconnected these factors are, the more complex and "rugged" is the landscape for achieving fitness. The vertical axis displays the interconnectedness of the organization itself—the internal complexity. For example, an organization that has a high degree of specialization and a high degree of interaction among its many organizational units would appear high on the vertical axis. For both axes, as the number and interdependence of different factors

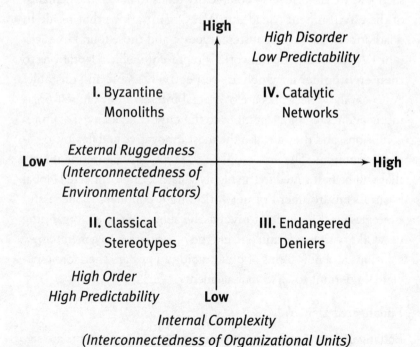

Figure 1.2. Fitness Landscapes for Organizations.

increase, so do the slopes of the fitness landscape. The strategic challenge for management is to characterize accurately the degree of internal and external complexity of an organization in order to select the appropriate strategy to achieve sustainable fitness.

Although reducing organizational fitness to four types is a vast oversimplification, it does help identify the range of strategic options confronting management in achieving fitness. The four quadrants and the organizational types within them represent idealized or extreme examples of organizational adaptation; associated with each type is a specific portfolio of strategies. Membership in quadrant III, representing "endangered deniers," is not desirable. These are organizations that are in immediate peril and in active denial. This outcome can be avoided only by moving toward a more stable environment (quadrant II) or evolving the organization in such a way that its level of complexity tends to match the demands of the environment (quadrant IV). Organizations that reside in quadrant II (the "classical stereotypes") and those found in quadrant IV (the "catalytic networks") represent viable adaptations to their environments, which are respectively stable and unstable. Auto-catalytic networks are of special interest: they are self-organizing and represent adaptations to the most complex type of fitness conditions, and they are also the most innovative and flexible organizational form. They may well be the type of organizational form that will be best suited to the highly volatile, interconnected global business environment of networks and e-commerce. Successful strategies for this quadrant involve the leveraging of self-organizing networks both inside and outside the organization to generate new solutions and new forms of order rapidly. They are therefore especially important to CAS management.

Endangered Deniers

Endangered deniers are organizations whose environments are significantly more complex than they can handle and whose extinction is a virtual certainty. Over thirty years ago W. Ross Ashby

(1963) formulated the law of requisite variety: when the variety or complexity of the environment exceeds the regulatory capacity of a natural or artificial system, the environment will dominate and ultimately destroy that system. In other words, the environment becomes too rugged for the system to search in real time. Rather than acknowledge the danger, the all-too-typical response is denial.

Classical Stereotypes

Classical stereotypes are simple and well adapted to a stable environment. Some examples are core organizational and economic processes and cultural, legal, political, and religious institutions that have seen little change. They are well adapted to their environment. Since they are simple and do not change much, they might be considered rigid. But they may embody a fundamental property that is key to forming more complex organizations; if so, they may be regarded as building blocks for more complex organizations. For example, premier venture capitalists are very good at recognizing and selecting for those core organizational and entrepreneurial processes that scale up and build large, successful organizations. They have a knack for selecting out the right kind of "DNA" to build large companies and even industries. The challenge for organizations in this quadrant is primarily scalability. Family businesses fit this model, as do partnerships and early-stage entrepreneurial businesses. If these forms of organization cannot be recombined into something more permanent and complex, then they too may become endangered deniers.

Byzantine Monoliths

Byzantine monoliths are organizations that are overorganized relative to the challenge of their environments. Examples are inflexible bureaucracies, monopolies, patronage-based systems, and companies that have never had to learn to be responsive to competitive or market forces. Such organizations can take on a surreal and malevolent nature as described by Franz Kafka in *The Castle*

([1922] 1995) and Terry Gilliam in his 1985 film classic *Brazil*. The equivalent in the animal world would be a domestic pet that is so inbred, protected, and indulged that it could never survive in a chaotic natural environment. Survival in this quadrant is highly dependent on the persistence of business environments that may be "unreal" and unsustainable. With changes in the business environment, such as deregulation, new competitive forces, or technological innovation, these monoliths can easily become endangered deniers because their internal order is not derived from interactions with a complex external environment but from their own self-referential internal interactions.

Catalytic Networks

When the complexity of the organization is equal to the challenges of interacting with its environment, the emergent organization, a catalytic network, can be a continuous and spontaneous source of innovation. It is in the ideal zone of fitness, the sweet spot at the edge of chaos. It cannot be managed in the classical sense of exerting top-down control. It can only be governed by setting standards, protocols, conventions, and rules that act to define the grammars of interaction and recombination for agents that can be inside or outside the organization. Management in this sense consists of setting in motion the actions of generations of agents, many of whom may be unknown, that will compete and replicate to produce results that further the fitness of the organization. The role of management is to set the fitness criteria and weed out those solutions that do not meet them.

The intentional use of self-organizing networks to generate innovations and to achieve organizational fitness is a relatively new approach. It builds on the notions of increasing returns and network externalities as a means of innovating and gaining acceptance in a marketplace. It represents a break with the traditional definition of the boundaries of an organization in that it uses forces and actors external to the organization to undertake activities that are traditionally performed within the organization. An example was the general ethos of the early Internet and the publication of open standards to devise an open system for mutual, self-organizing assistance in the development and maintenance not only of the Internet but also of many software and technical projects. This process of mutual "gift giving" seems to have been far more effective than many contractual or even transactional models in getting complex systems built, debugged, and improved. This exchange system, based on ancient principles of reciprocity that are found in most traditional societies, seems to be more deep-seated and efficient than many ever imagined. With the success of the Internet, this approach is gaining recognition and acceptance, and it represents a fundamental and far reaching advance in strategy. It may even succeed in unseating one of the most sophisticated and powerful monopolies of recent times.

In a wide variety of cases, innovation and fitness are achieved not through control or dominance but through directed coevolution. The Java platform movement and Netscape's decision to have its customers help debug its "giveaway" browser were early examples of this approach. Amazon.com's use of financial incentives to create a vast network of book recommenders—and hence, Amazon.com recommenders and loyalists—illustrates how catalytic networks and principles of self-organization can be applied to what otherwise would be considered franchising or distribution. The dramatic growth of the open source movement in spreading Linux, a free and efficient variant of the Unix operating system that is collaboratively developed by the user community, is an example of how a self-organizing network of sophisticated customers can drive innovation and market efficiencies, even at the expense of the alleged market monopolist, Microsoft. 3Com's vast network of self-organizing third-party developers for its Palm Pilot III product has given it a commanding lead, if not a lock-in, in the personal digital assistant (PDA) marketplace. This advantage could very well represent a challenge to PC manufacturers competing in the network and Internet computer appliance market in the future. This phenomenon has the aura of a sociocultural movement even broader than a business or commercial strategy. It may be the harbinger of a new form of socioeconomic organization that is "metacommercial."

Conclusion

Today's organizations have become too interconnected, too volatile, too big, and too complex to be managed by traditional top-down means. The science of complex adaptive systems offers a new mindset and a scientific basis for managing complexity using the principles of self-organization. The Internet, new digital technologies, and the application of the principles of self-organization have spawned a new generation of organizational and market strategies that make use of new protocols, standards, and values capable of creating complex, robust, and highly fit organizations.

2

The End of Economic Certainty

W. Brian Arthur

The story of the sciences in the twentieth century is one of a steady loss of certainty. Much of what was real and machine-like and objective and determinate at the start of the century, by mid-century was a phantom, unpredictable, subjective, and indeterminate. What had defined science at the start of the century—its power to predict, its clear subject/object distinction—no longer defined it at the end. In the twentieth century, science after science lost its innocence. Science after science grew up.

What then of economics? Is economics a science? I believe it is. It is a body of well-reasoned knowledge. Yet until the last few years it has maintained its certainty, it has escaped any loss of innocence. And so we must ask: Is its object of study, the economy, inherently free of uncertainties and indeterminacies? Or is economics in the process of losing its innocence and thereby joining the other sciences?

I believe the latter. In fact, there are indications everywhere these days in economics that the discipline is losing its rigid sense

---

Note: This essay was originally given as a talk at the conference Einstein Meets Magritte, Free University of Brussels, 1994. It is published in *Einstein Meets Magritte*, D. Aerts (ed.), Kluwer Academic Publishers, Dordrecht, 1998, and is reproduced here by permission.

of determinism, that the long dominance of positivist thinking is weakening, and that economics is opening itself to a less mechanistic, more organic approach. In this chapter I will show my own version of this loss of certainty. I will argue that there are major pockets of uncertainty in the economy. I will show that the clear subject/object distinction in economics often blurs. I will show that the economy is not a gigantic machine but a construct of its agents. These are not "anomalies" to be feared, they are natural properties of the economy, and if we accept them we will have a stronger, not a weaker, science.

High-Modern Economics

The fundamental ideas in economics stem from the thinking of the eighteenth century, in particular from the thinking of the English and Scottish Enlightenment. In 1733, at the height of the intoxication of Enlightenment thinking, Alexander Pope condensed its essence in one stanza of his poem *An Essay on Man:*

> All Nature is but Art unknown to Thee
> All Chance, Direction, which thou canst not see
> All Discord, Harmony, not understood
> All partial Evil, universal Good:
> And, spite of Pride, in erring Reason's spite
> One truth is clear, "Whatever IS, is RIGHT."

In this context "art" means artifice. It means technique or mechanism. And so, all the intricate wonders we see in nature, says Pope, are in fact a gigantic machine, an artifice like the mechanical automata figures of his time. All that looks unkiltered really has direction behind it. All that seems complex and discordant, like the movements of planets before the time of Kepler and Newton, has a hidden simplicity. All that affects each of God's creations adversely, in some unspoken way works to the good of the whole. Quoting Socrates, "Whatever is, is right."

These were not merely the ideas of Pope. They were the ideas that filled the intellectual air when Adam Smith was growing up. And Smith went on to enshrine them in *The Wealth of Nations*, that magnificent work that uncovered the hidden simplicity behind the traffickings of traders and manufactories and butchers and bakers. The economy was indeed Art, and its principles were now unhidden. The selfish interests of the individual were guided, as if by an invisible hand, to the common interest of all. Whatever was, was right. Two centuries later, the philosopher of science Jacob Bronowski was to comment glumly that economics never recovered from the fatally rational structure imposed on it in the eighteenth century. But we inherited more than Smith's rational structure. Deep in some recess of our minds, we inherited the thinking that the economy "is but Art," a gigantic machine, and that if we merely understood its parts, we could predict the whole. Certainly when I was studying economics in Berkeley twenty-five years ago, many economists hoped (as I did) that a "Grand Unified Theory" of economics was possible. From the axioms of rational human behavior, a theory of the consumer could be constructed. From this and a corresponding theory of the firm, we could construct a consistent microeconomics. From this, somehow, we could construct an aggregate theory of the economy: macroeconomics. All this would constitute a "Grand Unified Theory" of the economy.

There have always been two embarrassments to this hope of constructing a theory of the economy from its reductionist parts. One was that the economy relies on human beings, not on orderly machine components. Human beings with all their caprices and emotions and foibles. The second embarrassment was technology. Technology destroys the neatness because it keeps the economy changing. Human behavior was finessed in economics by the device of Economic Man, that perfectly rational being who reasons perfectly deductively on well-defined problems. And technology change was not so much finessed as ignored or treated as exogenous. And so to make an orderly, predictive theory possible, Economic

Man (the subject) needs to operate on well-defined Problems (the object). There should be no blurring of agent and problem. And the well-defined problems should have well-defined Solutions. And the solutions will make up the building blocks for the next aggregated level of the theory.

This approach works. But it runs into difficulties when problems start to involve more than one decision maker and any degree of complication. Then heroic assumptions must be made. Otherwise, well-definedness unravels, agent and problem become blurred, and pockets of uncertainty start to bulge.

Let me illustrate what I mean in the context of a typical micro-economic situation in modern economics (I have chosen it from the mid-1980s literature on industrial organization). Consider this problem: We have a circle that we might think of as a twenty-four-hour clock. A number of firms, say twenty airline companies, have to decide in which time slot of this clock their planes will take off, say from LaGuardia Airport to go to Washington. Of course the different airlines have different preferences about when to take off. They know their preferences and are going to book such takeoff slots. The choices will be made once and for all. But there is a trade-off (in every economic problem there is always a trade-off) between when they really want to take off versus not being too close to other airlines' choices of their time slots. So, given the airlines' preferences, which time slots will they choose? This is the problem.

We might feel uneasy about saying much with certainty here. But I want to show the modern version of the Enlightenment approach, where we find the Harmony of a solution within the Discord of the situation. This high-modern approach is called "rational expectations." I will first spell it out, then shine a bright light of realism on it so that it starts to unravel and pockets of uncertainty appear. Let's go ahead. In the modern approach, we begin by supposing we know the order in which the airlines will submit their choices. Now imagine that airline number 20, the last to choose, reasons like this: Knowing where the first nineteen airlines are, I will know where I will want to be. So regardless of any arbitrary choice of the first nineteen airlines, I will know which time slot to choose. This is an easy problem for me as the twentieth. What about airline number 19? Well, airline number 19, when choosing, will know the chosen positions of the previous eighteen airlines and can figure what it should do, given that the twentieth will choose an optimal position given the positions of the eighteen other airlines and number 19's choice. What about the number 18? Well, the eighteenth, knowing what the previous seventeen have chosen, arbitrarily can solve the problem of selecting an optimal placement knowing what the nineteenth will do, given that the nineteenth makes his optimal choice given what the twentieth will do as a result of number 19's choice. Getting complicated? Yes. But you can work the whole logic in reverse order by backward deduction, or more properly by dynamic programming, and deduce how all twenty airlines will place themselves.

Notice the properties of this procedure. The problem is well defined by making it sequential and assuming the airlines use logical backward deduction. The solution is precise and clean in a mathematical sense. The problem becomes a mathematical one. (Indeed, all such problems become mathematical. And economics in turn becomes mathematics.) Another property that we normally have in this kind of problem is that the individual act comes to good of the whole; that is, partial evil is universal good. It is not quite true in this case, but nevertheless this is a generic property that often holds in economics. However, the Solution comes with a lot of fine print. Airlines must know their preferences exactly. Not only that, they must know the preferences of all other airlines. Further, they must know that every other airline accurately knows the preferences of every other airline. They also must know that every airline knows that every airline knows the preferences of every other airline, and so on in an infinite regress. Also, each airline must be rational enough to work out the solution. Further, each airline must believe that every other airline is rational and will use perfect rationality to work out the solution. Further, each airline must know in an infinite regress that every other airline is using this rational way to work out the problem, because if one of these airlines fails to do so, it messes the solution up for every other airline. Further, the optimal placement of each airline using this backward deduction must be unique. If any link of this network of requirements breaks, the solution ceases to exist.

This type of multiagent choice problem is pervasive in economics. So let us take this solution approach seriously. What if we are airline number 3 and we feel uncertain as to what airline number 17 is going to do? As airline number 3, we might say: "I don't think the people of airline number 17 are that bright, and I'm not sure whether they are going to solve this problem by this rational method. And if they don't work it out in this way, then I am not sure what my optimal choice will be as the third bidder in the process." This is sufficient to upset the situation. But worse, airline number 3 may communicate its uncertainty to other airlines, and they may no longer rely on number 3 or number 17. The entire solution is starting to unravel. In fact the Solution as defined by rational-expectations theory is a function of airlines' expectations or predictions of what other airlines are going to do. The problem is that if I am a representative airline, I am trying to figure out what my expectations ought to be—I am trying to predict a world that is created by the expectations of myself and everybody else. There is a self-referential loop here. The outcome each airline is trying to predict depends on the predictions it and others might form. In other words, predictions are forming a world those predictions are trying to forecast. Barring some coordinating device by which an airline can logically determine the predictions of others (such as the tortured solution reasoning above), there is no logical way it can determine its prediction. There is a logical indeterminacy.

So it is in the economy. People are creating a world that forms from their predictions, but if they try to form these expectations in a perfectly logical deductive way, they get into a self-referential loop. There is a logical hole in standard economic thinking. Our forecasts cocreate the world our forecasts are attempting to predict. And if I do not know how others might determine their forecasts, mine are indeterminate. There are some cases in economics where it is pretty obvious that everyone can figure out what to do, where something like the above scheme does work. But otherwise the problem is fundamental. When our ideas and preferences cocreate the world they are trying to forecast, self-reference renders the problem indeterminate. The idea that we can separate the subjects of the economy (the agents who form it) from the object (the economy itself) is flawed. Pockets of indeterminism are present everywhere in the economy. And the high-modern form of economic determinism fails.

Economics Under Indeterminacy

There are two questions we want to ask now. One question is: Does it matter? Maybe all of this happens on a set of measure zero, maybe this difficulty is confined to some trivial examples in economics. The second question is: If there are pockets of indeterminism, how should we proceed? To answer these I want to turn to the field of capital markets, to asset pricing theory—an area of economics that does matter.

There is a well-worked-out efficient-market economic theory for financial markets, and there is a very different set of ideas that financial traders use. Let me first outline the standard theory. The standard efficient-markets theory says that any information hinting about the future changes of the price will be used by investors. By an argument very much like the airline argument, each stock's price is bid to a unique level that depends on the information currently available. Using past patterns of prices to forecast future prices (technical trading), in this view, cannot lead to further profits. Otherwise the information inherent in past prices could be used to make further profits, and by assumption investors have already discounted all useful information into current prices. So the standard theory says investors use all information available to form expectations. These will determine stock prices, which on average will uphold these same expectations. Rational expectations again. Thus there is no way to make any money, and the market is efficient. Traders, on the other hand, believe that the market can be forecast. They believe they can spot patterns in past prices that will be helpful in prediction: they believe in technical trading. They believe the market is anthropomorphic, that it has a psychology, that it has motives. "The market was nervous yesterday. But it shrugged off the bad news and went on to quiet down." Economists are skeptical of this, and so the two viewpoints sit badly with each other.

The standard theory is wonderfully successful. It has its own logic. And this logic is complete and has desirable properties, such as uniqueness of solution. But the standard theory must face some unexplained phenomena, or so-called empirical anomalies. Crashes and bubbles seemingly with no cause. The fact that the volume of market trades is an order of magnitude higher than theory predicts. The fact that econometric tests show that technical trading is indeed profitable statistically. The phenomenon of generalized autoregressive conditional heteroscedasticity (GARCH behavior), which means there are periods of high volatility in stock prices interspersed randomly with periods of quiescence. In sum, the standard theory does not explain about half a dozen major statistical "anomalies" in real markets. This has recently led to a great deal of modern theorizing, some using ad hoc behavioral observation, some more sophisticated modeling.

Let me now show, as in the airline problem, how the standard theory breaks down and leads to pockets of indeterminacy. Suppose investors can put some portion of their money in a single stock that pays a dividend every time period (a day, a year, say), and they cannot perfectly predict this dividend. The investors are buying the stock for the dividend plus any capital appreciation (tomorrow's price), and they face the problem of forecasting these. To make the standard solution work, we assume homogeneous, identical investors who have identical forecasts of the dividend at the end of the period and identical forecasts about the stock's price in the future—forecasts that are on average unbiased and are therefore rational expectations. A little economic reasoning then shows that today's price is equal to the common expectation of tomorrow's price plus dividend (suitably discounted and weighted). This yields a sequence of equations at each time, and with a pinch or two of conditional-expectation algebra, we can solve these for the expectations of future prices conditioned on current information and wind up with today's price expressed as a function of expected future dividends. The problem is solved. But it is only solved providing we assume identical investors who have identical forecasts of the dividend at the end of the period and identical forecasts about the stock's price in the future. But what if we don't? What if we assume investors differ?

Let us look at the same exercise assuming our investors are not homogeneous. Note that the standard theory's requirement of identical "information" means not just the same data seen by everyone but the same interpretation of the data. But imagine yourself in a real financial market, like the New York stock market. Then this information consists of past prices and trading volumes, moves made by large mutual funds or large pension funds, rumors, network news, the market sections of daily newspapers, what other traders are doing and what they are telling you, and what your friend's uncle thinks about what is happening to the market. All of these things constitute actual information, and it is reasonable to assume that even if everybody has identical access to all this information, they would treat this information as a Rorschach inkblot and would interpret it differently. Even if we assume that the people interpreting this information are intelligent to an arbitrarily high degree and are all perfectly trained in statistics, they will still interpret the data differently because there are many different ways to interpret the same data.

So there is no single expectational model. A given investor can still come up with an individual forecast of the dividend. But tomorrow's price is determined by this investor's and other investors' individual forecasts of the dividend and of the next period's price. And there is no way for our reference investor to fathom the forecasts of the others—to determine "what average opinion expects the average opinion to be" (to use Keynes's words). To do so brings on a logical regress: "I think that they might think such and such; but realizing that I think that, they will think this." Unless we assume identical investors, once again our agents are trying to forecast an outcome (future price) that is a function of other agents' forecasts. As before there is no deductive closure. Expectations become indeterminate, and the theory collapses.

Worse, expectations become unstable. Imagine that a few people think that prices on the market are going to go up. If I believe this and I believe that others believe this, I will revise my expectations upward. But then I may pick up some negative rumor. I will reassess downward. But realizing that others may reassess and that they too realize that others will reassess, I may further reassess. Expectations become fugitive, rippling up or down whether trades are made or not. Predictions become unstable. This is the way price bubbles start. If somehow people expect prices to go up, they will forecast that other people will forecast that prices will go up. So they will buy in, and once the bubble thus starts off, people can see prices go up and their expectations of upward motion fulfilled. Therefore prices may continue to go up. Similar logic applies to "floors" and "ceilings." If, for example, the price is 894, many investors may believe that at 900 there is some sort of membrane, a ceiling, and that when the price reaches this ceiling it will bounce back down with a certain probability or it may "break through." Such ideas seem strange at first. But it is quite possible that many investors have sell orders at 900, simply because it is a round number. So expectations that the price will fall if it hits 900 are likely to be fulfilled. Ceilings and floors emerge as partially self-fulfilling prophesies, held in place by their being convenient sell and buy places. We are now a long way from homogeneous rational expectations. Under the realistic assumption that traders may interpret the same information differently, expectations become indeterminate and unstable. And they may become mutually self-fulfilling.

To summarize all this: if we look at a serious branch of economics, the theory of capital markets, we see the same indeterminacy that we saw in the airline problem. Agents need to form expectations of an outcome that is a function of these expectations. With reasonable heterogeneity of interpretation of "information," there is no deductive closure. The formation of expectations is indeterminate.

And yet in every market, every day, people do form expectations. How do they do this? If they cannot do this deductively, is it possible to model their behavior in this area?

Economic Behavior and Expectations

In 1988, John Holland and I decided that we would study situations like this by forming an artificial stock market on the computer and giving the little agents—artificially intelligent computer programs—some means by which they could do the reasoning that is required. This was one of the very earliest artificial agent–based markets. Later we brought in Richard Palmer, who is a physicist, Paul Tayler, who is a finance expert, and Blake LeBaron, who is a financial theorist in economics.[1]

1. For a more detailed version of our study, see W. B. Arthur and others, "Asset Pricing Under Endogenous Expectations in an Artificial Stock Market," in W. B. Arthur, S. N. Derlauf, and D. A. Lane (eds.), *The Economy as an Evolving Complex System II*. Santa Fe Institute Studies in the Sciences of Complexity, vol. XXVII, Reading, Mass.: Addison-Wesley, 1997.

In this market there was no feed-in from the real stock market. It was an artificial world going on inside the machine. The artificial agents, the little artificial investors, were all buying and selling a "stock" from one another. The computer could display the stock's price and dividend, who was buying and selling, who was making money and who was not, who was in the market and who was not, and so on. The price was formed within the machine by bids and offers. Another program—a "specialist"—set the price to clear the market, as in actual stock markets.

The modeling question was: If the agents cannot form their expectations deductively, how are they going to form them? We decided to follow modern cognitive theory about how actual human beings behave in such situations. So we allowed our artificial agents looking at past prices and dividends to posit multiple, individual hypothetical models for forecasting and to test these on a continual, ongoing basis. Each of these hypotheses had a prediction associated with it. At any stage each agent used the most accurate of its hypotheses and bought or sold accordingly. Our agents learned in two ways: they learned which of their forecasting hypotheses were more accurate; and they continually tossed out ones that did not work and replaced these using a genetic algorithm. So they learned to recognize patterns they were collectively creating, and this in turn collectively created new patterns in the stock price, about which they could form fresh hypotheses. This kind of behavior— bringing in hypotheses, testing them, and occasionally replacing them—is called induction. Our agents used *inductive rationality*, a much more realistic form of behavior.

Very well then. But now the key question was: Did our market converge to the rational-expectations equilibrium of academic theory or did it show some other behavior? What we found, to our surprise, was that two different regimes emerged. One, which we called the *rational-expectations regime*, held sway when we started our agents off with sets of predictive hypotheses close to rational expectations. We could plot the parameters of all the predictive hypotheses on a chart, and, in this case, over time, we could watch them getting gravitationally pulled into the orbit of the rational-expectations solution, forming a "fuzz" around this point, as they made occasional predictive forays away from rational expectations to test different ideas. It is not hard to see why rational expectations prevailed. If the overall mass of predictions is near rational expectations, the price sequence will be near rational expectations, and nonrational expectations forecasts will be negated. So the academic theory was validated.

But there was a second regime, which we called the complex regime, and it prevailed in a much wider set of circumstances. We found that if we started our agents with hypotheses a little removed from rational expectations, or, alternatively, if we allowed them to come up with hypotheses at a slightly faster rate than before, the behavior of the market changed. Subsets of mutually reinforcing predictions emerged. Imagine, for example, that we have one hundred artificial agents, each using sixty different prediction formulas, so that there is a universe of some six thousand predictors. Some of the predictors that emerge are mutually reinforcing; some are mutually negating. Suppose many predictors arise that say the stock price cycles up and down over time. Such predictors would be mutually negating because they would cause agents to buy in at the bottom of the cycle and sell at the top of the cycle, mutually negating profits and therefore eventually disappearing from the population of predictors. But if a subset of predictors emerged by chance that said, "The price will rise next period if it has risen in the last three periods," and there were enough of these, they would cause agents to buy, which on average would cause the price to rise, reinforcing such a subpopulation. Such subsets could then take off and become embedded in the population of predictors. This was indeed what happened in the complex regime, endowing it with a much richer set of behaviors. Another way to express this is that our artificial traders discovered forms of technical trading that worked. They were using, with success, predictions based on past price patterns.

And so technical trading was emergent in our artificial stock market. This emergence of subsets of mutually reinforcing elements, strangely enough, is reminiscent of the origin of life, where the emergence of subpopulations of RNA in correct combinations allows the subpopulations to become mutually reinforcing.

Another property that emerged in the complex regime was the so-called GARCH behavior I mentioned earlier that occurs in real markets—periods of high volatility in the stock price followed by periods of quiescence—and that is unexplained in the standard model. How did GARCH become an emergent property? Well, in our artificial market, every so often some number of investors discovered a new way to predict the market better. These investors then changed their buying and selling behavior. This caused the market to change, even if slightly, possibly causing other investors in turn to change. Avalanches of change swept through the market on all scales, large and small. Thus emerged periods of change triggering further change—periods of high volatility—followed by periods when little changed and little needed to be changed—periods of quiescence. This is GARCH behavior.

Conclusion

Let me now summarize. What we found in our artificial stock market is that providing our investors started near the academic rational-expectations solution, this solution prevailed. But this was a small set of parameter space. Outside this, in the complex regime, self-reinforcing beliefs and self-reinforcing avalanches of change emerged. A wider theory and a richer "solution" or set of behaviors then appeared, consonant with actual market behavior. The rational-expectations theory became a special case.

In the standard view of the economy, which has an intellectual lineage that goes back to the Enlightenment, the economy is mechanistic. It can be viewed as a complicated set of objects (products, markets, resources, technologies, demands) with linkages between them. Subject and object—agents and the economy in which they perform—can be neatly separated. The view I am giving here is different. It says that the economy itself emerges from our subjective beliefs. These subjective beliefs, taken in aggregate, structure the microeconomy. They give rise to the character of financial markets. They direct flows of capital and govern strategic behavior and negotiations. They are the DNA of the economy. These subjective beliefs are a priori or deductively indeterminate in advance. They coevolve, arise, decay, change, mutually reinforce, and mutually negate. Subject and object cannot be neatly separated. And so the economy shows behavior that we can best describe as organic, rather than mechanistic. It is not a gigantic, well-ordered machine. It is organic. At all levels it contains pockets of indeterminacy. It emerges from subjectivity and falls back into subjectivity.

The result is not a chaos but an economy of complexity: an economy that is created by the minds of its agents—consumers, managers, decision makers. This economy is cognitive, not physical, and the theories that deal with it must recognize its cognitive nature. It is an economy that sits better with our perceptions of the actual world, and the problems it poses to its decision makers challenge their intuitive reasoning as much as their formal reasoning. It is an economy that sits well with the sciences of the twenty-first century.

3

Leadership and Influence

The Manager as Coach, Nanny, and Artificial DNA

Andy Clark

Markets, companies, and various forms of business organizations can all be usefully viewed through the lens of complex adaptive systems (CAS) theory. This chapter addresses a fundamental puzzle that confronts both the theoretician and the business manager: how to control and sculpt the behavior of such a system.

Many modern businesses exemplify new organizational forms that are dictated by the increasing importance of knowledge and information, the decreasing costs of sharing and transferring knowledge and information across business boundaries, and the need to be rapidly responsive to ever-changing customer demands and to the emergence of new market niches. The organizational forms that such pressures select tend to be diffuse, distributed, and nonhierarchically structured. They tend, in short, to be instances of complex adaptive systems.

A complex adaptive system is "soft-assembled" and largely self-organizing. This means that it is the emergent product of multiple, often very heterogeneous, interacting forces and that the crucial interactions are not controlled or orchestrated by an overseeing executive, a detailed program, or any other source of strict hierarchical control. There is thus a pressing problem: Are such systems "out of control" and beyond the reach of useful governance? This chapter argues that they are not. Such systems, though somewhat unfamiliar, can be led, influenced, and enhanced in a variety of ways.

This chapter begins by clarifying the nature of the problem: What is it about complex adaptive systems that makes control and intervention difficult? It then illustrates these issues with a biological example: the role of genetic factors in influencing mature form. It introduces some examples of new forms of business organization, shows how these new forms constitute complex adaptive regimes, and applies the biological lessons in this new realm. The chapter also pursues a speculative extension of these lessons, applying them to the task of understanding the subtle roles of tagging and explicit model building in nudging a complex nonhierarchical system in a desired direction.

Because complex adaptive systems cannot be efficiently controlled by overseeing executives, detailed plans, or other sources of strict top-down control, the manager must learn to act instead as nanny, coach, and "artificial DNA." The nanny creates and maintains an environment in which a child's own curiosity and intelligence will lead the child to learn and flourish. The coach looks out for difficulties and potential obstacles, trying various incentives and ploys to push the player onward. And DNA modulates, but does not fully prescribe, developmental processes. The way to manage the new organizational forms of contemporary business is similarly indirect. A manager must create the special conditions that enable flexible, self-organizing responses and must modulate the unfolding of intrinsic dynamics by the judicious use of tags, incentives, and other gentle forms of nudging. This requires burning the blueprints and actively supporting the natural processes that allow complex systems to adapt to fast-changing and unpredictable environments.

Aggregation, Soft Assembly, and Control

Aggregation is defined by John Henry Clippinger in Chapter One as a process in which multiple, often heterogeneous, elements interact so as to create a distinctive collective effect and in which the relevant interactions are not controlled or orchestrated by any distinct overseeing element. As an example, consider the way the individual, amoeba-like cells of the slime mold cluster together when food is short to form a mobile mass similar to a slug, called the pseudoplasmodium. This process does not, as was once believed, involve leader cells that issue a chemical call to aggregate. Instead, when food is low *every* cell releases a chemical—cyclic AMP—that attracts other cells into small local clusters. These local clusters now present even denser concentrations of cyclic AMP, which in turn attract more cells. The ensuing process of positive feedback, in which local clusters promote larger and larger clusterings, is an example of self-organization. In this process the higher-level pattern—the pseudoplasmodium, or slug—emerges from the interactions of multiple elements without the use of top-down control. (For a more complete account, see Ashworth and Dee, 1975; see also Resnick, 1994, p. 51.) What distinguishes soft assembly from the more general notion of aggregation is that soft assembly occurs when heterogeneous elements are temporarily recruited to form a coherent whole. A soft-assembled process is thus relatively easy to undo, allowing for subsequent aggregations in which a wholly or partially different set of elements are assembled into another, also temporary, whole.

Consider an infant learning to reach. Developmental psychologists Thelen and Smith (1994, chap. 9) argue that individual infants may confront very different problems in learning to reach. For a very active infant who thrashes about continually, the problem is to dampen and control the thrashing movements and to convert them into directed reaching. For a more passive infant, the main problem may be generating the initial burst of energy needed to overcome gravity and impart force to the limb. In each case, however, the problem that confronts the central nervous system is how best to exploit the existing dynamics of the system so as to increase the likelihood of successful reaching. To tackle this problem the central nervous system must find a solution that takes into account multiple factors and preexisting sources of order within the system. It has therefore been argued that the job of the central nervous system is not to generate a rich inner plan or explicit model of how to reach (Polit and Bizzi, 1978; Jordan, Flash, and Arnon, 1994; Thelen and Smith, 1994). Instead, its job is to learn how to modulate a few simple parameters in a biomechanical system of springlike muscles and masses. A modulation of limb stiffness, for example, may interact with the intrinsic springlike dynamics of muscles and joints so as to yield a brief oscillation whose resting point is on the desired target. The controller—the central nervous system—is not a locus of detailed blueprints for success. Rather it is a source of subtle prompts, nudges, and minor modifications that act on an ordered biomechanical system situated in an environmental context. The job of the controller is to modulate parameters (such as stiffness) that will then interact with the rich dynamics of the environment so as to yield a desired outcome.

Processes of aggregation and soft assembly thus suggest a more subtle, and powerful, role for the wider environment itself. Instead of seeing the environment as simply a source of problems and an arena in which problem-solving processes are played out, it becomes necessary to view aspects of the environment as equal partners in soft-assembled problem solving.

An example is the expert bartender. Faced with multiple drink orders in a noisy and crowded environment, the expert mixes and dispenses drinks with amazing skill and accuracy. But what is the basis of this expert performance? It does not at all stem from finely tuned memory and motor skills. In controlled psychological experiments comparing novice and expert bartenders, it becomes clear that expert skill involves a delicate interplay between internal and environmental factors (Beach, 1988; Kirlik, 1998).

The expert bartenders select and array distinctively shaped glasses when they receive the orders and use these external cues to help them recall and sequence the specific orders. Experts' performance plummets in tests involving uniform glassware, whereas the performance of novices, although not as good overall, is no worse in the face of such alterations. The expert has learned to sculpt and exploit the working environment in ways that transform and simplify the task that confronts the brain. Aspects of the working environment thus form part of what might be called our "cognitive scaffolding": the external sources of order and influence that enable embodied brains to solve complex problems.

This idea of scaffolding has its roots in the work of Lev Vygotsky, a Soviet psychologist of the early part of the twentieth century (see, for example, the recent translation, Vygotsky, 1986). Vygotsky stressed the way our interactions with external structures, including words, texts, and other agents, could reconfigure our problem-solving activity. The notion of scaffolding applied in this chapter is broader still, encompassing all kinds of external aids and supports, from simple environmental structuring, as in the example of the bartender, to the more diffuse and complex kinds of support provided by larger-scale linguistic, social, and economic factors. Such larger-scale factors include the words of our language, the conventions of politeness and social exchange, and the policies of powerful institutions such as the World Bank and the Federal Reserve. These factors likewise sculpt, simplify, and orchestrate the activities of multiple brains. Much of the distinctive power and scope of advanced human reason is rooted in these larger collective efforts. But the parallel runs deeper: some large-scale organizations, such as corporations and businesses, may themselves be usefully seen as adaptive entities that must respond rapidly and flexibly to changing environmental pressures and that may interact closely with a variety of extra-systemic forces. Multiple types of systems and actors thus exhibit the special kind of natural organization that allows them to adapt fluidly to changing circumstances and to exploit maximally a variety of external props and aids. These cases raise issues of control and guidance. Given such diffuse, multifactorial, self-organizing, and soft-assembled organizational forms, how can we (or nature) intervene to push such systems in specific desired directions? We have already seen some hints of an answer to this question in the discussion of the way the central nervous system might promote successful reaching. The next section describes the clearest natural example of successful intervention in complex regimes: the role of DNA in the production of biological form.

Genes, Coaches, and Nannies

According to a certain traditional view, genetic material constitutes a kind of detailed recipe for the form of an adult organism. If so, knowing the complete sequence of an animal's DNA would allow you to predict the full adult form (its shape, structure, and so on) given just a few assumptions (such as the presence of sunlight and sufficient food and vitamins). A participant in the Human Genome Project once asserted that the chromosomes in the fertilized egg constitute "the complete set of instructions for development, determining the timing and details of the formation of the heart, the central nervous system, the immune system, and every other organ and tissue required for life" (Delisi, 1988, p. 488).

It is now becoming clear, however, that such radical instructionism wildly overstates the role of the genes. What the genes actually encode looks more like a minimal instruction set whose effects depend heavily on a variety of nongenetic sources of form and order (Goodwin, 1994; Maturana and Varela, 1987; Kelso, 1995; Keijzer, 1997). These nongenetic elements do not merely feed a prespecified process; they play an active role in determining the form and characteristics of the mature organism.

A simple example is the way the sex of a Mississippi alligator is determined (Goodwin, 1994, p. 38). It is not the chromosomes in the fertilized egg that select the sex of the offspring but the ambient temperature of the rotting vegetation in which the eggs are laid. At 26 to 30°C, eggs all become female alligators; at 31 to 33°C they are mixed; and at 34 to 36°C the eggs all develop into male alligators. Thus instead of having sex distribution regulated directly via the genes, as with humans, alligators as a species benefit from a kind of external lottery that appears to serve them equally well.

The case of chick imprinting provides a slightly more complex example (Elman and others, 1996; Johnson and Bolhuis, 1991). Newly hatched chickens rapidly become attached to the first mobile object they see—normally the mother hen. This "imprinting" is not a simple, prewired response but instead the emergent effect of the interaction of multiple processes, some genetic and some environmental. One neural system first disposes the chick to prefer stimuli that resemble the head and neck configuration of a bird. This causes the chick to pay close attention to the nearest such item. A second neural system that operates only for mobile stimuli of a certain size then kicks in, allowing the chick to learn to recognize such objects in different lights, from multiple angles, and so on. It is the combination of these two genetically determined factors, along with the consequent hen-attending behavior of the chick, that creates the special conditions in which the chick learns to recognize the mother hen from any angle and to follow her around.

It has been estimated that a full molecular specification of a human body would require 5×10^{28} bits of information, whereas the human genome contains only about 10^5 bits (Calow, 1976; reported in Elman and others, 1996, p. 319). The entire human genome does not have enough coding capacity to support a detailed plan of the human brain, much less of the whole brain-body system. As a result, nature must rely on a variety of less direct methods, such as the provision of well-chosen prompts and nudges applied to a system (the developing organism) that has its own intrinsic properties and dynamics and that is embedded in a complex environment rich in natural order. (Think, once again, of how evolution makes use of varying environmental temperatures to help determine alligator sex distribution.) Mature form can thus only be explained and understood by looking at the complex interactions that take place between the genetic materials, the developing organism, and the wider environment.

The biologist Brian Goodwin studies those aspects of cytoplasmic and environmental order that, in close concert with various genetic prompts and nudges, yield the distinctive forms of plants and animals. His study of phyllotaxis, for example, shows that the arrangement of leaves on plant stems is not directly genetically determined but instead results from the interaction of stress patterns during growth and from the way that the emergence of one leaf alters the patterns of cellulose resistance, which affects the location of the next leaf, and so on (Goodwin, 1994, pp. 105–119). The most common pattern in nature involves leaves emerging in spirals at a rotation of 137.5 degrees. Goodwin explains this regularity by using a variety of modeling studies to show that, given typical initial conditions for stress, resistance, and rate of leaf formation, the 137.5-degree pattern will predominate; other possible but less typical natural patterns will arise systematically from other less typical initial conditions. In this example, one salient and robust feature of the mature plant (its leaf pattern) is controlled not by direct genetic specification but by the complex interactions between what *is* genetically specified (that is, some aspects of the initial conditions) and the results of mechanical stress and compensation.

The lesson is that perhaps DNA never constitutes a full, detailed blueprint of the structure of any complex life form. Instead, DNA appears to generate its own strategic nudges and influences that make the most of a variety of extrinsic sources of order, such as mechanical stresses, the normal ecological environment of a chick, or the temperature of the vegetation in which alligator eggs are laid.

But genes *do* matter. Genes are nature's way of exploiting and channeling all those complex, heterogeneous, and nonlinearly interactive sources of natural order. They work not by detailed plans but—like coaches and nannies—by nudges to the system at crucial points and by the active creation of the conditions under which external sources of order and form can be maximally exploited. We can think of genes not as full and detailed instruction sets but as catalysts (Elman and others, 1996, p. 351), seeds, or modifiers (Goodwin, 1994, pp. 16, 144). Indeed, there is a debate over whether genes should be conceived as codes or instruction sets at all. Perhaps it is proper to view the genetic contribution as a kind of minimal instruction set: a recipe that succeeds only given the reliable presence of multiple sources of extragenetic order and control. (For full discussions, see Clark, 1998b; Clark and Wheeler, forthcoming.) Intrinsically, a catalyst is inert; but placed in the proper context, a catalyst can have a dramatic effect—it can initiate and maintain a chemical reaction that would otherwise not occur. Thus the active contribution of genetic elements is twofold: the genes create and maintain the local conditions under which self-organization, aggregation, and soft assembly can occur; and they actively influence the unfolding self-organizing system at crucial points in its development. (For a more complete discussion, see Clark and Wheeler, forthcoming.)

New Organizational Forms

The common principle that unites all these cases is the nature of control: not as a top-down imposition of prespecified form but as the selective application of relatively simple forces to a highly complex self-organizing system. This common principle applies equally to new economic markets, companies, and various innovative forms of business organization, for these too are examples of complex adaptive systems. How, then, can we apply these ideas to the understanding of control and intervention in firms and business?

It is useful to begin with an example: the biotechnology industry. The sociologist and theoretical economist Walter Powell (1996, p. 197) discerns, in the biotechnology market, the emergence of a "new logic of organizing"—one that depends critically on the principles of aggregation, scaffolding, self-organization, and soft assembly. The key features of this new logic are

1. The exploitation of open corporate architectures capable of making maximal use of external resources

2. The use of minimal hierarchical control structures both within individual companies and between interdependent ventures

3. Acceptance of waste and redundancy as the natural cost of a continuing search for diversity and for productive collaborations with other ventures

4. The development of complementary or cospecialized skills and assets as a stable and productive mode of collaborative organization

Points 1 and 4 relate directly to the use of external scaffolding in processes of soft assembly; points 2 and 3 reflect the need for active creation of the conditions for soft assembly and self-organization. (This list is an attempt to distill the main lessons of Powell, 1996, and is somewhat influenced by the related analysis of Stark, 1996.)

The biotechnology industry operates in a high-technology, research-intensive, high-uncertainty market. The typical products are new biologically engineered drugs and vaccines. The development of such products is time consuming, expensive, unreliable, and highly knowledge intensive. Traditional pharmaceutical companies operated in a much more stable and less knowledge-intensive regime. The focus was on direct competition to discover drugs that would help with a few major ailments, and the research procedure was to choose a demographically promising disease, define a model of it, and then simply to take compounds off the chemists' shelves and screen for efficacy (Powell, 1996, p. 204).

The biotech companies depart from this methodology by probing deeper into the causal and genetic mechanisms of disease and trying to engineer "designer drugs." What seems to have emerged in the last decade is a kind of new, symbiotic organizational form in which big pharmaceutical companies such as Glaxo, Roche, and Ciba-Geigy outsource their research activities to smaller biotech companies, which in turn work in close synchronization with each other and with university groups. The big pharmaceutical companies shoulder the burden of funding and overseeing the extended clinical trials needed to get a new drug on the market and the complex business of promoting and marketing drugs worldwide. An example is the recent development of an animal model for Alzheimer's research that grew out of a "symbiotic collaboration between 34 scientists, two biotech companies, a pharmaceutical company, a federal laboratory and a university department" (Powell, 1996, p. 205).

What all this amounts to is a kind of environmentally scaffolded, soft-assembled solution to a daunting business problem. The expertise and equipment of other firms and groups can be seen as a rich surrounding environment, ripe for exploitation by those businesses whose organizational forms and boundaries are sufficiently porous and responsive to allow them to profit from this potential scaffolding.

Biogen displays the full flavor of such a soft-assembled organizational mode. It is a biotechnology firm with 410 employees and at least thirty-seven close ties to outside groups that span the big pharmaceutical companies, university departments, and hospitals. More members of the core Biogen workforce work on products outside the firm, collaborating at other sites with members of other firms and research teams, than within it (Powell, 1996, p. 200).

Biogen displays all four of the key features sketched earlier. First, it is not a traditional self-contained drug discovery and marketing operation. Instead, it exemplifies an open corporate architecture in which crucial functions are easily and flexibly offloaded to external ventures capable of scaffolding its business activity—just as genes exploit environmental features, extracting maximal benefit from minimal internal encoding.

Second, such flexible reorganization is encouraged by a loose internal control structure that favors self-organization and involves minimal hierarchical control. To this end Biogen is organized around shifting project teams, and individual researchers are granted a great deal of freedom to pursue their favored lines of research, with merit pay for publication. Such researchers are encouraged to seek out and to form the external links required for their own specific projects. No strict hierarchy prevails among the various collaborating groups.

What forms is a "complex, multiparty web in which it is exceedingly difficult to pinpoint the center or starting point" (Powell, 1996, p. 209).

Third, Biogen is tolerant of the inevitable episodes of overlap, such as when several teams are pursuing closely related projects, and of failure. Waste and duplication inevitably accompany such a policy of "letting many flowers bloom." Biogen accepts this as part of the price for the kind of diversity and flexibility that bring other benefits. Stark (1996) stresses the way new organizational forms foster innovative research at the inevitable expense of on-the-spot optimality and efficiency. By maintaining an open organization tolerant of multiple, overlapping, even dead-end efforts, a company increases the likelihood that when some new environmental opportunity arises, it will be more closely positioned to benefit from it. To borrow Stark's example: it may be efficient in the short term to seek food where you have found it before; but it is a mistake to lock in that efficiency by suppressing the capacity to explore new territories, because in the long run the distribution of rewards may well change. Extensive internal diversity thus provides for rapid self-organized response to new opportunities and is one key to long-term adaptability and fitness.

Putting all this together, we derive the fourth and final feature (really a summary of the other three): Biogen has developed a kind of internal expertise that is specifically adapted to allow it to participate in multiple, collaborative ventures. The company is built to engage in soft assembly, to foster aggregation, and to self-organize in response to environmental opportunity. Considered in isolation from its many collaborators, Biogen might look like an impoverished unit; but in fact its interactive nature is one of its greatest strengths. It is highly specialized so as to maintain the specific skills and capacities that enable it to optimize new opportunities and derive maximum benefit from the economic and business environment.

The immediate task of management in such new knowledge-intensive and information-driven ventures is to create the internal conditions that allow the creation and maintenance of multiple collaborative endeavors. The manager's task is to facilitate these collaborative links; to encourage exploration; to promote internal diversity; to tolerate overlap, redundancy, and failure; to catalyze rather than dictate. The goal of management is not to draw up detailed blueprints for performance or change but to foster decentralized adaptation and create the broad conditions necessary for deriving maximum benefit from multiple sources of environmental order and opportunity.

Models, Tags, and Explicit Control

Whereas genes have matched their contributions by trial and error over evolutionary time to the reliable extragenetic features of a stable, normal ecological backdrop, the matching and externalization taking place in various high-technology markets and endeavors is happening in an environment of continuous change and instability. (See also David R. Johnson's discussion in Chapter Ten of the Internet as a self-organizing domain.) Nature's solution to the problem of coping with a rapidly changing, unstable environment must surely be identified as the brain, and especially the human brain—the kind of brain most strongly marked by cortical plasticity and flexible learning. Several adaptive features distinguish advanced human cognition: our capacity to learn in order to make the most of new environmental opportunities (as when a sailor first learned to use canvas and the wind to propel a boat); our ability to employ a variety of reflective tricks, such as the use of deliberate practice (taking sailing lessons, for example); and our penchant for creating highly scaffolded environments (the schoolroom or the consistently arranged and clearly priced shelves of a supermarket, for instance).

In a new business world that is an interacting web of fuzzy-boundaried, soft-assembled, self-organizing coalitions, it initially seems unclear what kind of role our more direct and deliberate attempts at management and control could play. Such things as computer models of the market, the imposition of tags, logos, trade-marks, symbols, and labels, or the articulation of explicit instructions, incentives, and game plans may at first appear not to have a useful purpose. Yet such practices, carefully conceived and flexibly implemented, can in fact greatly enhance the efficiency and flexibility of the newly emergent organizational forms.

We can begin by considering the fundamental and underappreciated process of tagging—providing a label for some salient object, feature, or procedure. (See also Chapter Four and Dennett, 1995.) Tags for products, teams, qualities, and the like support easy recognition and thus simplify communication. More important, they facilitate model building, thought, and problem solving. Recent work with a breed of small chimpanzees called pan troglodytes involving their ability to solve puzzles that require the detection of higher-order relations (that is, relations between relations) provides a striking example (Thompson, Oden, and Boysen, forthcoming). Spotting a situation in which there is a simple relation (such as the relation of sameness between two identical cups) is a first-order task well within the reach of chimps and other animals. A higher-order task would be, for example, to match one pair of identical items (the two cups) to a different pair of identical items (such as two identical shoes) or to match a pair that satisfies the relation "different" (say, a shoe and a padlock) to another pair that satisfies the same relation (a banana and a cup). The higher-order task is to match not the physical objects but the abstract relations between the objects.

Thompson, Oden, and Boysen show that the higher-order task is tractable only to chimps that have been trained to associate concrete tags (here, in the form of plastic shapes) with abstract features. Thus, for example, a plastic circle is a tag for the notion of "sameness," and a plastic square might tag "difference." The authors conclude that the practice of tagging itself opens up new problem-solving horizons to the tag-trained chimps.

The experience of tagging may provide the chimps with something closely akin to a new perceptual modality, like vision or touch

(Clark, 1998a). Tagging depicts certain features of our world as salient; it makes them pop out into our consciousness. What may be called "perceptual tuning" occurs when we learn to treat complex sensory patterns as specifying objects, which can then be attended to in ways that reveal patterns among them (much like the relations between relations in the case of chimps). Experience with the tags allows the chimps to treat the sameness of two items as a simple object: the complex, or abstract, relation is replaced by the simple, or tangible, tag. This effectively reduces the higher-order task of spotting relations between relations to the lower-order and easier one of spotting relations between tags. Such a process can be iterated: with the help of tags, an organism sensitive to several higher-order relations can treat them all as new objects and extend its search space to ever greater levels of abstraction and complexity. Human science is a testimony to the power of this process of iterative labeling and search.

In sum, tags play a dual role. They aid communication and interpersonal understanding, and they contribute to the fundamental processes of thought and reason, by providing new domains in which thought may operate. (Clark and Thornton, 1997, provide a more rigorous computational analysis of this idea.) The cognitive benefits of tagging are not, however, confined to individual thought. Any group, team, or company confronting a problem is also a system within which tags may play a fundamental and not merely communicative role. This role is somewhat parallel to the genetic case, for the tags, like DNA, do not participate in detailed plans and instructions that rigidly guide systemic activity; instead, the tags act in a variety of more subtle, modulatory, and catalytic ways. In particular, tagging can

Help create and maintain adaptively valuable diversity

Help create and stabilize the multiple external alliances characteristic of the new organizational forms

Participate in processes of diffuse control

Promote the kind of systemic self-understanding that underpins effective indirect intervention and control

Each of these points is discussed in turn below.

Create and Maintain Adaptively Valuable Diversity

Consider Stark's anecdote (1996) concerning the roadside rabbit breeder whose sign reads "Pets and Meat." This is a case in which a single resource is tagged twice, allowing it to participate in two very different economic regimes. Similar tag-driven diversity, Stark notes, is common in the emerging markets in Eastern Europe, where a company's survival can depend on its capacity to account for itself according to multiple standards. For example, a company may be eligible for central support only if it employs mainly local workers, but it may at the same time be assessed by potential investors in terms of net worth and market share. Companies operating in economies subject to rapid change and reorganization are often compelled to maintain a variety of identities and self-justifications, switching from one to another as opportunity and politics dictate.

Create and Stabilize External Alliances

Tagging can also help create and stabilize the kinds of powerful intergroup alliances highlighted in the Biogen case. The role of tagging here is to keep the collaborative elements in the sweet spot between too much disorder and excessively rigid order (see Chapter One). If the collaborations are becoming too complex, costly, and inefficient, it may be fruitful to allow only a few highly successful units to seek out new collaborative ties. Such units will be tagged, within the company and for the benefit of outside interests, as "effective collaborators." The use of tags to thus stabilize specific interactive regimes may be somewhat parallel to the role of the tags in the chimp experiments described above. In each case, the process of tagging creates a simple entity that is easy to identify and manipulate and that can subsequently participate in increasingly complex regimes. An example of this might be a university department and a company's project team becoming known as an effective extended unit and being jointly recruited into a new collaborative venture.

Participate in Processes of Diffuse Control

Tags and guidelines can also contribute to diffuse control. For example, they could be used to destabilize a system that has strayed from the sweet spot toward too much order. If, for instance, the number of successful external ties is low and stagnant, it may help to create new project teams and issue new labels and guidelines that encourage experimentation and reward attempts at collaboration as much as already successful joint endeavors. In such cases, tags and explicit guidelines function not to instruct the system (the company) directly but to modify the background conditions against which processes of diversification and self-organization operate according to their own intrinsic dynamics. The use of tags and guidelines thus constitutes a potent method of diffuse control, rather like the way the release of a certain chemical or neurotransmitter can bathe a whole population of cells, temporarily altering their overall behavior.

Promote Systemic Self-Understanding

A good set of tags is essential to explicit systemic self-understanding and self-analysis. The extent to which such self-understanding is possible within a complex adaptive system is yet unclear; the simplifications and distortions self-understanding inevitably imposes may well be intolerable in the context of a system of multiple nonlinearly interactive parts. Nonetheless, it seems clear that some attempt at self-modeling (perhaps with the help of computer simulations of the business and the market) is often fruitful and can play a role in successful intervention.

Creating Effective Tags

At this point, however, the lacuna in our story looms large. The question of how to create useful tags is surely one of the major unsolved problems in contemporary cognitive science (see, for example, Dennett, 1994, 1995; Clark and Thornton, 1997; Deacon, 1997). The survival of a company in an evolving, volatile market may depend on its adopting the right tag for its products, as when telephone companies began to identify themselves more broadly with information and telecommunication or when entertainment companies were reborn as media and communications giants. But the process by which a good tag is discovered or created remains ill understood, and there is still no substitute for human intuition and creativity at this point.

We can, however, keep one caveat in mind. The best tags will emerge from the interactions that currently characterize the workings of a system. It is not likely that tags simply imposed by high-level management will be sufficiently up-to-date and in touch with real operating procedures to effectively modulate the flow of activity. A better strategy is for management to observe actual working practices closely and to pay special attention to the vocabularies, groupings, and procedures that emerge from these real-world interactions. (See Chapter Five for some examples.) New tags should be inspired by—not imposed on—these emergent organization forms. In the case of the Internet, recent attempts by the government to fix the number and ownership of domains appears to be a case in which this caveat was not heeded and in which top-down imposition threatens to undermine—rather than sculpt and streamline—effective emergent practice.

In sum, tags are powerful and not yet fully understood tools for the analysis and control of complex adaptive systems. Such resources cannot simply be seen as imposing order on some relatively plastic base, as in traditional top-down models. Instead, the tags themselves constitute subtle forces that nudge systemic self-organization in certain directions. They are not mere shorthand for existing dynamics, but they are not elements of static blueprints either. It is best, perhaps, to see them as seeds or anchor points around which new organizational forms can soft-assemble: cheap but effective parts of the environmental scaffolding that supports complex problem solving and flexible response.

Conclusion: Management as Artificial DNA

Complex adaptive systems cannot be efficiently controlled by over-seers, detailed plans, or other sources of strict top-down control. Instead, the role of management must be to create the conditions for flexible, self-organizing response and to modulate the unfolding of intrinsic dynamics by the use of diffuse influences and the judicious application of simple forces and nudges. Here are a few key points to remember:

In businesses where knowledge, information, and innovation are at a premium and where the business horizon is marked by great uncertainty, flexible soft-assembled responses and the simultaneous cheap exploration of multiple options may be the key to success.

Management should aim to create the conditions that will allow the business to self-organize in response to environmental shifts and opportunities and should make timely use of outside resources, including other firms, as effective scaffolding for its activities.

Open or porous corporate architectures with minimal hierarchical structure and maximal inner diversity encourage boundary-crossing aggregation and collaboration and foster easy self-organization and exploratory groupings.

Do not underestimate the power of gentle interventions, such as the provision of new tags: this form of scaffolding and modulation can greatly increase the capacity for action and recombination within a complex regime.

Resist the urge to try too hard! The well-evolved business organization, not the manager, knows best. Listen to the system and try to intervene in ways that respect and maintain the successful strategies that emerge from the ground up.

Central to this theoretical picture is an image of individual companies as increasingly dependent on a process of matching themselves to an evolving set of external sources of order and opportunity. As in the biotechnology case, the best shot at market success may involve matching a given company's expertise and resources very closely to what might be termed a collaboration niche. In such a niche, a company contributes an essential, sometimes unique, set of skills and knowledge to a project that spans multiple companies and institutions, but its contribution is not, by itself, sufficient. An individual company is thus rather like the expert bartender, its successful performance depending not on internal resources alone but also on the way those resources are adapted to exploit a variety of powerful external sources of order and problem solving. As a result, the boundaries between core systems, whether companies or biological organisms, and the wider environment become more flexible and less clear-cut. This blurring of boundaries has practical, moral, and legal consequences. It affects our conception of the very nature of individuals and businesses, raising deep questions concerning accountability, reward, and the basic units of moral and economic significance. For example, it may be unclear whether it is the biotechnology firm or its loose academic partners, or the temporary union of both, that should be held accountable for some costly mistake or fatal error. Moreover, given the picture we develop, we cannot assume that a relevant boundary, once established, will always stay in the same place. Instead, we may confront a kind of fluctuating nexus of organization and order.

4

Tags

The Power of Labels in Shaping Markets and Organizations

John Henry Clippinger III

W hat's in a name? Everything: identity, power, prestige, stigma. To name, or tag, something is to exert power over it. Language, the ultimate tagging mechanism, gives us the power to create markets and organizations and to shape nature in our own image. Tagging is so much a function of who we are that it is virtually invisible to us.

In recent years, science has come to learn an enormous amount about the power of tags and "languages" across a variety of disciplines from genetics to evolutionary biology, sociobiology, cognitive and neural psychology, and especially linguistics. In *Consilience: The Unity of Knowledge*, E. O. Wilson (1998) argues that we are the beneficiaries of the confluence of a number of scientific discoveries. We are breaking out of our specialist enclaves and are on the cusp of achieving a coherent and unified scientific understanding of diverse physical, biological, psychological, and sociological phenomena. The complex adaptive systems (CAS) perspective is part of this larger trend, and the focus of this chapter is to draw on this new knowledge to show how tags are powerful instruments of order and selection in organizations and markets. Tags are the indispensable tools of management; tags, in a sense, are the "invisible hands" of management.

Tags are the outward displays—verbal, olfactory, sensual, visual—of internal conditions. The interpretations of those displays are the actions to be taken in response to them. These displays and responses in effect define the limits of community by prescribing the rules and protocols for shared activity. Tags stand for something that is recognizable to both the giver and the recipient, and therefore they are the building blocks of all systems of communication and exchange. Tags are the "currency" of social activity. Tags emerge from the interactions of different agents and act to bind together these agents around the shared meaning of the tags. Hence, tags act to define a community of interest or activity. These definitions, like the definitions of words, can be constantly changing and evolving. John Holland (1995) compares tags to DNA: "the capacities of an agent are completely determined by a small set of strings, the *chromosomes* defined over a finite alphabet . . . called *resources*. One class of chromosomes are 'tag' chromosomes, and these determine an agent's external-phenotypic characteristics—that is, what it displays to the world, which in a communications sense is what is transmitted. The other type of chromosomes (condition chromosomes) determine the conditions or responses that agents make to other agents' external or phenotypic tags."

Unless these two classes of chromosomes are coordinated, there cannot be even the simplest form of social organization. In 1986, Holland created a simulation model in which behavior consisted solely of trading, fighting, and mating (Holland and others, 1986). Each of these three types of social exchange had its own tagging system, and collectively these could be considered the "culture" of the group. Through this simple definition, Holland achieved in a scientifically explicit and measurable way a definition of culture covering a broad range of behaviors, from genetic behavior to all forms of social behavior (Holland, 1995).

Holland's approach offers a way of accounting for how natural selection applies to cultural and business organizations. For instance, in order for self-organizing behavior to emerge from a collection of independent agents, the focal point of selection is not the individual physical agent but the tags and conditions shared among all the agents. In other words, selective pressures are exerted on the expressiveness and the effectiveness of the tagging systems not on the physical or genetic attributes of the individual agent. Consequently, an organization that has unfit individuals, but a highly fit and effective tagging system, can perform more effectively than one that is made up of fit individuals but that lacks a good system of tags. Neither material circumstances nor even genetic fitness determines cultural or organizational fitness. It is, rather, the fitness of the system of tags serving all the individuals that really matters. In this sense, companies that may not have extensive capital, material resources, or even highly talented individuals can effectively compete if they have highly developed competitive corporate cultures and "teamwork."

The objective of this chapter is to show how tags can provide a wide range of powerful techniques for implementing bottom-up strategies to manage complex organizations. Building on the discussion of tags in Chapter One, this chapter delves into the mechanics and "grammar" of tags in driving self-organizing behaviors, examining the different types of tags and how the "semantics" of tags (what they refer to and how they are categorized and organized) are critical to achieving fitness and order. The discussion also draws on recent research in linguistics to describe the "DNA" of tags—the universal means by which tags encode their meanings. The chapter then shows how an understanding of the mechanics of tags can be used to provide new approaches for addressing typical problems in managing complex organizations. These problems include corporate culture and change management (how managers can use tags and self-organizing processes to evolve new corporate cultures and drive adaptive change management processes); managers as market makers (how managers can use the principles of tagging and self-organization to create markets for skills and knowledge); and tags and emergent markets (how managers, by viewing new markets as emergent tagging systems, can better identify market risks and effectively shape the course of market formation to reduce product introduction risks).

The Grammar of Tags

Scientists in fields as diverse as sociobiology, anthropology, and evolutionary biology have concluded that there is a kind of universal "grammar" that accounts for a wide variety of adaptive processes, from protein and immunological evolution to the formation of cultures, personalities, and markets (Wilson, 1998; Durham, 1991; Kauffman, 1993). Kauffman suggests that parallel-processing "neural networks" using such grammars are universal to all forms of complex adaptive behavior. He says that these neural networks "are somewhat like Holland's problem-solving algorithms called classifier systems, in which rules cast as binary strings trigger the firing of other rules, attain a fitness or 'strength' dependent upon the payoff in a mock economy, and co-evolve with other rules by mutation, recombination, and selection. In Holland's case the couplings are governed by match criteria by which the action part of one rule acts on the message condition part of another rule" (Kauffman, 1993). Such classifier systems are also known as genetic algorithms (see Chapter Eight).

Such grammars help us answer the primary question of this book: How does one manage between order and disorder to keep an enterprise in the "sweet spot" of optimum fitness? (See Chapter One for a discussion of the concept of the sweet spot.) One way of thinking about this problem is to think about how to find the right kind of tags to reconcile the need for diversity with the need for order in a particular context. The choice and application of these tag grammars is management's central task. Management uses tags to affect the supply and demand of critical skills and resources within the enterprise and, through marketlike mechanisms, to select for behaviors that enhance overall competitiveness. Tags are also the means by which management organizes and communicates the culture, experiences, and goals of the enterprise. Strong companies develop their own systems of tags for handling key business issues, and many of the newer high-technology systems companies have made the management of these cultural tags a critical component of their competitive advantage.

There is a deep correspondence between the organizing principles of language and those of genes. An insight into the processes and rules by which tags are formed elucidates the role tags play in forming organizations and markets. A manager who understands the mechanics and dynamics of self-organizing tagging systems has the means to design tagging systems that result in fit organizations, just as a scientist who understands gene sequences (the syntax, or grammar, of genes) and gene function (the purpose, or semantics, of genes) can create new gene-based therapies and technologies.

The Semantics of Tags

As a species, we are unique in our ability to symbolize and communicate. Through language we are able to create rich, diverse descriptions of our world and thoughts and to share and modify them with others. We are able to categorize and define the things around us according to how they make sense to us. Every human creation is a creation of language. We have specialized vocabularies for building systems of laws, precise technical languages for technologies and sciences, and richly symbolic and personal vocabularies for artistic, cultural, and religious expressions. All are variants of the same underlying generative principles that create all languages. Language is a rich, species-specific tagging system that defines the universe of potential human actions and expressions.

Whereas language could be considered just a form of "tag chromosome" because it does not necessarily entail any concrete action or behavior, what are called tagging systems in this chapter include both a set of actions and a set of labels (tags) that are, by their very definition, closely associated with the actions. The meaning of a tag in this sense is not just linguistic but behavioral as well. The semantics of our general language can be quite abstract and may entail no action or response. By contrast, tagging systems are a specialized sublanguage that semantically binds thoughts to actions.

The semantics of business-based tagging systems have a special operational character. Things, people, roles, actions, and processes are defined as they relate to behaviors; hence, to change a label entails a behavioral change or consequence. In the tagging systems of business, distinctions in categorical frameworks are made not in deference to abstract principles of knowledge and objectivity but as a means to effect concrete changes. A failure to clarify a job title or to characterize a task fully can result in management failure, not because the staff does not understand the "meaning" of the words but because the actions associated with the title are unclear or unknown. Likewise, a failure to define a new product or product category fully can result in market failure, not because the definition is incomplete or vague in linguistic terms but because it does not clearly specify an action that can be taken in terms of the product or category. Without a definition that clearly denotes an action, the buyer does not know what problem the product solves, an investor does not know how to categorize a company to price the shares, and a supplier does not know how to supply the right kind of components. The choice of tags can have strong sociocultural implications as well. Certain types of tags are pejorative, both because of the way they characterize an individual or a people and because of the consequences associated with those tags, such as ridicule, discrimination, or even murderous "ethnic cleansing." The power of a pejorative tag is to give the party assigning it implicit (or explicit) powers over whatever is tagged, and these powers can and do have material consequences.

Many of a language's greatest and most subtle powers are invisible to those who use it. They reside in the hidden assumptions behind the language we use: the implicit, the tacit, and the unexamined presuppositions. Since our languages and tagging systems are the consequence of tens of thousands of years of evolution, how we make sense of the world today still has its origins in how we made sense of it over forty thousand years ago. Times have changed, especially in the twentieth century, but our tagging systems are still captive to old categories (Deacon, 1997). Although it is commonly thought that all languages are equally expressive (that you can say in one language anything you can say in another), in fact there are distinct differences in how different languages categorize, or tag, their respective worlds. This becomes most apparent when comparing the semantic tags of cultures very different from our own with the semantic tags we use. The Dyirbal of Australia, for example, have a category called *bayi* that includes men, kangaroos, opossums, bats, most snakes, fish, fishing equipment, insects, the moon, storms, rainbows, boomerangs, some spears, and the willy wagtail bird. The Burmese have a classifier system (a grouping of nouns) that tags as equivalent the sun, airplanes, the ocean, and needles (both examples Beaken, 1996). Neither tagging system makes much sense to a Westerner or seems to have any explanatory value, unless one is familiar with the foundation myths of the culture from which the implicit tagging categories were derived.

The DNA of Tags

In Chapter Three, Andy Clark argues that management should act like DNA by instructing rather than attempting to determine specific outcomes. The study of genes provides a rich source of other analogies that are helpful in understanding the uses of tags. For example, we now know that genes alone do not determine the final expression or physical form of an organism. Rather they handle complexity by incorporating external environmental factors—what Clark calls "scaffolding"—into an organism's growth and differentiation. Clark points out that there are only an estimated 10^5 bits of information in the human genome whereas a full specification of a human body would require 5×10^{28} bits of information. Hence, there is no way that DNA itself could fully specify an outcome; instead, extensive use is made of the scaffolding of the external environment to provide the requisite additional information needed to create a mature adult. That information comes across in the form of tags.

From the perspective of tag management, this use of scaffolding means that tags evolve new meanings in new contexts and that the tag grammar for creating these new meanings is the key to adaptation. DNA has just four tags, or building blocks: adenine (A), thymine (T), cytosine (C), and guanine (G). These can be combined into "sentences" (such as CACGTGGACT . . .), each of which code for a specific tissue or cell type. Language has many similarities to DNA and its four building blocks. The building blocks, or universal tag categories, can be used not only to translate across different language groups but also to recognize how languages change and adapt to add new terms and meanings. Pustejovsky (1995), Moravcsik (1998), and their colleagues have explained that the equivalent of DNA for tags is a lattice-like structure that provides a universal grammar by which to recognize the different ways in which things are tagged and explained.

Tags, like words, can be defined according to what Pustejovsky (1995), borrowing from Aristotle, calls their "qualia." Every tag or word is functionally defined by four distinct criteria (qualia): formal (its "dictionary" definition); telic (its purpose); constitutive (what it is a part of or related to); and agentive (how it came into being). Associated with these four qualia are syntactic and semantic contexts that capture certain types of grammatical expressions containing the four different types of explanations or descriptions about the tag and its object. The formal definition (essentially the "dictionary" definition) of the tag *hammer*, for example, is "a tool for pounding." The telic definition (purpose) is determined by how the thing represented by the tag is used, its purpose or its goal; in the case of *hammer* "to strike and drive in nails." The constitutive definition (what the tag is part of or related to) derives from what the object to which the tag refers is made of. The constitutive definition of a hammer is "a metal head and a handle." The agentive definition (how it came into being) has to do with how the tagged object came into existence: hammers are made by people or manufactured by machines; they are not "natural" objects but artifacts of human effort.

Not all tags have all their slots or qualia filled out. Many are underdefined or underspecified. Many word or tag meanings are inherently ambiguous; tags only take on specific meanings or expressions when they occur in highly specific contexts. Whereas technical and scientific terms, for example, are highly specified and unambiguous, general vocabulary terms and tags are inherently underspecified and "promiscuous" in the meanings they can take on.

Brands are tags that acquire their meaning through the interactions of the product, the company, the customer, and the public. Good, durable brands are not imposed from above but emerge and evolve from the customer's experience with the product. The formal definition of the brand (that is, the name given) can be constant, but the meaning of the brand (the constitutive, telic, and agentive definitions) may change dramatically. Since brands acquire their meanings over time, they may become stale and fail to reflect new values of the market. Many well-recognized consumer brands, such as Coca-Cola, Levi Strauss, Nike, or Procter & Gamble, have had to reinvent the underlying definitions or semantics of their brands as consumer tastes and demographics have changed. In some cases, the formal tag name (say, Betty Crocker) may be so closely associated with a highly specific and dated definition (agentive), that the formal name cannot survive the change in values and tastes. In the case of other consumer brands, such as Coca-Cola, the formal name has proved to be highly durable and has readily acquired new meanings without having to be changed. Coca-Cola as a company has been a master of brand management for its different beverage lines—Diet Coke, Classic Coke, Mountain Dew, Sprite, PowerAide—by preserving the continuity of the formal name (the brand tag) while adapting it to new meanings and definitions. For example, Mountain Dew has acquired a new telic definition (how it is used) associating it with consumption by active youth, while its constitutive definition (the recipe) and its agentive definition (who makes it) have remained unchanged. The BMW brand of quality and "the ultimate driving machine" may be less affected by fad, but they are vulnerable to any failure of the product to perform as expected (any change in its telic definition).

Brand managers need to understand the contexts and the qualia conditions under which their products are tagged and retagged. They must be concerned about having tags and words acquire highly specific meanings, and they must understand how tags take on or discard certain meanings. The reason is that tags will necessarily assume and shed meanings. The better that managers understand this, the better they can manage the tagging systems that influence the complex organizations for which they are responsible.

An example of how this works is the straitjacket imposed by "legacy tags" in the corporate world. Consider the Regional Bell Operating Companies, which in the midst of rapid technological change and deregulation are struggling to redefine themselves in terms of a competitive environment and a new technology base. But the old tags hamper them as they keep attempting to reduce the new to the old and the familiar: new technologies and services are priced, packaged, and sold under the old labels. For example, distance-based pricing no longer bears any relation to costs or to customer value, but it hangs on as a legacy of the old regulatory environment. The dysfunctional legacy tags of pricing, market definition, and related noncompetitive habits subvert innovation. At the time of the PC revolution in the mid-1980s, IBM made a similar mistake, but it recovered; Prime, Apollo, Wang, and DEC did not.

Corporate Culture and Change Management

Making cultural changes entails changing how groups within a company tag and respond to events and to one another. Shared meanings are essential to achieving shared and coordinated goals. Yet as the principles of complex adaptive systems tell us, it is counterproductive to impose tag definitions from above; they must emerge from the interaction of the parties who are involved in implementing and expressing the change. To bind groups together and create a coherent identity, tags need to evolve out of the interactions of the participating groups.

The role of the manager is thus to provide the right combination of context and fundamental grammars to shape the outcomes of the self-organizing processes and achieve the desired strategic goals. Managers also need to appreciate the different grammatical rules that different functional and professional groups have. Often a tag such as "innovation," with the same formal definition to everyone, may have a very different interpretation and meaning (the telic definition) for a marketing group than for a research group and thus may invoke a different kind of behavior in each group.

The ability to master different types of tagging systems and to affect how tags are assigned to you and your peers may be critical to a successful career in any large enterprise. Job titles are tags, as are performance evaluations, professional qualifications, social and educational status, and personal reputations. Getting stuck with the wrong tag can be career limiting. Corporate promotion can be as much about a proficiency in dodging the assignment of undesired tags as it is about achieving performance targets. Every company has not one but many cultures, each with its own jargon and tagging conventions. The rising manager must know at which level he or she is operating, and in which culture, and read the tags correctly. Those who can read multiple types of tags—the corporate cultural codes—become effective participants, and those who cannot, even though they may be formally designated as members, remain outsiders. In some cases, the rules of one group are almost the inverse of those of another. For example, technical staff, engineers, and programmers may tend to be highly explicit and outspoken in their exchanges, without the subtlety and indirection that are often necessary at the higher levels of an enterprise. By contrast, at the senior-management and board level, what is not said can often be more important than what is said. Those not familiar with such rules may erroneously conclude that implied action is inaction. But through their very avoidance of being explicit and direct, senior managers and board members can launch processes that would be impossible to initiate directly.

The power and survival value of cultural tags is dramatically illustrated in the formation and survival of military cultures. Many military histories focus on the evolution of weapon technology as the driving force of military success, but in many cases, from Alexander the Great to the Vietcong, it was the "soft stuff" of tags that enabled armies that were outnumbered and outgunned to defeat "superior" opponents. It is tags, in the form of commands that derive their meanings from training and drill, that tell soldiers what to do. Military cultures are organized around tagging systems that give a coherent sense of membership, purpose, status, value, and even protection in exchange for loyalty, skills, and obedience. The British, Roman, Macedonian, and Ottoman militaries succeeded in great measure through their ability to achieve a coherent organizational identity. The decisive military advantage in each of these cases was neither sword nor shield, but culture—systems of tags that functioned brilliantly to serve the needs of the individuals, bind their loyalties, and advance the overall purpose of the dominant culture.

Languages are themselves self-organizing. They are forever spawning new vocabularies, jargons, and rules; new sublanguages emerge to give a new symbolic order to a culture, profession, or subculture. Language systems grow by combining categories and by differentiating them. The combination of two established categories into a new semantic type is called a "complex type" in linguistics (Pustejovsky, 1995). Although the resultant category may appear to be a composite of two prior categories—for example, horse and carriage—it may reflect something entirely new, such as the "horseless carriage." Even if it is "logically" wrong, a new category has to have a starting point within, or be connected to, an established category. However, it is often difficult to break the attachment to prior categories; the first horseless carriages were equipped with buggy-whip holders. If well adapted to its environment, the new category will rapidly evolve away from the old ones, just as, over time, the category of horseless carriage evolved into the autonomous category of the automobile. Hence, we see that tags must sometimes shed meanings as well as acquire them in order to survive, and the manner in which they do this indicates the selective pressures being applied to the tag.

The Manager as Market Maker

Organizations have the same self-organizing and emergent properties as languages. One way of thinking about organizations is as a collection of coordinated internal tag markets organized around functional areas. How might these internal tag markets work for knowledge management, project management, or product innovation? The simplest and most unobtrusive approach might be to use popularity or demand for some knowledge, product, or skill as a surrogate tag for market value. How far and how fast an idea travels through an organization is often indicative of its value. So by providing a tag that makes visible to everyone in a group or division what is hot and what is not—sort of a "top 100" list of skills by category—a manager can identify which skills are in demand. Others can respond by developing those skills to meet the demand. The manager should not have to organize a skill database actively or recruit people for projects, because if the rewards are identified, workers can refer to the tags to self-select and self-organize to obtain the skills, thus satisfying the demand.

Intranets where all workers have their own Web sites can be powerful vehicles for implementing such an approach because of the ease of measuring click-throughs and downloads and of tagging transactions and content. Jobs, for example, could be tagged and rated not only in terms of salary and promotion prospects but according to other more contextual criteria, such as flextime or degree of interest, challenge, and fun. Workers in the system could use tags to rate the attractiveness or the likelihood of rewards for certain jobs, in much the same way that vendors in electronic auction systems such as eBay are rated by purchasers.

Such an approach, although unobtrusive and a natural by-product of how people work, still does not utilize the full potential and power of a market mechanism. A spectacular supplier of innovations or knowledge cannot, for example, accumulate "capital" or credits for outstanding performance and cash them in for money, prestige, free time, or new work opportunities. Nor can a manager who wants to increase the supply of certain forms of knowledge, and discourage the production of others, manipulate how the credits are assigned. Making the transition to this next level of self-organization, where the process behaves more like a market, requires issuing a new "currency" of tags specifically designed to increase the supply of the desired type of intangible corporate resources, such as knowledge, skill sets, favors, and innovations. As the issuer of this tag currency, a manager can influence the supply of certain types of knowledge by tagging the knowledge object by type and pricing it sufficiently high to attract suppliers. By giving buyers of knowledge products tag currency "budgets," the manager can initiate a process that does not involve micromanagement. Rather, the manager would act like a miniature version of the chairman of the Federal Reserve, heating up or cooling off the knowledge market by manipulating the cost and supply of credits and adjusting the "conversion rates" for specialty tag currencies into other currencies or perquisites.

Managers may be able to use their authority in order to give and collect favors and credits—in effect to monopolize and direct the markets of knowledge, skills, and credits to their own ends. Such market mechanisms could be used to depoliticize certain management practices and align them better with the overall interests of the enterprise and its shareholders. A tangible measure of success would be the degree of liquidity achieved in these specialty internal markets. Liquidity indicates the important CAS properties of diversity and flows; thus it may also be a good predictor of fitness.

It may seem that to introduce such tagging mechanisms into a corporation or organization is something of a contrivance and contrary to the natural character of organizations. However, markets are merely a more deliberate, developed, and numerically explicit implementation of the natural methods of exchange that characterize all social groups. All societies have elaborate tagging and typing conventions to ensure that the appropriate exchanges take place. At the core of these social exchange systems are kinship systems that evolved over tens of thousands of years to support the stable exchange of goods and to form coalitions for defense and warfare. To decode the tagging conventions of kinship systems is to understand how a culture governs its primary exchange systems. The "currency" of kinship-based exchange systems is a set of codified obligations and ritualized exchanges. The exchange between parties is not set by price but by fixed conventions and role relationships. In contemporary organizations such as corporations and bureaucracies, exchange systems are no longer governed by kinship tags but by legal, professional, and operational tags that can also carry their own legal requirements and privileges. Exchange systems are ubiquitous and fundamental to all forms of social organization.

Formal exchange systems and tags, however, tend to become dated, out of touch, and dysfunctional. Under such circumstances, informal systems often emerge from below and self-organize to fill the void. Such informal networks have their own rules and tags and are often not even acknowledged by the official organization. The challenge is to recognize that this is a natural process and that tagging systems are being invented and abandoned all the time. Rather than fight this process, companies should capture it and cultivate it to their desired ends.

Some companies are already starting to do this. For instance, in many high-tech companies, technical support for computer problems is often better performed through an informal channel of quid-pro-quo's than through formal technical support channels. In some companies, the official channels *are* the informal ones. John Seely Brown (1997), chief scientist and director of Xerox Parc, documented similar subculture self-organizing effects among the sales and technical support staff at Xerox. Xerox Parc anthropologist Lucy Suchman said that "formal office procedures have almost nothing to do with how people do their jobs" (Brown, 1997). The informal language and subculture of the salespeople and support personnel is what really works, even in the face of management's efforts to eradicate it. People on the front lines, close to the customer, often know what works better than their bosses do. Brown (1997) concludes: "If local innovation is as important and pervasive as we suspect, then big companies have the potential to be remarkably innovative—if they can somehow capture this innovation and learn from it. Unfortunately, it is the rare company that understands the importance of informal improvisation—let alone respects it as a legitimate business activity." One of the goals of this book is to make this less rare, to unlock the powers of self-organization.

Managing Organizational Markets Toward the Sweet Spot

Understanding the role of tags and other CAS principles, a good manager will monitor the behavior and structure of the markets and tags to see how well they are generating and allocating the supply of goods, services, knowledge, cooperation, or other needs. The manager should look to see if the market is too chaotic: perhaps it has too many categories, too many suppliers, too many changes; perhaps it lacks the stability and order necessary for stable relationships to develop, roles to form, and exchanges to take place. Then the manager would reduce the number of categories and supplies and introduce greater order by simplifying roles and relationships. Or the manager may find that the market is too ordered and rigid; that it is failing to recognize the important characteristics of new terms; that it has not introduced the requisite variety into the organization. In this case the manager would intervene by adding tags and relaxing the selection rules, thereby increasing the number and diversity of tags and relationships. The manager should act to achieve the right balance between too much order and too much chaos, using tags to help keep the organization in the sweet spot. Application of these principles to a variety of settings is illustrated in Chapters Five and Ten, and elsewhere throughout *The Biology of Business*. Following are a few more examples.

Consider a large computer hardware company trying to innovate in a mature product line, say printers, and finding that few genuine innovations are forthcoming. The suppliers of the innovations and the rules for supplying acceptable candidate innovations are limited to the individuals and roles that have historically been involved in the process. There are too few suppliers, the specification of what is to be supplied is too narrow, and the incentives for entering the market are too low to attract creative product innovators. The CAS manager who takes note of these facts will realize that the flows of ideas, proposals, and prototypes have become highly constrained: a few people act as gatekeepers and perpetuate a pattern of relationships that have begun to fail. The manager discovers that the labels being applied are legacy tags that no longer reflect the tags of the customer or marketplace. Finding no emergent tag types that combine existing tag types into new tag types, the manager determines that there is very little real innovation. To foster the needed innovations, the manager does not have to call meetings and individually instruct, cajole, inspire, and direct all players. Rather, the manager systematically deregulates the process by expanding the number of supplier tags, relaxing the rules that govern who can contribute, changing the underlying specifications for candidate innovations, and using new tags to change the flows among participants. Customer tags are brought into the design process, and the incentives and rewards are raised to attract innovative players from elsewhere in the firm. The manager fosters an environment of managed chaos.

Consider the contrary case, more typical of a smaller and newer high-technology company trying to survive in a highly competitive, highly innovative market driven by three-month product cycles. The danger here is that the chaotic, competitive, and quick-changing marketplace can render the product innovation process chaotic and dysfunctional. The result can be a pathology called the Red Queen Effect, in which everything goes faster and faster but makes no forward movement (Ridley, 1993). In such hypercompetitive environments, where competitors are tightly coupled to one another in reciprocal product cycles, the challenge becomes not letting the competitor's tags dictate the terms of the competition, like a runaway arms race, but rather to retain control over the product and the customer tags. As in a competitive sport, the goal is to make your opponent play your own game, to govern the reciprocal product interactions so that the rules favor your core competencies. You would not want to compete, as for example Netscape did with Microsoft, on capacity and resources, for even if you win against a larger foe, your victory could be Pyrrhic. To succeed under these very difficult circumstances requires the selective enhancement of order in the product development process. If there is too much order, the product may not be responsive and timely; but if there is too little order, things may become chaotic and ill defined, letting the competitor dominate the market. Here the manager needs to be attuned to the origin and nature of the tags: Do they reflect the customers' criteria or those of the competitors? Are they genuinely innovative? Do they build on the company's core competitive strengths? In hypercompetitive conditions, the objective must be to build your brand and to not let your competitors dilute it. This, again, entails a knowledge of how to manage the processes by which tags indicating quality are assigned and valued.

Tags and Emergent Markets

Standard economics embodies a mechanistic view of human and market behavior. With the rise of the Internet, the knowledge economy, and especially e-commerce, this deeply ingrained view is rapidly being challenged by economic theories better suited to the new digital, knowledge economy. In Chapter Two, W. Brian Arthur proposes an organic view of markets that represents a radical departure from classical economics. He argues that most economic circumstances cannot be characterized by rational models; instead, economic analysis must take into account the manner in which beliefs and preferences are tagged and how markets self-organize around these beliefs. Arthur argues that "the economy itself emerges from our subjective beliefs. These subjective beliefs . . . are the DNA of the economy. [They] are not deductively determinable in advance. They coevolve, arise, decay, change, mutually reinforce, and mutually negate." How do you represent those actors' beliefs that Arthur calls the DNA of the economy? How is it possible to have an economics of subjectivity? The answer is tags, which also coevolve, arise, decay, change, mutually reinforce, and mutually negate. Beliefs are expressed through tags. Markets are constructed and transacted through the interchange of tags. Expectations about price are but one form of tags that shape market behavior. In markets that are driven by young technologies yet to be developed into marketable products, a language model provides a more accurate way of describing and predicting market behavior. Markets emerge through the interaction of many agents, each of whom is attempting to establish stable and mutually agreed-upon product categories, value propositions, and buyer-seller roles and relationships. In early markets the DNA of tags (the various subtle definitions, or qualia) is not yet fully formed. The different participants do not yet know how to value or price the product; how to relate it to known product categories; how to establish viable and sustainable buyer-seller, supplier, and distributor roles. Rather than being a series of "rational" choices, early market activities are more like multiple conversations in which the participants are trying to agree on terms and definitions. Just as traders probe capital and currency markets to discover prices, so do product market innovators probe emerging markets to help define new product categories and market relationships. The objective of these probes or conversations is to find those "mutually reinforcing relationships" that Arthur (Chapter Two) says are "reminiscent of the origin of life, in which the emergence of subpopulations of RNA in correct combinations allows the subpopulations to become mutually reinforcing."

The challenge is to bring emerging markets to life. Rather than allowing this to be a random process of blind natural selection, one can employ a more detailed understanding of the self-organizing properties of languages and tags to make it a more managed or "bioengineered" process. Just as the grammars that govern the emergence of new languages and sublanguages parallel genetic evolution, so similar laws and grammars govern market behavior.

Nowhere are the forces of emergence and complexity more evident than in Internet markets. Neither capital nor product markets have quite figured out what the real Internet market categories and business propositions are. There is enormous debate about the appropriate business models for the Internet. How do you make money? How do you price your goods and services? The frictionless nature of transactions on-line and the ease with which individual needs and preferences can be addressed have shifted enormous bargaining power to the consumer. In some cases, near-perfect market information has given the consumer the power to drive down the margins in e-businesses. Information and software are being given away. On-line retailers (such as Buy.com) are even selling products below cost on the expectation that they can make it up on advertising.

Internet capital markets are fueled by expectations about future earnings. Because no one can predict who will win and who will lose or what the business models will be, valuations are completely expectation based. Given the absence of reliable pricing models, price is subjective and vulnerable to the bubble effects of mutually reinforcing expectations. Until a new order emerges—a new grammar of product categories, market roles, and relationships—the Internet market will continue to be inherently speculative. This is not to say that Internet and digital technologies will not transform the global economy; they are already doing so. However, product categories and valuations are unlikely to be stable or sustainable for the near term. Who can say yet whether Internet portals constitute a viable product or service category? Who can say yet that the hypercompetition among on-line retailers will not result in many Pyrrhic victories? An enormous amount of capital is being invested to achieve an advantage for an unknown future. Just as the one who frames the argument or who speaks the mother tongue has a disproportionate advantage, so do the first movers into emerging markets. However, it is not yet clear where, precisely, a market can or will emerge. In 1997, no less an authority than Kevin Kelly, author of *Out of Control* (1996) and *New Rules for the New Economy* (1998), pronounced definitively on the cover of *Wired* that Push technologies were the transformative technologies of the Web (Kelly and Wolf, 1997). Push technologies were the received wisdom, and those in the know anointed them and invested in them. Pointcast, as the leading Push vendor, was the darling of the digerati. Push technology was thought to have solved the pricing problem for the media companies, distributors, advertisers, and software companies. Channels on the desktop, mimicking television and other known media models, were the answer.

However, for as much as big players pushed to make it happen, Push technology did not: neither the technological innovation nor the value propositions (tags) materialized to make Push technology work. Push technology was imposed, not organic, and it never took root and grew. The tags were not right for consumers, content providers, advertisers, or distributors. They did not catalyze into a self-organizing, self-sustaining process. The Web is too different to mimic old mass media. Instead, "search engines," which soon became "portals," displaced Push technologies and channels as the means by which consumers could be aggregated. Challenging the portals are the auction and community-building services such as eBay, GeoCities, Tripod, and Hotmail. These suggest that the new and stable commerce and business models that will emerge from the Web are likely to build on the powerful one-to-one, many-to-one, and one-to-many aspects of the Web.

The Web will select for its own grammar that derives from its unique architecture. It is proving much stronger than even its greatest advocates thought possible. It has not been folded into more traditional business models but, rather, is in the process of folding virtually every business and form of human organization into itself. The Web has produced a new business ecology and thereby introduced new criteria for fitness and survival.

Conclusion

As we move away from objectivist models of markets and organizational behavior, tags assume a deeper, more important role in our understanding and control of both markets and organizations. Tags are the tools of the invisible hand: they allow for management influence without excessive management intrusion. Proficiency in the creation and selective application of tags will characterize the CAS manager of the next millennium, who will abandon attempts to exert managerial control and turn instead toward achieving organizational balance.

5

Complex Adaptive
Knowledge Management
A Case from McKinsey & Company

Brook Manville

That we now live in a "knowledge economy," in which knowledge represents an ever-increasing share of the value of products and services, is understood by more and more business leaders (Micklethwait and Wooldridge, 1996; Drucker, 1993). A new discipline of knowledge management has arisen, which can be broadly defined as a systematic approach to fostering the creation, sharing, and application of knowledge for enhanced organizational performance (Manville, 1998; Davenport and Prusak, 1998). This chapter explores one key dimension of knowledge management—the classifying of knowledge for easy access by workers seeking to build knowledge and apply learning to business problems—with a new perspective drawn from the evolving theory of complex adaptive systems (CAS).

The vehicle for the discussion is a case study of the international strategy consulting firm McKinsey & Company, where I am a partner. I compare the firm's approach to knowledge management over the last decade to one informed by CAS theory and argue that CAS theory offers a better approach than the one the firm originally followed and a better approach than those taken in knowledge management programs in many other companies today. The chapter concludes by describing a new intranet community initiative based on a self-organization or "complexity" model, whose early results support the argument that this is a superior way to manage the knowledge of an organization. (Knowledge management at Mc-Kinsey & Company has been treated by several commentators; the best recent discussion is Bartlett and Ghoshal, 1997.)

Knowledge Management

"Knowledge management" has become a controversial concept, partly for the confusion the term has engendered and partly for its over-hyped promise. The phrase means different things to different people and has become conflated with other concepts of the knowledge economy such as "competing on competencies," "building a learning organization," and "leveraging intellectual capital." (See, for example, *California Management Review*, 1998.) The over-hyped promise stems from the claims of various providers—and the quick assumption of many observers—that knowledge management offers a single technique for curing all the ills of ignorance in an organization.

Clearly, there can be no "silver bullet" for managing knowledge in the broad-based and rapidly changing new economy, and whether we talk about competing on competences or about building a learning organization, it is fundamentally true that knowledge is more important than ever to companies. How then, in this new economy, can a business maximize this important asset? Silver bullet or not, pragmatic approaches are needed, and for the last several years, many companies have vigorously pursued knowledge management programs.

The first generation of approaches shared a common assumption that knowledge was essentially the same as information: codified, structured data in a meaningful context, such as market research, customer contact information, news reports, and "lessons-learned" checklists (Davenport and Prusak, 1998). Strategies in this early phase of management application merely continued the information management approaches of previous years—building databases, installing technology, and collecting, disseminating, and retrieving information, to enhance sharing and access by "knowledge workers." The second generation realized that much of any organization's knowledge (arguably the most important part) is based in its people and cannot be readily collected or disseminated. Judgment, experience, skills, the previous learning of workers—so-called tacit knowledge—became the target of management approaches that sought techniques and processes to make the implicit explicit: to "extract" knowledge from people and codify it for dissemination and use by others (Polanyi, 1966). A third generation faced the difficult task of extracting knowledge from people who might not have even realized they had it. This generation developed techniques for fostering learning and exchange through more social approaches, such as expert networks, team-based organizational design, structured storytelling, and so on (Nonanka and Takeuchi, 1996; Wenger, 1998).

The Classification Challenge

In every generation of management approaches, the issue of classification and cataloging of knowledge remains a central challenge (Davenport, 1997). Whether the knowledge is published information, experience that can be codified, or tacit judgment, identifying and marking it so others can find and use it is a precondition for deriving value from it. The human mind cannot find and take advantage of what others know without some structure to organize and categorize; in the oceans of knowledge in any organization, where does one begin, and how does one select, without some guide to the universe?

Creating a guide—a classification scheme—for any body of knowledge is notoriously difficult. How does one find the right categories to sort the knowledge? Knowledge is not static but continues to grow and change. So how does one keep categories alive and flexible but still sufficiently standardized to facilitate easy recognition? There is also the relativism problem: the labels and language one person uses to describe a concept will be different from those of the next person. As for knowledge that is tacit or unspoken, how does one find the right categories and put what is found into the appropriate bins?

Despite the obstacles, the value of categorization cannot be denied. Thus, knowledge classification schemes abound, and every knowledge management program in use today has at its base some kind of framework. Whether it is customer knowledge (for example, key accounts, other U.S.-based accounts, the rest of the world), knowledge of processes (for example, treatment of paper or leather), knowledge of products (equity derivatives or fixed income derivatives), knowledge of people's skills (competence in basic materials, competence in microchip design), somebody in charge of organizing a company's collective knowledge has had to develop a method for classifying and cataloguing that knowledge.

At the same time, everybody using a classification system, even the person who developed it, will be quick to acknowledge its frailties. There are always a few cases that just do not fit or some new concept or type that was not around when the system was implemented. Every scheme has some "miscellaneous" categories; nobody is very happy with that, but we all live with it. Every classification scheme represents an imperfect model of reality.

Imperfection is partly the nature of the beast, but it is also perhaps partly a reflection of an outdated mindset that is often brought to the task. Implicit in the usual process of developing a classification system are a few key assumptions: that someone in a central position in the organization can understand enough of all the rest of the organization to devise all the categories that might matter to anyone; that categories can be determined with sufficient permanence that the scheme will not need constant revision; and that even if some people in the organization do not buy into the categories, they can and ought to be forced to accept them.

Many knowledge management programs are based on these assumptions, which might be labeled an "engineering mindset." From this perspective, the organization is seen as a kind of machine.

When pursued with an engineering mindset, knowledge management is akin to the development of a list of parts and a set of operating instructions.

If, by contrast, the knowledge management task of classification were based on the CAS principles of self-organization, different assumptions would prevail: that nobody in a central position can really understand enough to develop all the relevant categories for any large organization; that good classification is by nature impermanent; and that when people in the organization do not buy into some categories, this is not a problem but an opportunity to foster a richer diversity of knowledge in support of innovation and adaptability.

A CAS perspective offers a more organic view of the organization. Rather than seeking to diminish the complexity of the many moving parts (the knowledge workers), a CAS approach embraces the complexity. This organic model seems attractive, but it calls into question management per se. Is there something practical one can do to "manage" knowledge while embracing complexity? Or is it simply a matter of not managing at all? Does embracing complexity mean that there should be classification schemes consisting of millions of categories? If so, would this really be an advance? Even if it pleased all the dissenters, would anyone ever find anything?

McKinsey's Early Efforts at Knowledge Classification

To answer these questions, I turn now to the case of McKinsey & Company, where I helped develop the first knowledge management programs. In 1987, I was asked to join a new project at McKinsey intended to enhance the building and sharing of knowledge. This first knowledge management initiative was the result of a worldwide diagnostic exercise performed by some of the firm's consultants. It found that McKinsey was missing huge opportunities for serving clients better by not taking advantage of what we collectively knew. A subsequent report recommended the implementation of new programs and infrastructure such as databases, directories, and dedicated coordinators of information to make our internal market of knowledge sharing work better.

The initiative also set as a goal the establishment of a catalog of key words that could adequately encompass and describe our firm's management research and consulting work with clients around the world. The goal of this "knowledge architecture" was to label specific kinds of management consulting experiences, such as codified reports of engagements conducted with different clients and documents of multiclient research projects, so that consultants seeking to leverage what was done before could more quickly get up to speed on what the firm as a whole already knew. Our codified experience was collected in a few central databases. The keyword system was intended to help the firm's generalist consultants find reports, summaries, and documents more quickly and thus get help from other experienced consultants whose names were listed on the documents, to answer such questions as: What is the right way to approach restructuring a bank? What do we know about organizational design for oil companies? What is our latest thinking about market segmentation strategies for large-scale retailers?

Functional Classification

All of our reports and documents could be relatively accurately classified on the industry level. Standardized classification schemes for industries existed, and apart from the debates about nuances (such things as the difference between the travel and transportation industries or health care versus health delivery), the frameworks worked fairly well, needing only occasional updating and tuning. The trickiest part of our task had to do with "functional classification," which involves themes that apply across specific industries. In the example of restructuring a bank, that would mean the "restructuring" part of the problem rather than banking per se; in "organizational design for oil companies," it would mean organizational design rather than the industry context of the oil business.

Functional classification is difficult and uncertain; it has bedeviled all classification efforts. This kind of knowledge is at the heart of a management consultant's problem solving, but attempting to codify and classify it represents a mare's nest of controversies. What one consultant calls "organizational design" may be called "change management" by another; what is "marketing strategy implementation" for some may be known to others as "channel management tactics." Adding to the complexity of our earliest efforts to develop a functional classification system were the bits of jargon and shorthand McKinsey consultants would use for particular kinds of engagements. For example, a special cost reduction process was called AVA (for "activity value analysis"). If one is trying to capture and classify all the consulting experience that the firm builds, what are the right words to use in a context where people refer to similar things in so many different ways? Could a standardized framework for this kind of knowledge be devised? If so, who would decide what the right words would be? These were the challenges my colleagues and I faced as we worked on our knowledge management program in 1987.

Such dilemmas are similar to those faced by any organization trying to capture, codify, and classify its unique experience in ways that create value for its clients or customers. The same issues of language, standardization, and common versus unique terminology are relevant to, for example, engineering firms, HMOs, pharmaceutical research and development organizations, or manufacturing enterprises. The approach currently accepted as the best for addressing these problems is the one I developed for McKinsey: to create a relatively limited list of keywords, with a limited hierarchy of subterms, that most people buy into; to test and revise candidate terms with various outspoken practitioners and users; and to find an appropriate authority within the organization to resolve conflicts and provide a stamp of approval for the final framework. Add to this solution the safety valve of a robust thesaurus of synonyms so that those who type in a favorite term will still be led to the authorized one. Implement any of the increasingly sophisticated "intelligent" technologies that use semantic recognition and patterning, to lead those using one word to the constellation of others related to the same concept. When all else fails, promise to revise and update the authorized list periodically so omissions and missteps can be corrected.

This overall approach did add value at McKinsey in the ensuing years, and the firm's current version of the framework, many times revised, continues to assist consultants and researchers in finding their way through the firm's knowledge base of experience more quickly and accurately than before. New semantic search technologies have also helped, as have the gradual acceptance of the framework and enhancement of the thesaurus by teams of researchers within the firm.

Nonetheless, certain problems have not gone away, and there is a persisting uneasiness about the classification system that anyone who has to support it always feels. New terms continually crop up, and older terms become dated and irrelevant. But how is one to distinguish between fads of the moment and longer-range, systemic changes in the business landscape? Despite the best efforts to keep the terms succinct while covering all relevant categories, words chosen for the scheme inevitably have some semantic overlaps with one another—for example, "organizational design" and "organizational culture." Is there no way to avoid such messy redundancy? There is also the frequent lobbying of this or that zealous subgroup of consultants who want their particular favorite term used or made more prominent in the hierarchy of the framework. How is the administrator to avoid the pressure of special interests and preserve an overall consensus that best serves the greatest number of firm members?

In reviewing this case history, I realized my knowledge management group in those years was blinded by its own engineering mindset. Among my colleagues were many librarians and technologists, and others easily influenced by the librarians and technologists, and we were all working from the perspective of "scientific management" (see Micklethwait and Wooldridge, 1996). In our efforts to create a firmwide, authoritative classification system that categorized the elusive functional knowledge of work around the world, we were driven by the assumptions of a centralist, mechanical vision. We paid lip service to an organic set of processes all around us, but at the end of the day we tacitly believed that the company was like some great machine and that our job was to sketch and label a blueprint of its knowledge. We spoke about the importance of conversation-based learning and about how experience in people could be found through the pointers of words in our directories and databases. But underneath we still clung to the idea that important knowledge could be codified and classified, that it was sufficiently static to fit into a framework, and that some central, omnipotent authority could and should decide what the right word for this or that should be. We were not alone in the prejudice; the market of practitioners seemed to want the same. Consultant after consultant would call to demand that someone at corporate headquarters make it easier to find what he or she was looking for.

A Different Perspective: Complex Adaptive Systems

A CAS perspective on the challenge of a knowledge architecture offers a different approach to its design. If we think of a large, multiheaded organization of thousands of loosely linked, independent management consultants not as a unified and predictably coherent machine but as a complex, living, adaptive system, the ways in which we identify and describe its collective knowledge might be very different. We would represent that knowledge not as contained in the organization but as something emergent from it. But it would be messy, redundant, and never static, and our system of classification would not obscure that. We would expect and even embrace multiple representations of what is known across a broad collection of small communities within the enterprise. In this light, the various problems we faced in creating a knowledge architecture might be recast as opportunities for a more market-sensitive approach to knowledge building and sharing.

To flesh out this approach, let's begin by examining the strategies of creating such an architecture with the aid of the principles of complex adaptive systems, borrowing from the work of Holland (1995), Clark (1997), Arthur and Arrow (1994), Kauffmann (1993, 1995), Clippinger (Chapter One), and others. The discussion that follows does not challenge the notion that it is valuable to categorize what the organization knows. Rather, this analysis examines whether a new approach to categorizing knowledge may be more helpful and effective in light of how knowledge is actually created and used.

Fitness Strategy

The starting point is to see the task of classifying knowledge for the firm as part of an overall "fitness strategy" that can help the enterprise to adapt and survive in an ever changing environment. Creating, sharing, and applying knowledge effectively will require the firm to seek and maintain a point of equilibrium between excessive chaos and excess order—the "sweet spot" where the organization is maximally responsive to the variety of its environment but still sufficiently structured that it can act and perpetuate itself (see Chapter One). As Andy Clark has argued in *Being There* (1997), complex systems sample and "invent" their environments through representations that are indexed to certain actions in certain situations; complex adaptive systems are conditioned to "see what they want to see," that is, what they have been successful in representing and acting on in the past. From this viewpoint, classification of a consulting organization's collective knowledge can be seen as a representation of how its practitioners saw problems and solved them for clients in the past. The ongoing sampling and creation of solutions to business problems, drawing at least partly on previous experience, is the adaptive strategy that determines McKinsey's success and survival. The suitability of the match between its knowledge and the problems in the environment in which it operates thus defines its degree of "fitness."

Given all this, what would be the best way to design and implement knowledge classification to increase the fitness of the organization? To answer the question pragmatically for a manager, it will be necessary to look more deeply at the origins, nature, and situation of knowledge within the organization and to reframe traditional concepts using the principles of complex adaptive systems (nonlinearity, diversity, models, building blocks, aggregation, flows, and tagging). A different metaphor of how knowledge creates value will enable us to take a fresh look at the potential use and benefits provided by a schema of classification and at the same time may provide a solution to the knowledge management problem that is more in step with today's turbulent competitive environments.

Complex Adaptive Systems Are Nonlinear

The first principle to consider is nonlinearity. The enterprise lives and operates in a world in which the future is not a linear projection of the past. In such a context, the successful complex adaptive organism will itself also exhibit nonlinear assumptions and pursue nonlinear strategies. We can accordingly redefine the knowledge of a global and diverse consulting organization not as a static entity but as something in continuous, unpredictable motion. In complex adaptive systems, small, incremental changes can provoke sudden, unexpected "threshold changes." On the negative side, these could be rapid mismatches with a nonlinear, "rugged" market environment, leaving the consulting firm exposed—out of touch with the issues with which clients are wrestling. On the positive side, these changes could be sudden innovations, such as new ideas or new approaches to management problems, arising anywhere, anytime, and potentially useful in meeting the new needs of clients. At its best, a "complex adaptive" consulting enterprise fosters random, even explosive, innovation but is also able to sense any sudden lack of adaptation in an unpredictable environment.

Complex Adaptive Systems Are Diverse

Closely related to nonlinearity is the principle of diversity. The more rugged the fitness landscape—the more unpredictable the environment of clients or the greater the potential complexity of problems, for instance—the greater the need for diversity of response and anticipation. As Holland (1995) and others have explained, diversity can be regarded as a form of economic wealth: the greater the diversity (that is, the greater the number of different agents, such as individuals, ideas, and enterprises, and the more interaction there is among them), the greater the economic activity and thus the greater the potential for growth. Diversity leads to richness of innovation, and thus a higher upside potential, for both adaptation and the creation of new wealth-generating niches. A consulting firm defined as a prosperous complex adaptive enterprise would be rich with an innovative diversity of ideas and knowledge.

Complex Adaptive Systems Use Models

A third principle of complex adaptive systems is that they create models; that is, they externalize and objectify implicit understandings. There is a lively debate about the degree to which the implicit knowledge of an organization can become or needs to become explicit and the degree to which it can be separated from actions and the knowledge containing "scaffoldings of the environment." Without wading into this debate, we can agree that whether in application, codification, or both, the knowledge of the firm's consultants eventually gets translated into various kinds of models that frame, and at the same time represent solutions to, the business challenges faced by clients. The consulting process can be considered a continuous process of modeling and refining solutions to create desired outcomes. The consulting firm is constantly building and refining new models, testing previous ones, and discarding those that no longer work.

Complex Adaptive Systems Use Building Blocks

Because models in this sense are highly tailored to individual situations, it would be prohibitively expensive—and not competitively advantageous—for consultants to create solutions to business problems from scratch every time a solution is needed. In the face of constant demand for innovation and tight deadlines, consultants ideally draw on existing wisdom. In doing so, they mirror another principle of complex adaptive systems: using building blocks.

Fitness in a rugged competitive landscape is enhanced by having a repertoire of reusable responses. A finite number of subelements can provide, flexibly and quickly, the means for creating a nearly infinite number of innovative models at a higher level of aggregation (as, analogously, software development today increasingly draws from libraries of code objects). In a consulting firm that provides value to clients by applying models of knowledge to problems, building blocks might be defined as pieces of previous experience whose lessons are relevant to addressing a current challenge in the marketplace.

Since solutions themselves are highly case specific, the most transferable pieces of experience for management consultants are actually not the answers but the means of getting to the answers. This will include versions of generic questions, derived from the issues that frame various types of problems. It will also include the approaches and methodologies that help the consultant move toward the solution in a particular case more effectively. Stated otherwise, the building blocks of knowledge in a complex adaptive consulting firm are bundles of issues and tools practitioners use to diagnose problems and develop solutions. Because most work for clients involves a multitude of related problems, issue bundles and tools enable the consultant to identify, disassemble, and resolve "management messes." Different issue bundles and tools, in different combinations, are used in different situations, depending on the client opportunity at hand. These building blocks help create the models of applied knowledge that constitute the consulting process. However, to understand more about the source and creation of building blocks, we need to look at two more principles of these complex systems.

Complex Adaptive Systems Are Aggregations

"Aggregation" refers to the notion that from the interactions of individual agents, properties and behaviors can emerge that are distinct from, and larger or more complex than, the mere sum of the individuals' actions. The important implication for classification is that organizational knowledge is a collective phenomenon—indeed multiple collective phenomena—embedded in communities.

It is common shorthand at McKinsey to say that "the most important knowledge is in our people." The same can be said for virtually every professional service or knowledge-based business. It is an imprecise shorthand because the most valuable knowledge is not so much in specific individuals as it is in groups of individuals who, in aggregate, create solutions and collective understandings that are greater than the sum of their parts. Innovations and break-through ideas are almost always the fruit of multiple collaborators or of a process of testing and refining that includes many passive and active contributors, such as team members, officemates, clients, and others. In the consulting firm, groupings may be formal, informal, or some combination of the two: engagement teams; practitioners sharing a geographic location; client service teams that work with the same client organization over time; or industry or functional "practice groups," that is, communities of practitioners devoted to the collaborative development of problem-solving approaches.

If we assume that consulting knowledge is an emergent property of groupings within the enterprise, we can view knowledge creation as an adaptive process that is, to use Andy Clark's phrase, "soft-assembled" (Chapter Three) in ways that respond to local contexts.

Various groups, formal and informal, are in constant motion, seeking to create innovations and solutions to serve clients. The emergent outcomes of their efforts represent a portfolio of potential adaptations, some of which survive and some of which do not. For example, practice groups at McKinsey devise various new approaches and ideas, with varying degrees of success. A few are widely adapted by fellow practitioners and applied to their various clients successfully. Others "die on the vine" for any of a number of reasons, indicating lack of fitness: they are poorly expressed, are too narrowly defined, lack the tools or language of application, or are just not current or robust enough to suit today's problems.

Since outcomes of knowledge creation are nonlinear, predicting success is difficult. Similarly, creating aggregations of specific people to generate new knowledge offers no guarantee of innovations. One can put together specific groupings in the hope of stimulating knowledge breakthroughs, but CAS strategy is much more about facilitating self-organization. Following a CAS approach, one would create the context to allow groupings to form and perpetuate themselves and would replace hierarchies with internal "markets" that produce knowledge that will either succeed or fail for all to see.

Complex Adaptive Systems Consist of Flows

A precondition for enabling an enterprise to self-organize is to understand the organization in a way that differs from the way many managers today would understand it: not as a well-structured machine of different functions but as a series of "flows." The complex adaptive system, by contrast to the traditional model of a company, can be conceived as a series of constituent flows of resources, information, people, goods, capital, and so on. As discussed in Chapter One, the structure and character of an organization are essentially defined by the direction, rate, persistence, and type of flows that exist within an enterprise. Instead of causally related units, complex adaptive systems are made up of "state spaces," or networks of nonlinear relationships among, for example, agents with no prescribed future that can reorganize and configure themselves without any predetermined plan.

McKinsey, like many other professional service firms, can be seen as a series of flows. Loosely organized around geographical business units, its consultants are highly mobile and belong to multiple formal and informal networks simultaneously: practices, special initiatives, client service teams, regional collaborations, and so on. Staffing coordinators with no real predetermined plan assemble and broker an ongoing variety of groupings in the form of engagement teams to work with different clients, week after week. Consultants frequently cross the boundaries of geographical organization to work in different parts of the world or on projects sponsored by various practice groups that are themselves cross-boundary "virtual organizations." With its "up or out" policy (be steadily promoted for skill growth or be asked to leave) and its massive recruiting program, the firm takes in large numbers of new people and loses almost as many experienced people every year.

With so many people moving around and often leaving, the firm is challenged to capture and continue to build on the experience of previous work. The engineering model of management would imply the process that we ourselves followed in the late 1980s: top-down, hierarchical codification and labeling of what has been learned by groups or individuals, before they break up or leave the firm. A CAS perspective, by contrast, would understand learning and knowledge as more dynamic, as part of the flows of the enterprise. In this view, knowledge would require not top-down codification but mechanisms to categorize and communicate in real time what is being learned, on an ongoing basis, by the formal and informal groupings and subgroupings of the organization.

Complex Adaptive Systems Use Tags

This brings us to the CAS principle of "tagging." The mechanism by which self-organizing behaviors are launched in an enterprise is the flagging or labeling of something as significant, which invites aggregations of resources or people to join around a common theme. Tagging something gives it an identity and a role in a process of selection.

The consulting firm can be seen, in a CAS perspective, as a huge market, with the "buyers" and "sellers" of knowledge and experience in constant interaction. The "buyers" are always looking for help and knowledge to solve their immediate problems for clients; the "sellers" are always seeking to increase the value of what they know and to enhance their personal reputation based on knowledge and experience. The enterprise can be construed as an ever shifting set of flows of self-organizing groupings, some looking to buy knowledge, and others looking to sell knowledge, for the needs of clients. Enterprise fitness depends on adaptability, which is based on innovation as displayed in the application of knowledge and models. In such a system, the tagging of knowledge becomes a critical determinant of success, for tagging represents the identification of building blocks within the process of market selection. It is difficult to imagine anyone or any group of people at the center of the enterprise sufficiently knowledgeable about all models to tag every building block wisely and comprehensively. More reasonably, following a CAS perspective, those who build and apply the models should do the tagging themselves.

Tagging a piece of knowledge within a consulting firm—if done by those creating and "owning" the knowledge—is an invitation to self-organization. It should draw in those looking for ways to solve a problem or those with an interest in developing and refining the knowledge further. Tags are the beginning of a conversation among those who connect via the idea that the tag represents. Knowledge is built and refined through such conversations, and groupings are formed on the basis of conversation and knowledge exchange.

Accordingly, if the enterprise is represented as a series of knowledge flows, then tagging becomes the catalyst that generates groupings and signals an entry of new knowledge into the competition for successful market application. At the building block level, tagging can be seen as a cry of market participants to others throughout the enterprise: "We have a way to frame the issues of this problem and some tools and techniques that can help in solving it." The tag can stimulate others to join the group that created these building blocks and can invite conversation with, and use of those building blocks by, others in need of consulting assistance. Tags can be new, but in order to be effective they must be defined in terms of, or have some reference to, things previously known.

Applying CAS Thinking to Knowledge Classification

What all this means from a practical perspective is that the messiness and redundancy of our original knowledge architecture, and the continuing insistence for this or that term by particular groups of consultants over the years, are not so much problems as opportunities. If, when we were trying to design the original keyword list, we had abandoned our aspiration of static neatness and had understood that consultants' lobbying for some particular word to describe a piece of knowledge was actually a sort of "tagging flare," shot up from the flows of the internal marketplace of ideas, we would have designed a system of functional business terms very differently. We would not have tried to create a monochromatic, hierarchical list of terms that represented the best (yet imperfect) compromise for everybody. Instead, we would have embraced the complexity of the marketplace and encouraged the identification of a rich diversity of terms, not necessarily consistent or coordinated in any centrally logical sense. We would have done so based on a background assumption that we were in a self-organizing enterprise in which interactions between groups and competition for acceptance of building blocks were fostering a richness of diversity in knowledge creation and thus greater potential fitness.

By this approach, individual practice groups, offices, client service teams, and other ad hoc or informal groupings would each be encouraged to create its own language and terminology for the knowledge it was creating and using. But if all we are saying is that the knowledge architecture should be a market free-for-all, in which every community and subcommunity labels its own building blocks and from which self-organized, value-adding order might eventually result, a question arises: Will order result fast enough, or efficiently enough, to satisfy knowledge seekers within the firms who are wrestling with client problems under tight deadlines? Complexity theory holds that maximum value is created when the adaptive system finds an equilibrium point between order and chaos—the sweet spot. Is there a tagging strategy that would help the organization find the sweet spot where it is responsive to the fast-changing needs of the environment and of the internal market that seeks to serve clients but where there is enough order that consultants can take effective action within harsh deadlines?

I would argue that the answer is yes and that an appropriate tagging strategy would find its own sweet spot between order and chaos. The top-down engineering approach we tried to apply erred too much on the side of rigid formality; leaving words and nomenclature completely up to individual actors would push the firm too far in the other direction. A sweet spot might be achieved not through the top-down best-compromise approach but through a program that defines success as facilitating, in a way more orderly than the market, the creation of new tags and the ongoing retirement or replacement of those tags that no longer achieve market success. Such a program would be more about establishing context for community-driven tagging than about providing answers to those communities; more about educating actors than about deciding the terms and syntax for them; more about creating vehicles and pathways of communication among communities and fostering cross-organization transparency in general than merely disseminating from center to periphery the latest edition of the keywords.

A New Role for Knowledge Managers

In this worldview, the role of the knowledge manager working in a complex adaptive organization is that of developer of communities and subgroupings and builder of the infrastructure and vehicles of communication. The knowledge manager is a thoughtful educator about the process of tagging, an illustrator of the value it adds, and a sharer of best practices from grouping to grouping about labeling and identifying ideas. This manager invests time in working with groupings and communities to make the implicit explicit via the creation of "maps" that help show the rest of the marketplace what the grouping or community knows and how it thinks about the particular problems it works on. The "mapmakers" would ideally have at least one foot in the knowledge-creating communities themselves and would pursue as their professional development path networking and community building with other "mapmakers" in other groupings around the enterprise.

A chief knowledge officer in such an organization could aspire to create "maps of maps" and a community of community builders, each representing his or her own subgrouping of knowledge and experience, each of which in turn has its own tags for, translations of, and links to, the tags of other communities. In the technology realm—the physical representation of knowledge for many organizations—the goal of the chief knowledge officer is to create not an enterprise-wide intranet (currently popular with many technologically enthusiastic companies) but a network of intranets, each with its own knowledge architecture and tagging, representing the experience and expertise that are the building blocks of each particular subcommunity. Each subintranet would bring with it its own form of tagging. Hypertext linking, if vigorously used, then becomes a core process of self-organization at the logical level. Each Web site linked to another is a potential flow of knowledge, a potential enhancement of the fitness of the organization.

A Current Experiment with a CAS Model

A new model for creating a classification system is emerging as a potential new best practice at McKinsey as the result of a pilot intranet project begun in 1998. The effort, nicknamed "the Genome Project" (by analogy to the biomedical research mapping project), was intended to map a knowledge base for our Organization Practice. The project aimed to examine the books, articles, and communities of practitioners that collectively represent a competency in solving organizational problems for our clients.

The original goal of the project was to create one big knowledge base of readings on a Web site. However, after working for a few months, we came to several realizations that shifted the effort in a "complex adaptive" direction. First, "organization" was such a broad topic that it was really better represented not by one big Web site but by several smaller ones (on "leadership," "organizational design," "organizational culture," "management processes," and so on). Second, knowledge about organization was inherently overlapping and messy: organizational design was hard to separate from organizational culture, which in turn was hard to separate from leadership, and so on. Third, a great deal of what the firm collectively knew in such arenas was not, and could not be, codified; the tacit knowledge in our people was as important as, or even more important than, anything published. Fourth, there was no single simple way of creating an all-encompassing classification scheme (the obstacle was again functional terms); every hierarchy anybody devised was countered with multiple reasonable objections and plausible alternatives. In light of these realities, how could we build the knowledge base?

Our revision to the project expanded the solution space and embraced the apparent complexity. Instead of pursuing the intranet as one large project, we broke our team into multiple smaller teams, each one with responsibility for a subdomain of knowledge. We encouraged each subteam to join together with, and reach out to form, communities of practitioners and encouraged each community to devise its own map of terms for the knowledge in which it had a professional interest. We embraced the inherent redundancy of Web technology. By encouraging each subteam to create links to relevant sources (and people, via personal home pages), we allowed for multiple overlapping networks of knowledge. By creating a working philosophy of team culture, ongoing revision and change, and continual feedback from the "market" via usage reports, we allowed for a process of organic self-organization. Networks of links grew and expanded; they also, from time to time, collapsed and died for lack of use. What started as a sort of Web-based library evolved into a dynamic, "living" array of both codified and people-based knowledge, a sort of loose constellation of consultants and resources self-organized around different relevant topics. The constellation has become, in the aggregate, a collective competency regarding organization.

In this knowledge base, the classification scheme has grown and defined itself organically as well. Each subcommunity chooses its own terms and builds its own maps, based on real terms and questions from the market. Aware of what other subcommunities are doing, each subcommunity also regulates itself to create appropriate links to others, thus maintaining a process of intraorganizational tagging, flows, and creation of building blocks. A self-appointed steering committee, drawn from all of the communities representing different domains of knowledge, works to maintain some feasible limit on the overall number of terms and maps. However, there is enough flexibility for completely new domains of knowledge to arise and be linked to the project, based on the initiative of an interested community (as was the case with a group working on "performance management"). Similarly, domains may consolidate and recombine following the "voice of the market" (as was the case with "organizational design" and the "role of the corporate center").

In less than a year, this intranet has become one of the largest and most popular Web sites of the whole firm, and many firm leaders are pointing to the project as a potential model for all of McKinsey's intranets. It is still too early to declare the project an unambiguous success, but it is clear that the self-organizing model of knowledge and community-led development will be a strong example for the next generation of knowledge management tools at the firm.

General Implications

The theory of complex adaptive systems, combined with our experience at McKinsey, has much to suggest about knowledge management in other companies. Though this case study is deeply rooted in the way McKinsey works and serves its clients, many principles seem to have broader potential application. The challenge of organizing knowledge in large, complicated enterprises, in which much of what is known is based in people and where different subcommunities of people each see the world in their own particular way, is not unique to McKinsey or even to professional services firms. Product manufacturing companies, with their multiple different functions, as well as the increasingly prevalent joint ventures and collaborative alliances among groups of companies, need to classify and access what is known. All of these cases pose daunting challenges to any group of people with a central, engineering mindset who think that they, by themselves, can know enough to do all of it alone. These are arenas in which tagging, building blocks, flows, and nonlinear approaches represent promising alternatives. As we begin to see our companies not as hierarchies and structures but as aggregations of communities, markets, and loosely affiliated networks of knowledge workers, it stands to reason that we must think about management in different ways. Let fitness be the new reward for those who dare to experiment.

Seven Levers for Guiding
the Evolving Enterprise

Philip Anderson

Anyone who has ever been a senior manager in a complex organization knows how difficult it is even to understand what is
happening in the ranks, much less to change behavior. It is hard to
find the levers of control, and often when they are pulled, either
nothing happens or unintended consequences overwhelm the
intended ones. Organizations that once ran smoothly become dysfunctional and must be reorganized. Paradoxically, an enterprise's
very success can break its organization because growth leads to
increased complexity. Increasing scale allows people to specialize in
different functions. For example, in a small organization, everyone
may have to type his or her own documents, but as the organization
reaches critical mass, it may be more efficient to hire a typist. As
they grow, simple organizations with few specialized parts transform
into complex ones that have many specialized components.

Complex organizations frequently clank and flounder despite the
organizing skills of their managers. For instance, the technocrats of
the old Soviet Union were often superbly trained, but the complexity of Soviet enterprises outpaced their ability to understand
and direct them. Once an organization expands beyond the number of specialized parts that an administrator can grasp, it develops
its own inherent dysfunctions. Systems that used to work in simpler
times begin to break down.

The paradox of organization is that the very things that lead to efficiency tend to undermine adaptability. Because organizations divide labor and standardize tasks, they tend to respond poorly to changing environments. Dividing labor is efficient, but it also divides up signals from the environment into small packets. So no one in the organization understands what the market is saying about the enterprise as a whole. Standardizing best practice is efficient, but routines become grooved, institutionalized, and inflexible.

Confronted with dysfunction and disarray, those who manage complex organizations typically engage in a never ending round of change efforts. They spot defects and fix them, only to find that the cure creates new, unanticipated problems. Change initiative follows change initiative, eventually leading to cynicism about change management in general. Reorganizations eliminate one set of issues only for another to surface.

This chapter begins by describing how firms overcome this tendency for organizations to break down, using evolved (rather than engineered) solutions derived from the principles of self-organization. It explains what it means to say that self-organizing enterprises evolve via variation, selection, and retention. Next, the chapter explores how viewing the organization as a network of connected agents can lead to fresh insights. It examines four guidelines for diagnosing self-organizing systems, then explores how managers lead self-organizing enterprises. Seven levers for guiding evolution are described, and their application is illustrated by a study of the case of Capital One, a fast-growing financial services company.

Combating Disorganization: The Engineering Solution

Business process reengineering (BPR), a popular movement launched in the late 1980s, was put forth as an antidote to the inevitable decay of complex organizations. Its premise is that organizational processes descend into a hodgepodge of special cases and quick fixes built up over time on design principles that fit outmoded technology. Reengineering specialists argue that they can eliminate the clutter, using modern networked computing, by designing processes for the smoothest possible flow, cutting costs and enhancing quality dramatically (Hammer and Champy, 1993).

BPR principles dictate that firms organize around processes or groups of activities required to produce something for a customer. BPR advocates believe that *doing* work has become less problematic than *coordinating* it (managing handoffs and handling exceptions), and so one person should execute as many steps in a process as possible. Generalist jobs replace specialist ones, enabled by information systems that let workers see a bigger picture than specialists do.

Many workers and middle managers came to despise reengineering because to some extent the rise of BPR coincided with a wave of downsizing in American firms: "reengineering" was seen as a code word for layoffs. It also happened because people often were not asked to reengineer their own jobs; instead, outsiders steeped in industrial engineering and information technology did most of the design work. Finally, reengineering lost its luster because it was associated with extensive software creation efforts that always seemed to be late, over budget, and full of bugs. By the mid-1990s, the tide of managerial opinion seemed to have turned mostly against BPR, and many partially completed reengineering efforts were abandoned.

However, a great deal of reengineering continues to take place when a firm implements an enterprise resource planning (ERP) system. ERP software is designed to integrate the information systems that support a firm's most important processes. If the division of labor creates efficiencies but tends to defeat itself, why not minimize specialized tasks? If complex organizations are difficult to understand and control because so many separate parts interact, why not standardize the way all the parts in an enterprise operate and use software to automate as much coordination as possible? If subunits tend to suboptimize by pursuing their own goals, why not use software to facilitate more global optimization, and to hold each subunit more accountable for its actions? In a sense, ERP turned reengineering on its head. BPR projects typically redesigned a work process, then developed custom software to support the new work and information flows. ERP systems are packaged software with thousands of predefined business processes embedded in them, taken from what their authors regard as best practices culled from many industries. Companies that implement ERP systems typically alter their processes to fit the software, instead of writing software to fit their processes.

ERP began proliferating rapidly in the early 1990s; the leading vendor (SAP) grew at a 35 percent rate per annum throughout the decade. ERP software promised to eliminate redundancy and get incompatible corporate systems to communicate with one another, reducing information technology spending. Unlike much custom software, these packaged systems were relatively well documented and bug free, and they could be maintained by a variety of suppliers. Many firms that had built a variety of incompatible packages for mainframe computers or minicomputers found moving to ERP less painful and costly than trying to integrate those systems, fix "year 2000" bugs in them, and move them to cheaper client-server computing platforms.

However, early ERP installations gained notoriety for taking much longer and costing much more than expected. The systems themselves were quite complex, difficult to learn, and difficult to install. Political and change management issues proved even tougher to resolve. For example, if an entire corporation had to standardize on one "best practice" for each process, which division's procedures would prevail? Such problems became even more acute for firms that participated in the merger wave of the 1990s, because ERP systems forced them to standardize the core processes of subunits with different traditions, histories, and cultures.

In addition, it proved very difficult to implement ERP systems incrementally, one piece at a time. Streamlining and integrating one business process throughout a company or a number of business processes locally is hard because these processes are interwoven with so many others. It seemed to many early adopters that ERP had to be implemented company-wide and mandated by top management because reengineering processes for ERP usually meant reinventing the entire corporate approach.

Only time will tell whether the shiny new ERP systems of the 1990s will become the outmoded, troublesome legacy systems of the next decade. For example, SAP's popular R/3 enterprise resource planning software is based on late 1980s client-server technology and treats the desktop essentially as a dumb terminal with a graphical user interface. It does not use modern object-oriented design, and its huge, integrated model may prove difficult to migrate to pure object code.

Perhaps more important, ERP systems may freeze their adopters into the best practices of the late 1980s and early 1990s. It is difficult to change these systems one element at a time because their processes are so tightly intercoupled. Firms that wish to change a core process significantly may well find that a cascade of consequences forces them to reengineer many other processes. ERP systems are designed to institutionalize and integrate a common set of best practices, not to change those practices in order to keep up with fast-paced shifts in the business environment. As the culmination of the BPR movement, ERP represents one approach to the organizational paradox described earlier. It is the ultimate expression so far of the idea that managers, given the right tools, can control and intervene in complex organizations the way they can in simple ones.

Combating Disorganization: The Evolutionary Solution

Self-organization is an interesting concept because complex organizations often appear to be chaotic, constantly disrupted, and difficult to control. One message from the emerging science of complexity is that order arises spontaneously all the time from complex, irregular, and chaotic states of matter. It is no accident that the chaos of the Big Bang evolved into atoms, molecules, elements, stars, and galaxies; it is no accident that life eventually organized into cells, tissues, organs, organisms, species, and ecological communities. A defining feature of complexity is that order arises naturally from the evolution of vast aggregates of simple subunits.

The second law of thermodynamics tells us that closed systems tend to spin down into maximum disorder. By contrast, open systems, which receive energy from the outside, tend to produce order, not disorder: they self-organize. Interactions among a collection of objects tend to produce aggregates that have stable spatial patterns or temporal rhythms. Higher-order behaviors emerge from the interactions of many simple components, and they do so without a central controller. No agent does the organizing; structure arises even though none of the interacting units has a plan or a goal for how the overall system should behave.

In nature, as Stuart Kauffman (1993) reminds us, order is often provided free of charge. Patterns arise spontaneously when large numbers of components interact in a nonlinear way instead of additively. Because nonlinearity leads to positive feedback loops, some interactions are reinforced and crowd out others, creating order. For example, when a fluid is heated, many different modes of vibration are superimposed on one another. The pattern with the largest rate of increase in velocity damps out the others, which is a positive feedback loop: the more common it becomes, the more the other patterns are suppressed. The result is that once the rolling motion of convection starts, billions of molecules fall into a pattern. Positive feedback, not the design or direction of some controller, explains why.

Organization can arise, given such patterns, because nature has orderly building blocks with which to work. Order is not the same as organization; orderly things are merely arranged in some regulated condition whereas organization involves differentiation and specialization. An array of identical cells is maximally ordered but has no organization. Given order to work with, natural selection produces organization because systems that exploit divisions of labor have higher fitness than systems that do not.

Furthermore, adaptability appears to arise naturally in complex systems. When a system is inertial and difficult to alter, large changes in input produce small changes in output. When a system is chaotic, small changes in input produce large changes in output. Somewhere in between lie systems at the "edge of chaos," where small changes in input can produce any size of output. Smaller changes in output are more common, but larger ones also occur.

To summarize, as organizations become more complex, they tend to develop dysfunctions that cannot be explained through managerial ineptitude. In simple structures, a manager's skill at dividing labor, specifying procedures, and integrating subtasks directly influences the organization's effectiveness. However, in complex structures, pushing the levers of control either produces nothing or produces a cascade of unintended consequences. Complex structures appear to decay into either inertia or chaos.

Complexity theory suggests that in natural systems, order emerges as long as a system has an inflow of energy, enough parts, enough interconnections, and positive feedback loops. Organization arises from order because divisions of labor are efficient, and systems tend to evolve to a state in between inertia and chaos, called "self-organized criticality" or "the edge of chaos" (Kauffman, 1993).

Evolving Behavior: The Self-Organizing Enterprise

Self-organization proceeds from the premise that effective organization is evolved, not designed. It aims to create an environment in which successful divisions of labor and routines not only emerge but also self-adjust in response to environmental changes. This happens because management sets up an environment that encourages rapid evolution toward higher fitness, not because management has mastered the art of planning and monitoring work flows.

Managers are sometimes confused by the term "self-organization" because they focus on either organization charts or power relationships. Self-organization does not mean that workers instead of managers engineer an organization design. It does not mean letting people do whatever they want to do. It means that management commits to guiding the evolution of behaviors that emerge from the interaction of independent agents instead of specifying in advance what effective behavior is, then encouraging the agents to conform to the standard.

Self-organization focuses on evolving productive interlocking behaviors. What evolves is a set of behaviors, not an organization chart. The social psychologist Karl Weick (1979) defines organizing as a set of recipes for assembling interlocked behaviors. An organization takes puzzles and processes them through a set of interpretations and procedures that people associated with the organization share. As a result, these people invoke a set of interlocking behaviors.

An organization evolves when the recipes for assembling behavior shift. As a consequence, the repertoire of behaviors that are evoked in response to puzzles changes. Self-organization means that a new behavioral pattern emerges from the interaction of separate agents, who adapt what they do in response to what they believe to be the consequences of their actions.

The Process of Evolution

The psychologist Donald Campbell (1965) has argued cogently that all evolutionary systems depend on three elements: variation, selection, and retention. Consider the giraffe. First, through some form of mutation, a giraffe with a longer neck than usual is born. This is *variation*. Second, such a giraffe is able to reach food sources that other giraffes cannot. As a consequence, it is likelier to breed successfully. This is *selection*. Third, this unusually successful giraffe passes on the genes for longer necks to its descendants so that they too have longer necks. This is *retention*. Over many generations, the population of giraffes increasingly comes to consist of the longer-necked variety because longer-necked giraffes breed more success-fully than do shorter-necked ones.

Evolution does not require genes; retention of positively selected variants can proceed in other ways. For example, a pan of heated liq-uid forms a stable collection of so-called Benard cells, hexagonal units within which convection rolls circulate the liquid from bot-tom to top and back again. As the liquid begins to heat, variation occurs: some molecules start moving faster than others, and these fluctuations self-amplify. Then, the most vigorously growing fluctu-ations are selected at the expense of others, in the sense that mole-cules tend to migrate from slower flows to faster ones. Finally, fluctuations interact with each other to form an interlocking grid; the extent of a single convection cell is bounded by the emergence of neighboring cells. Retention occurs because the presence of each cell reinforces the conditions of existence for its neighbors, not because convection cells pass on genetic material to their descendants.

Evolution occurs within self-organizing enterprises via these same three processes. New behaviors emerge spontaneously from the interaction of separate agents or from changes in an organiza-tion's architecture. Those behaviors that appear to be associated with the agents' definition of success are reinforced. Repeated behaviors are retained and become routines because agents learn and form habits. Behaviors are also retained because they form an interlocking, mutually reinforcing structure: people do what they do in organizations in order to meet others' expectations.

Analysis of the Self-Organizing Enterprise

Why are some organizations so much more effective than others? How does superior organization arise? Instead of focusing on whether some managers institute more effective routines than oth-ers or partition work better than others, complexity theory suggests that some organizations are configured to evolve faster and more effectively than others. Differences in the pace and direction of evolution arise directly from the architecture of the organization. Effective managers guide evolution indirectly, by shaping this architecture to influence behavior instead of specifying behavior directly. They do not tell organizational agents what to do; rather, they manipulate the structure within which variation, selection, and retention operate.

Complex adaptive systems solve problems by breaking them into small pieces so that small segments of an organization can adapt to them locally. Interesting behavior arises because these small sections interact with one another in accordance with a set of interconnections among them. The configuration of these interconnections determines what interactions there will be and which behaviors interlock in response to a puzzle posed by the environment.

Complex adaptive systems can be modeled in a number of ways, but viewing them as a network of connected agents is particularly useful. Such a network is defined by tags, which define how agents connect (see Chapter Four for more detail). The structure of a network fundamentally constrains how fast it can evolve and in what directions.

Managers can guide the evolution of a self-organizing enterprise more effectively if they learn to analyze the firm's network structure. Today, a typical manager knows a great deal about his unit's objectives, its financial and accounting performance, its organization chart, its chief initiatives, and its upcoming deadlines but has no picture of its pattern of connections and flows. When an organizational puzzle arises, who goes to whom to interpret what the environment is saying? Who provides advice? Who contributes to assembling a response? Who attempts to defeat the winning response? Who observes the outcome and updates his or her recipes accordingly?

Social network analysis is a well-developed and fast-growing area of organizational sociology, and it provides many tools and concepts for analyzing organizations as networks (Wasserman and Faust, 1994). However, there has been little research on the dynamics of networks, how they evolve, and what configurations lead to more rapid and diverse evolution. The study of complex adaptive systems has not yet produced a widely accepted theory of network evolution, but it has generated a number of useful analytical insights concerning the pace of evolution in tightly or loosely connected networks. Maximally connected networks evolve slowly and in constrained ways.

It is faddish to suggest that empowering people in organizations means eliminating social divisions. Confronted with breakdowns in complex systems, managers frequently prescribe increased communication. The notion driving such behavior is that the more richly connected any network is, the more paths there are; hence the more potential ways there are to solve problems. However, analysis of neural networks suggests that some networks perform below par because there are too many interconnections among the nodes. When a neural network starts out with too many connections, the overall system tends to show confirmation bias. This is to say that the network does not update its preliminary conclusions. Selection and retention overwhelm variation because positive feedback loops reinforce the first set of successful connections that emerge, tending to lock the pattern in. A set of neural networks performs best when, early in their training, communication between the networks is limited. Each network is given time to build its own interpretation before being exposed to the conclusions of others, so some solutions are allowed to emerge that do not initially seem as successful as others.

This insight helps explain why savvy managers often isolate innovation teams from the rest of the organization during the formative, exploratory learning period. It also explains why new joint ventures or acquisitions tend to perform better when they are loosely integrated with the rest of an organization at first. In general, when a network appears to be producing too much convergence and order, managers can tune it by breaking some of the existing connections, especially ties between newer nodes and those with a great deal of experience inside the network.

Evolution proceeds more rapidly when networks are partitioned.

The Nobel Prize–winning economist Herbert Simon (1996) has shown that complex systems evolve from simple ones much more rapidly if they are "nearly decomposable." In such systems some elements interact very strongly, and these form subsystems. The linkages between subsystems are much weaker than the linkages within subsystems. A cluster of elements that interact strongly with each other can serve as a building block that can be invoked by a relatively small number of signals from the rest of the system. Systems that are assembled from such stable intermediate building blocks evolve much more rapidly than those that are not.

Networks tend to form partitions so that distinct modules perform tasks that have highly correlated patterns of constraints. Organizations become modular when the work they perform is modular. Chunking work into pieces that can be performed relatively independently is a prerequisite for building fast-evolving networks.

Examining the profile of connection strengths within a network leads to useful insights. Strong connections should cluster so that all the elements of a subsystem are powerfully tied to one another. Weak connections should also cluster and should predominate. Connections should generally be symmetrical: if one agent invokes the other frequently but the converse is not true, then agents may not be properly grouped into subsystems that have strong internal ties and weak external ones.

Chaos may signal that a network is too richly interconnected.

Stuart Kauffman (1993) has conducted extensive simulation experiments with a family of networks consisting of N agents, each connected to K other agents. His results suggest that networks are chaotic when every agent's output is influenced by the actions of many other agents. Simply put, when an agent cannot hold anything constant but instead responds to input from many other agents, orderly patterns do not emerge from agent interactions.

In such situations, order emerges when the amount of input to each agent is reduced. In particular, aggregate order arises spontaneously when each agent responds to input from just two other agents. Networks that are connected in this way congeal into islands of change, partitioned by walls of stable behavior. They squeeze themselves into a relatively small corner of all the states they could occupy; without such retention, evolution cannot occur.

A slow rate of evolutionary improvement may reflect too much interdependence.

Kauffman's studies suggest that when the performance ("fitness") of an agent depends on the performance of many other agents, it is easy for individuals to become trapped in suboptimal performance. In such cases where K—the number of connections—is high, the overall fitness landscape has many peaks and valleys. When an agent reaches a local peak, it finds that other peaks are relatively far away, and that most changes depress performance instead of improving it.

Assembly lines illustrate this problem well. A product comes off the line without defects only if no errors arise at any stage of manufacture. As a consequence, a major change introduced at any step of the process tends to disrupt many other activities. Management theorist William Abernathy (1979) called this trap the "productivity dilemma." His studies suggest that in search of efficiency, Ford's assembly lines became so tightly integrated that significant innovation in automobile technology became impossible: even small annual model changes could only be implemented by shutting down factories for weeks for the changeover.

It is more important to identify the worst-performing element in a network than the best-performing one.

Self-organization arises when the fitness of the worst-performing element in an adaptive landscape is raised. This contrasts with the BPR approach to managing complex organizations, which focuses on identifying best practices and standardizing them across the enterprise. By contrast, Per Bak's research (1996) has shown how systems that constantly replace the least-fit element naturally evolve to a state of self-organized criticality. Such systems are neither inertial nor chaotic; changes in the network can result in large or small shifts in the network. Small changes are more common than large ones according to a power law.

Consider, for example, the operation of a "genetic algorithm," as described by John Holland (1995). (See also Chapter Eight.) Genetic algorithms evolve effective software instead of designing it. First, a population of candidate solutions is generated randomly. Then, from among the pool of better performers, two are selected, and a child solution is generated containing code from both. The child solution is subjected to mutation, and if it is superior, it replaces the worst performer in the population. The process continues until the child solutions that are generated no longer improve on the least-fit solutions in the pool. Systems built this way naturally evolve to the state that Stuart Kauffman (1993) has termed "the edge of chaos," poised at a phase between order and chaos.

Diagnostic guidelines based on the theory of complex adaptive systems such as those just presented allow managers to visualize the organization in new ways and diagnose whether the enterprise is configured to evolve rapidly and flexibly. In addition, managers can intervene in a number of ways to increase the likelihood that a self-organizing enterprise will evolve effective behaviors. Self-organization does not imply that managers are passive. In self-organizing systems, managers intervene indirectly. Instead of engineering behavior, they influence the environment that shapes behavior.

Managing the Self-Organizing Enterprise

If complex systems naturally self-organize, why do we need managers and what is their role? The term "self-organization" disturbs many executives because they believe it means "no management necessary." Actually, it simply means "no central controller necessary." Managers do not add value to self-organizing enterprises by orchestrating routines or specifying how labor should be divided. In self-organizing systems, managers are stewards of the evolutionary process, not directors of activity. They govern instead of executing, because they understand that evolved behaviors and recipes generally outperform designed ones. Accordingly, as they progress in their careers and are placed in charge of complex organizations, they must develop skills in tuning a network instead of directing traffic on it.

To understand what managers do in self-organizing enterprises, it is useful to ask why management exists at all. Suppose every agent in an organization were exposed directly to a market for his or her services so that the cost and revenue of every action were known. The invisible hand of prices would coordinate interlocking behaviors, eliminating the need for supervision. Why are transactions ever conducted outside markets? Three conditions lead to organizing. One is the presence of transaction costs. It would be inefficient to negotiate a new contract for every activity, ensure the contract is fulfilled to the letter, and adjudicate each possible dispute. Another is team production: when a task cannot be carried out by a single agent alone, it can be difficult to price each individual's contribution correctly. A third is social dilemmas: when individual and collective interests are at odds, agents may find themselves unable to reach an achievable outcome that would leave everybody better off. If each agent worries that he will cooperate but others will not, each may choose behaviors that are individually rational but collectively irrational.

Because agents cannot always see an accurate cost-revenue calculus for their individual actions, organizations may set up indirect selection systems meant to fill in at least some of the missing information. Organizations substitute incentive systems for market feedback. Selection becomes vicarious. Agents pursue rewards, and if rewards are highly correlated with market outcomes, evolution hones the behavior of individual agents to fit the demands of markets they cannot observe.

Many evolving systems in nature develop vicarious selection systems of some sort because they lower the costs of trial-and-error learning. For example, most animals have evolved tasting and smelling systems that send discomforting signals to the brain when the animal encounters something poisonous or diseased. Such mechanisms originally arose as mutations and were quickly selected because they helped animals predict in advance what to avoid in the environment. Evolution would proceed if animals that ate poisonous things died out while those that avoided poisons did not, but it progresses more rapidly when taste and smell produce avoidance without an expensive and possibly fatal trial. As the philosopher Karl Popper (1966) pointed out, indirect selection makes it possible for our hypotheses to die in our stead.

Managers in a self-organizing system operate an indirect selection system based on what Peter Drucker (1994) has termed their theory of the business. When management's internal model effectively represents the organization's external environment, then variation, selection, and retention can operate on ideas, prototypes, and preliminary steps, instead of committed organizational actions. More effective organizations are able to detect and avoid, better than less effective enterprises do, things that will not work in their markets. Early and cheap failure is an advantage in evolutionary competition.

Consider, for example, how organizations develop new products. When an agent has an idea for a new product, that individual first builds support for it. It competes in a marketplace of ideas, which is a vicarious selection system. Metaphorically, other agents smell and taste the proposal to see whether it fits their model of what is likely to succeed in the firm's external markets. Most ideas are winnowed out inexpensively at this stage, but some become new product initiatives, usually in a modified form. Such projects develop along a series of milestones, and at each intermediate point, a vicarious selection system asks whether the initiative is still meeting its intermediate objectives, whether it still smells and tastes good. The new product is exposed to trials that stand in for the verdict of the external marketplace: What do focus groups say? How do beta-test users react? How many third parties agree to support it? How well does it sell in test markets? Through such indirect selection mechanisms, prospective products evolve through dozens of cycles of variation, selection, and retention before they enter the market.

This process evokes thousands of interlocked behaviors. Like the nodes of a neural network, agents activate recipes that have worked in the past and establish novel connections in response to feedback. Managers do not operate the network; they influence the feedback that causes the network to self-organize. Agents seldom are exposed directly to the voice of the customer. More typically, they interpret what the voice of the customer will say, based on performance data provided by indirect selection systems.

Managers help structure the context within which self-organization takes place. They provide governance, not control. As stewards of networks that evolve effective behaviors, managers carry out a series of critical functions.

Selecting the External Environment

Self-organizing systems structure themselves to fit their environments. Managers decide what environments to occupy, and these choices place a fundamental constraint on what the organization can do: some environments are much more conducive to rapid evolution and growth than are others. A network does not choose an attractive domain or niche to occupy; managers choose those for it.

The quality of the models that underpin vicarious selection systems depends largely on the environment. As Andy Clark (1997) argues, good models are simple. The best representation of the environment is the environment itself. Environments provide external scaffolding that simplifies internal models, allowing them to focus on a few controllable parameters.

Some environments provide better scaffolding than others do. For example, consider two predators of the same species that operate in different patches of a prairie. The first occupies a hunting ground where prey congregate at a watering hole; the second patrols a range where prey are spread out, no likelier to be at one place than another. The first predator will probably prove fitter than the second. It can breed more rapidly and with less risk because it can spend less energy hunting yet still enjoy a higher probability of success. The environment provides richer external scaffolding for the first predator. Unlike the second, the first predator does not need a complex internal model telling it where to search for prey, because the environment has structured a simple, highly predictive correlation: the prey are at the watering hole.

Similarly in business, some environments provide better scaffolding than others do, allowing vicarious selection systems to operate more effectively. Organizations that focus on serving coherent market segments do not need to filter out as much noise as organizations whose customer needs are weakly correlated. Organizations whose beta users and test markets are representative of the most attractive growth segments can develop good predictive models. Organizations that control key industry standards can formulate plans without having to guess how these standards will evolve. By choosing which environments to occupy, managers implicitly define what processing will be done by indirect selection mechanisms and what can be offloaded onto the environment.

The environments that managers choose today govern which environments their organizations will be able to enter tomorrow.

For example, a recent study by Dong-Jae Kim and Bruce Kogut (1996) examined which semiconductor firms have been able to diversify into various branches of the industry. Firms that entered the industry by producing memory chips (DRAMs) were able to use the know-how gained in this environment as a springboard for making many other kinds of chips. By contrast, firms that started out making digital signal processors (a specialized type of semiconductor) were stuck in that domain, largely unable to leverage their skills into other forms of chip manufacture.

By setting strategy, choosing what markets to serve and how to win in them, managers define the context for self-organization, channeling the rate and direction of evolution. Networks can achieve structure without central control, but the kind of structure that evolves is very much a function of strategic choice. The first role of the manager is to determine what business the organization is in.

Defining Performance

Complex systems adapt by changing their behavior to move "uphill" in a rugged fitness landscape. Given a performance metric, they will move toward higher fitness without a central controller. But who defines what performance is? Managers do.

For-profit organizations in capitalist society supposedly maximize long-run profitability. Meeting this goal does not necessarily mean maximizing short-term revenues and minimizing costs. Many intermediate performance measures can be targeted in the belief that they lead to the ultimate goal of survival and wealth creation. In the short run, organizations pursue multidimensional objectives. The feedback a network uses to hill-climb depends on what performance metrics agents use and how one is traded off against another.

One fundamental choice managers make defines for the network what the accepted discount rate will be, governing how agents will value long-term versus short-term returns. Another is defining whether growth or cost cutting is more important at a given point in time. For example, the managers of many Internet start-up companies believe they live in a world of increasing returns, so that the first company that gains a critical mass of a market will go on to dominate it. This theory of the business leads them to reward revenue growth over cost cutting, and their networks emphasize this dimension when evaluating in which direction higher performance lies. Managers also define the firm's risk-return frontier, influencing agents' willingness to hazard losses in search of gains.

Managers shape networks' behavior by emphasizing indicators that they believe will ultimately lead to long-run profitability. For example, some managers have embraced a theory of the business suggesting that organizations must lead the market in total quality, or they will ultimately fail. Others make expensive investments in human capital, depressing short-run profits, because they believe the long-run health of the business depends on attracting, motivating, and developing the best people available. Others believe their companies must expand globally, even if they lose money initially, because only global enterprises will thrive in the future. In each case, managers stress some dimension of performance other than today's profitability because they think that dimension is a more important determinant of tomorrow's results.

Even if managers knew exactly what indicators were most strongly linked to long-term profitability, they would still have to ensure that the firm survived and was permitted by society to operate in the future. Organizations must be legitimate as well as profitable, and managers must define performance in ways that maintain legitimacy. For example, because the electric utility industry failed to maintain social approval for nuclear power, every other dimension of performance for nuclear power plants has become irrelevant.

Managers support political candidates to shape the laws that govern competition. They donate to charitable causes because they believe that to survive and thrive, they need to maintain high social status in their communities. They contribute to public education because they believe their future health depends on being able to tap a skilled workforce. All these investments put a damper on short-run profits, whatever the firm's discount rate, risk-return profile, or emphasis on quality. Organizations make such investments because managers must define performance in more than financial terms to ensure the long-run health of the enterprise.

Complex adaptive systems strive toward better fitness as defined by managers. Part of operating a vicarious selection system is telling the agents which way is up on a rugged fitness landscape. Scholarly models of fitness landscapes assume that performance can be measured and evaluated; in business, performance is more open to interpretation. A self-organizing system can only evolve functional behaviors when managers tell it what functionality means.

Managing Meaning

Theories of self-organizing networks argue that by applying local rules to input from the environment, agents can create aggregate order without a central controller. Usually, we assume that signals from the environment are unambiguous, if perhaps noisy. In reality, most input—be it from the environment or from other agents—can be interpreted in different ways. Members of organizations tend to see what their culture conditions them to see. Who propagates the culture that shapes competing interpretations into a consensus? Who tells agents drowning in ambiguous signals which ones deserve their attention? Managers do.

The Santa Fe Institute's Murray Gell-Mann (1994) has argued that complex adaptive systems evolve through variation, selection, and retention of mental models and implicit theories, not just behaviors. First, he suggests, agents compress previous data into a schema that extracts regularities from experience. Then, the agents choose how to behave in the present by confronting their schema with current data, in just the same way that the development of individuals arises from the interaction of their DNA coding with the environment. Finally, the consequences of these behaviors lead to the survival of favorable schemata.

Where do these models come from? Algorithms for compressing experience into a schema are neither automatic nor neutral. One can usually interpret events in several ways, and as Ernest May

(1973) reminds us, the lessons drawn from history often are at odds with known facts. Individuals and groups struggle to legitimate their points of view, contesting for a greater share of mind, not just a greater share of resources. Managers adjudicate these contests, shaping behavior indirectly by directing attention and influencing beliefs. A vicarious selection system operated by managers determines which symbols and ideas proliferate and which die out.

Managers help guide the evolution of self-organizing systems by managing meaning. As organization theorist Jeffrey Pfeffer (1981) argues, they get more done by managing symbols than by managing things. They propagate mores and values through tools such as stories, myths, and rituals. Managers influence the production of interlocking behaviors they can neither control nor fully understand, by socializing agents instead of telling them what to do.

In the language of complex adaptive systems, managers manage meaning by tagging and retagging flows through a network (see Chapter Four for an in-depth discussion). In a real sense, management consists in part of asking agents, "What do you think you are doing?" This perspective is quite congruent with Karl Weick's notion (1979) that organizing is a set of recipes for reducing equivocation. These recipes are validated because a consensus forms around them. Weick asks, "How can I know what I think until I see what I say?" Agents in self-organizing systems may well add that they cannot know what they think until they have learned to read the tags.

Choosing People

By choosing to evolve solutions instead of plan and direct them, managers rely on agents to adapt locally. Unexpected aggregate patterns emerge from the interaction of the agents. But who chooses the agents? Managers do.

When scholars simulate evolving networks, they often treat agents as if they were all the same. In reality, some agents have a broader repertoire of actions than others do, some have more capacity to store and process information, and some operate more quickly than others do. In addition, some agents are more likable than others, more persuasive, more creative, better able to manage diversity, more prestigious, and so on.

Attracting the most capable agents to the enterprise is only part of management's task. Organizational demography matters as much as individual capability does. If a collection of agents is insufficiently diverse, it may not generate enough variation for behaviors to evolve. Even if a network is diverse in aggregate, the universal tendency for people to associate with others like themselves can segregate the network into excessively homogenous clusters. Hiring new agents from outside the organization who bring in new rules can stimulate variation, but they must be linked to well-connected, veteran agents or their new ideas and recipes will not propagate.

Reconfiguring the Network

Models of self-organizing systems drawn from nature sometimes allow nodes and connections to be added or eliminated. More commonly, however, simulations hold the number of agents fixed or introduce new agents randomly. Connections strengthen or atrophy as a function of network traffic. By contrast, many business organizations frequently add and drop agents or reorganize, altering the pattern of flows. Who reconfigures the network? Managers do.

We should draw a distinction between directing network flows and changing the network's architecture. Managers who favor evolving over designing an organization reject the former and embrace the latter. Flows along a self-organizing network are directed by tags, not by a central authority. Such networks resemble the Internet, where messages reach their destination via a series of hops guided by the information in their headers. Each packet that flows onto the Internet knows where it is supposed to end up. The Internet constantly reconfigures itself because hundreds of routers (computers that read packet headers and send messages on their next hop) and thousands of nodes are added or dropped every day.

Because it relies on tags and not a central switching table, the Internet self-organizes and constantly finds new ways to cope with its own congestion.

In organizational networks, managers alter the node structure when they add or delete roles. For example, downsizing efforts in the early 1990s dramatically reshaped many organizational networks by eliminating middle managers and outsourcing "noncore" functions. More recently, some firms have tried to generate innovation by creating new positions, such as chief knowledge officer, Web master, supply chain coordinator, dean of a corporate university, or evangelist. When managers establish strategic alliances, sponsor new ties to university scientists, join research and development associations, create programs to attract value-added resellers and complementary asset providers, form temporary virtual organizations, or build user communities, they create new sources of variation that can alter the organization's evolutionary path.

Managers may also reshape network flows by making or breaking connections between nodes. By linking internal communities of practice or external communities of customers over the Internet, they establish new ties among former strangers. By holding conferences and innovation fairs and training workshops, they introduce people who might not ordinarily meet. By placing people together in temporary, cross-functional teams, they alter these individuals' interaction patterns. By creating "skunkworks," moving offices that were formerly at the same location, or changing reporting relationships, they interrupt existing linkages and make some nodes more isolated than they once were.

These actions allow managers to make the networks they govern more or less tightly coupled, more or less modular. They also allow managers to rearrange the social proximity of agents. Researchers examining cognition have concluded that the brain organizes its network of neurons so that similar vectors representing similar things are close to one another. Reasoning by analogy generates insight when the brain perceives a resemblance between things that were previously categorized as different. In a similar way, organizational innovation often occurs when managers bring formerly separate agents into close social contact. For example, Sony's former chairman, Akio Morita, was an inveterate source of fresh connections between people working in different organizational compartments. When Morita connected two groups at Sony—one that had created a new set of headphones and another that had invented a small portable cassette player—he planted the seed that grew into the Walkman.

Managers in self-organizing systems frequently adjust to change by reconfiguring networks instead of telling agents how to adapt. For example, telephone companies have bought Internet service providers to learn how to cope in a world where voice and data both travel over a single network. Advertising companies have acquired Web design boutiques, pharmaceutical companies have established joint ventures with biotechnology start-ups, and banks have purchased brokerages to absorb new routines and business models. In this way, as Christopher Meyer suggests in Chapter Eight, managers can organize processes of exploration and adaptation instead of committing in advance to a specific course of action. Such efforts to induce change work best when the parent stays loosely coupled to the new venture so that agents in both organizations are allowed to evolve their organizations in accordance with models that are in line with the rules of the market.

Self-organizing networks that evolve effective behaviors are dynamic. In part, this reflects the natural tendency of connections to strengthen or wither in response to positive and negative feedback. In part, the dynamism of networks is engineered by managers who add and subtract nodes, make and break connections. As yet, research has produced little guidance for managers who would like to move beyond rules of thumb when deciding when and how to guide evolution this way. Providing new theory and tools to help managers take such actions more rationally should be high on the agenda of scholars who study complex systems.

Evolving Vicarious Selection Systems

Managers can accelerate the rate of evolution in self-organizing systems by operating vicarious selection systems. This proves functional when indirect selection mechanisms are good predictors of environmental feedback. When a system's vicarious selection mechanisms fall out of alignment with the environment, its fitness decreases and its survival may be threatened. Who selects vicarious selection systems? Managers do.

As Donald Campbell (1974) has shown, vicarious selection systems often form a nested hierarchy: each system is itself modified by a higher-level system. For example, managers use reward systems to simulate the voice of the market, winnowing initiatives so that investments in those unlikely to succeed can be terminated quickly. Reward systems in turn evolve through variation, selection, and retention, as organizations try out new incentives, keeping some while discarding others. Managers develop theories about which reward systems work best, and these theories become a vicarious selection system for a vicarious selection system. Theories about reward systems are themselves the subject of selection systems; for example, managers may consume research aimed at testing competing theories about reward systems.

As one vicarious selection system pyramids on another, managers run the risk that their theories will become far removed from the environment, causing vicarious systems meant to help evolution along to retard it instead. Managers must be vigilant for signs that vicarious systems are no longer predicting the environment well. To keep these systems honest, executives must constantly strive to improve them, generating variations, testing them empirically, and propagating the ones that have the most predictive power.

The problem managers must combat is that indirect selection systems tend to become institutionalized. What once was a means to an end becomes an end in itself. For example, David Halberstam

(1986) has recounted how General Motors' system for evaluating the projected financial performance of new cars devolved into an elaborate game during the 1960s. The goal of the exercise became manipulating projections to justify what one wanted to do, not predicting whether a new model would succeed in the marketplace. For the "finance guys," maintaining the system allowed them to exercise control over the product portfolio; for their opponents, the "car guys," manipulating the system was an act of honor, undertaken in order to save the company from its own dysfunctional review procedures.

In the end, the best way for managers to keep indirect selection systems from spiraling out of control may be to operate several of them in competition, even if some inconsistencies result. This contrasts with the example of many capital budgeting systems, which suffer from the "abominable no-man" syndrome: one thumbs-down verdict anywhere along an approval chain can terminate a project proposal. Better is the approach of companies such as Ore-Ida, the potato processor, which has given many different people, designated "Ore-Ida fellows," the ability to seed innovations with grants. In this way, different vicarious selection systems run in parallel, providing more than one means for variations to propagate. In the spirit of self-organization, managers are likely to find that evolving vicarious selection systems is superior to designing them.

Energizing the System

Ilya Prigogine (1980) demonstrated that "dissipative systems," into which energy flows, tend toward spontaneous order, unlike closed systems, which wind down into disorder due to entropy. Who keeps energy flowing into organizational systems? Managers do.

Because people are motivated by factors other than money, management must do more than align incentives with market forces. They must energize agents by providing inspiration and challenges. By setting aggressive goals, managers create a perceived mismatch between the performance presently achieved and the performance required. If agents accept the objectives, the gap motivates a self-organizing network to redouble its search efforts.

When a system is stuck on a local peak in a rugged fitness landscape, the only way to improve performance is to drive search behavior beyond the normal zone of comfort. For example, when Jim Clark persuaded the developers of the original Netscape Navigator that the market demanded that version 1.0 of the browser be completed in five months, they invented a host of new solutions that allowed them to achieve what most had thought nearly impossible. Such stories of extraordinary achievement are common when management sets aggressive goals and convinces agents that reaching them is not only possible but imperative.

Management also pumps energy into the system through vision and leadership. Great leaders convey to those who work with them a sense of excitement about the enterprise in which they are engaged. For example, Sun Microsystems has stimulated thousands of third parties to embrace its Java programming language by promulgating its vision of "write once, run anywhere." Through its evangelism, Sun has generated tremendous momentum behind Java because programmers have understood why it creates exhilarating new opportunities.

Incentives alone do not explain why people go above and beyond their job descriptions or why third parties rally behind a standard. The energy flowing through a self-organizing system depends in large part on the way managers motivate its agents and partners. Such systems do not need central controllers, but they do need executives who add momentum to the evolutionary process by providing the spark of inspiration.

In summary, management plays a strong role in determining why some organizations are more effective than others. They propel evolution forward and push it in interesting new directions by manipulating the context of behavior. A look at one highly effective self-organizing system—Capital One, a credit card issuer that specializes in direct marketing—will make these seven management functions more concrete.

Capital One: Self-Organization in Action

Capital One is one of the great American growth stories of the 1990s. Formed as a division of the Bank of Virginia (later Signet Bank) in 1987 by Rich Fairbank and Nigel Morris, this financial services firm was spun out of its parent as a public company in 1994. With $17 billion in managed assets, Capital One has become one of the top ten credit card issuers in the United States; between the end of 1992 and the middle of 1998, it grew from 1.5 million to almost 17 million cardholders. In fewer than six years, Capital One established a presence in more than 10 percent of American households through internal growth, not significant acquisitions.

Capital One has not only grown but has also enjoyed above-average profitability. Return on equity was 23 percent in 1998, despite 50 percent annual growth in the firm's marketing budget. As a consequence, its value has soared; a share of stock that sold for $16 in November 1994 fetched $125 by the end of 1998.

The original insight underpinning Capital One's growth was Fairbank and Morris's recognition that low-cost information processing would enable them to create a new kind of company that operated like a scientific laboratory for mass customization. In 1987, credit card companies had devised information systems to support billing and detect fraud but had not built systems capable of targeting direct-marketing credit card offers to customers in a sophisticated way. Capital One's founders believed that through constant testing of direct-marketing offers, the company could evolve the right product to deliver to the right customer at the right time and at the right price, for many different sets of customers.

The technological foundation of Capital One's business is a unique, proprietary set of information systems that support targeted direct marketing. Capital One conducts dozens of experiments each day: 14,106 in 1997, up from 335 in 1989. Any individual test includes a bundle of parameter settings—for example, in credit cards, whom to target, what pricing to offer, what initial interest rate to present, what credit policies to apply, and so on. In addition, when customers or potential customers call Capital One, its systems project immediately the costs and benefits associated with that customer, allowing the firm to experiment with different real-time responses and offers. The information system allows managers to measure all costs and revenues associated with a particular group of tests, which are analogous to the results of scientific laboratory experiments. Through a set of proprietary algorithms, Capital One is able to identify very quickly whether a particular test is exceeding or falling short of projected results.

The result is a Darwinian environment for ideas. The five thousand credit card products that Capital One offers today are the hardy survivors of intense competition for attention and resources. Its managers estimate that at least 99 percent of Capital One's tests fail. Capital One is poised at the edge of chaos, in the sweet spot where the population of experiments produces many failures, fewer small wins, fewer large wins, and the occasional stupendous revenue-generating concept. Its strategy of highly parallel experimentation is perfectly suited to its catalytic-network position (see Figure 1.2 in Chapter One). In a rugged fitness landscape with many profitable peaks whose locations are difficult to predict, Capital One's ability to try thousands of concepts and cull the winners helps account for its extraordinary performance.

Capital One's first breakthrough innovation was the balance transfer offer, introduced in 1992. The firm deployed its information systems to identify customers who used most of their credit lines but were unlikely to become delinquent in paying. Armed with this information, it was able to send these customers targeted direct mailings, offering a low initial "teaser" rate if they took out a

Capital One credit card and used it to pay the balances on their other credit cards.

Eventually, competitors caught on and began imitating Capital One's practices, in some cases copying the very text of its mailings. Capital One's response was to accelerate its pace of testing, moving into new markets faster than competitors could copy them. In addition, the firm honed its ability to identify very early which tests were proving to be extraordinarily successful and to exploit these offerings rapidly. The Capital One recipe was to generate many fast, cheap failures and massively reinforce successful experiments. By the time competitors realized what profitable product-customer-price combination Capital One had discovered, the pioneer had already blanketed the niche with direct mailings, leaving slim pickings for imitators. It was able to exploit success rapidly because it had developed the capability (via an information architecture based on reusable components) to turn small, prototype information systems into industrial-strength applications with astonishing speed.

Capital One's portfolio of product offerings constantly mutates. The goal is to keep the proportion of products invented within the previous two years above 80 percent. New offerings in its core product lines emerge from the interaction of many loosely coupled units that focus on local experimentation. At the same time, a small group of managers focuses on growing entirely new lines of business. For example, Capital One has become the largest direct marketer of cellular telephone services in the United States. It did not enter this industry through top-down planning; cellular service was one of at least eighty new business concepts that the firm tried during its first four years, most of which failed.

How do such variations arise? Capital One has no formal organization chart. Managers at Capital One are given areas of responsibility and charters to innovate, not rigid roles or job titles. Furthermore, part of everyone's job is to manage organizational white space, defined as the things an employee is not assigned to do. Employees are formally evaluated on how well they worked to spot white space opportunities and jump into them when appropriate. George Overholser, vice president of new business development, comments, "It's a scary management style, because senior managers often have little idea of what people are doing day to day" (personal conversation, date n. a.).

Although managers do not exercise hands-on command and control, Capital One is far from chaotic. Its systems substitute for executives' monitoring; as Overholser says, the market is the boss. Capital One's employees are expected to be stewards of ideas that are competing for the right to be tested in the marketplace. The fifteen thousand experiments Capital One conducts in a year must win in the marketplace of ideas the right to a trial. When an idea steward's superior does not support an idea, the originator of the idea may take it elsewhere within Capital One, seeking out the best home for the concept. The currency employed in this internal marketplace consists of one part evidence and one part enthusiasm. The more passionate an idea steward is and the more data that person can provide to buttress the idea, the higher the probability that the idea will win some of the resources allocated to experimental test cells.

The firm's overall adaptability arises from the complex interaction of many people at all levels of the organization who engage in locally selfish behavior. According to Overholser, idea stewards are told that they should be willing to lie down in front of trains on behalf of their ideas. In fact, they are encouraged not to do jobs they are asked to do by individuals who are not as close to the ideas the steward is championing. The emergent outcome of this intense, narrowly focused competition of ideas is profitable because, in the end, the voice of the marketplace, expressed with statistical rigor, is the ultimate arbiter of success or failure.

How does one manage a corporation whose product portfolio and lines of business evolve through thousands of trials? Managers at all levels of Capital One have mastered the art of indirect selection, providing an environment that encourages experimentation, rigorously culls ideas, and rapidly institutionalizes information systems to support the winners. The organization's information systems work because the firm's organization, culture, recruitment, and reward systems have been configured to evolve profitable behaviors faster and more effectively than rivals can. Overholser explains, "We as managers create an environment that fosters the innovation and competition of ideas, to recognize and roll out rapidly the best ones. The product mix is self-organizing. As a management team, we do not tell people what to test, but we do select which tests won."

To understand what managers do in a self-organizing enterprise such as Capital One, it is useful to revisit the functions of management described above.

Selecting the External Environment

Capital One's senior managers did not dictate that the firm would diversify into cellular telephone service or auto financing, but they have established clear guidelines for the kind of environments toward which experimenting is directed. The firm's managers who are charged with pursuing growth opportunities look for four touchstones: a flexible product to facilitate testing, direct marketing to allow actuarial evaluation of experiments, an industry structure where marketing companies can enjoy high returns, and the commitment of smart, entrepreneurial problem solvers. Says Overholser, "The types of businesses that work for us have many possible product configurations that can be tuned to fit the marketplace at any given time. For example, in credit cards, you can manipulate the interest rates, teaser periods, targeting algorithms, and ways you deal with risk. In the cellular telephone business, you can give away free minutes, you can work with different times of day, and you can decide whether to cross-sell when customers call for service."

The firm's managers recognize that internally generated experiments will not be enough to maintain the firm's growth rate at its present size. Accordingly, they have established partnerships with private equity firms to tap into experiments conducted by a vast pool of entrepreneurs. Sometimes, deals that are turned down by venture capitalists may have been rejected because of flaws that Capital One's direct-marketing prowess can solve or overcome. By choosing to examine thousands of entrepreneurial business plans, management does not dictate how the firm's business portfolio will evolve, but it does propel the firm into growth opportunities that would otherwise be overlooked.

Once it enters a business, Capital One selects environments that rivals are neglecting. For example, in the credit card industry, half the households in the United States receive over fifty credit card offers a year, while the other half receive only six. The firm's chief information officer, Jim Donehy, says, "We're not testing where everybody's radar screen is focused; we're testing where everybody else is not looking." Through such policies, senior managers do not control which experiments the firm conducts, but they direct it toward unusually promising niches.

Defining Performance

In self-organizing enterprises, managers shape networks' behavior by emphasizing or de-emphasizing indicators that they believe will ultimately lead to long-run profitability. Managers do not dictate the outcomes of experiments, but they do choose how to keep score.

At Capital One, the single most important metric by which an experiment is evaluated is the predicted and realized net present value of a customer over that customer's lifetime. Because the firm's systems are set up to identify customer lifetime value, this common metric provides an important benchmark for comparing different experiments. Allocation of marketing dollars is most heavily influenced by lifetime net present value per marginal marketing dollar, subject to several constraints that limit the number of test cells and create competition among ideas. The marketing budget and global earnings targets help determine the number of test cells executed in a given year. So does management's goal that 80 percent of the organization's products should be no more than two years old.

Capital One uses a balanced scorecard to communicate performance expectations to employees. Overholser describes the concept:

> Our senior managers have spent years popularizing something called the "big yellow square" as an antidote to the evils of "monovariabilitus." People walk around with "big yellow square" buttons pinned to their shirts. The "big yellow square" is really a graph that reflects how well we are performing against four competing desires: economics, customer satisfaction, internal people satisfaction and growth. Progress on each of the dimensions is depicted as the distance of each of the quadrilateral's respective corners from the center; at any given time, we want to make sure we see a square. If it stops being shaped like a square, we're willing to retreat on one area of progress in order to restore the balance.

Managers also focus attention on other measures, such as the ratio of losses to assets, a key metric employed by outside investors. The bonus pool (which is split among approximately the top one hundred employees) depends on a complex formula that takes into account a number of factors, such as recruiting, innovation, and customer service. However, the most important measure is the year-on-year sum of earnings plus marketing investment per share. By comparing marketing investment plus earnings to the previous year's results, top management removes the incentive to downplay long-term investment in order to maximize compensation.

Because its complex selection environment defines performance as a trade-off among various goals, Capital One maintains a focus on customer value while encouraging innovations that improve performance in other dimensions as well. Without dictating which experiments win, top management has channeled Capital One's evolution by defining what "winning" means.

Managing Meaning

Top managers indirectly influence self-organizing firms by channeling their attention toward a particular set of signals. One reason that Capital One's Darwinian environment succeeds is that individuals are expected to fail and are not penalized for failure. As Overholser says, "If you have 15,000 tests and most of them fail, you can't have career paths based on keeping your nose clean."

Instead of measuring individuals by the financial results of their experiments, Capital One assesses twenty-four key competencies, such as communication skills, recruiting ability, and effectiveness in project management. Each employee's performance in each of these twenty-four areas is evaluated twice a year by several managers, and bonuses are determined by ratings for these "behavioral anchors." Overholser explains, "If someone exhibited the right behaviors in stewardship for those ideas, their careers can move along at a great pace, even if they presided over spectacular failures."

The result is a clear sense among employees of what is wanted, what the firm stands for. One younger executive describes what employee and employer value at Capital One: "This company values expertise in an employee over anything else. Seniority, pedigree, and achievements are not valued as much as being really good at your job. People feel good about being competent, and being able to do their work well. I hear talk about work issues around the water cooler, because people are proud of what they do."

Choosing People

By consciously deciding which agents to bring into a network, managers influence the network's evolution indirectly. Overholser estimates that senior managers at Capital One spend at least 20 percent of their time on recruiting. He contends that their primary need for growth is the ability to attract talent into the company, especially knowledge workers. This investment is necessary to build a group that runs itself.

Historically, the company has hired exceptionally bright recent college graduates and MBA's to staff existing business units. Over-holser explains, "We must test ideas that have never been tested before, so we have a very young company. We want to defy conventional wisdom, so we like to hire people who are wet behind the ears." Grueling interviews of top candidates weed out ninety-eight of every hundred applicants. The small number of people who are asked to join the firm are expected to be great problem solvers who can behave autonomously. Extraordinarily intelligent young managers (the average SAT score of Capital One's marketing and analysis managers in math is 760 out of 800) are given responsibility much earlier in their careers at Capital One than at most rivals. It is not uncommon for employees in their twenties to run multi-million-dollar businesses.

Capital One chooses different kinds of people when it needs to enter new industries. When they go into a different industry or innovate at a higher level of the organization, they don't bring in novices but people who are savvy, sophisticated, and networked.

Reconfiguring the Network

The firm's top management keeps the enterprise from sliding into too much order by frequently changing the network of nodes and relationships across which behavior flows. When new employees join the company, they are seldom recruited for a specific job. Rather, they join the organization of whichever manager makes the best case to them and thus attracts their commitment.

Capital One makes a point of assigning people to areas where they have not already demonstrated competence. For example, a junior manager who has never led a project might be assigned one where he or she can hone project management skills in a forgiving environment. New hires must move among several different jobs so they can get to know the organization. No rules constrain an employee from looking for openings anywhere in the organization, and when someone's business plan is rejected, that employee simply finds another team to join.

Capital One constantly creates and breaks up teams to encourage the emergence of unconventional wisdom. Project groups are constantly taken apart and put back together in support of various tests. If a group appears to be engaging in repetitive behaviors, it will be disbanded and its members encouraged to seek other opportunities with longer-term impact. In some groups, such as Overholser's, employees are required to move elsewhere in the organization after a year.

Evolving Vicarious Selection Systems

Capital One's vicarious selection systems are the bedrock of its emergent behavior patterns. By aligning the laboratory environment as closely as possible with changing markets, the firm is able to predict outcomes and detect failures from a few data points. Capital One has invested heavily in algorithms that provide "early election returns"—predictions, based on a few months' data, of what the results of a test would be were it allowed to play out to the end.

The company's proprietary models enable it to forecast what lifetime net present value of customers will flow from every marketing dollar spent on a program. Capital One's uniform emphasis on lifetime net present value per dollar invested provides a common basis for comparing ideas that compete with one another. As a result, across different businesses, the company can decide which test cells to commission, and it can evaluate the results of each experiment.

Another vicarious selection system is the set of hurdles that idea stewards must cross to champion concepts in which they believe. Any new concept can only get off the ground if someone is willing to start promoting it without any assistance. Access to people who provide systems that support a test is not granted automatically; passionate advocates must win support instead of commanding it.

Resources naturally pull away from projects that appear to be foundering, without a central authority deciding to pull the plug, because other projects are constantly bidding for attention.

Energizing the System

Spontaneous order requires a constant flow of energy into a system. Part of the emotional motor that powers Capital One is the sheer excitement of seeing one's ideas win in the marketplace. Another part is the satisfaction that high performers experience when they earn the respect of their peers. The time that senior managers do not spend in command-and-control activities is devoted instead to motivating, coaching, and rewarding outstanding performance.

Capital One's compensation practices also inject vigor into the organization. Managers earn salary and stock options, with heavy incentives to load up on the firm's stock. On several occasions, the firm's top managers have exchanged stock options that were in the money for more options that would vest only if shareholder performance significantly improved. Cash bonuses can range up to 60 percent of salary, as can options on a face-value basis.

Although high performers are richly rewarded at Capital One, perhaps the most powerful incentive is inherent in the open nature of the firm's laboratory environment. The managers who are competing for test cells meet on a regular basis and together watch the results of the competition as results begin to flow in from experiments. Because everyone knows which hypotheses are panning out, idea stewards push hard to get their tests to work. For the puzzle solvers Capital One has tried so hard to attract, the pleasure of proving an idea right publicly is the most powerful motivator of all.

Conclusion

Capital One illustrates what it means to say that effective behaviors emerge and self-adjust to environmental change in a self-organizing system. Capital One is managed quite effectively. The company's spectacular growth arises from behaviors that are evolved, not designed—this is the essence of self-organization. Self-organization does not mean giving people a mission, standing back, and seeing what happens. Capital One moves forward because it stimulates thousands of experiments, selects those that clear the firm's vicarious selection system and perform well in test markets, and retains the successful concepts through a high level of automation and service.

Our world is becoming more complex because it is becoming more interconnected, and ubiquitous connections allow communities of specialists to flourish. In addition, the best minds, particularly among younger people, are increasingly likely to participate in networks that give them considerable local autonomy. In such a world, designed enterprises will find it increasingly difficult to compete with organizations whose behaviors are evolved, not planned. The question that readers of this chapter can expect to confront is not whether their firms will embrace self-organization but how their firms will survive competition from companies like Capital One if they do not.

7

Heterarchy

Distributing Authority and Organizing Diversity

David Stark

The epochal transformation taking place in the societies of Eastern Europe and the former Soviet Union offers an extraordinary social laboratory to study processes of organizational change. Standard accounts tend to emphasize discontinuities. Indeed, the surprising rapidity of the collapse of communism throughout the Soviet bloc, the election of democratic governments who face an entirely new array of political challenges, and the sweeping embrace of market mechanisms and private property all made it seem that the world had changed in the moment of a breath. Exhale communism, inhale capitalism. Now, however, after nearly a decade of developments, including war in former Yugoslavia and stalled reforms in Russia, some analysts are attuned to continuities. The outbreaks of ethnic rivalries, the persistence of nondemocratic political forces, and the continued power of entrenched economic interests all reveal lasting legacies of the old order. From that view, the more things change, the more they stay the same.

But there are alternatives to seeing these postsocialist phenomena either as evidence of a revolutionary (albeit democratic and capitalist) rupture or as indicators of a glacial stasis. What we need is a framework that can take into account discontinuities and continuities, shearing from the former its facile optimism and from the latter its morbid pessimism while replacing both with a pragmatic realism.

The alternative adopted in this chapter is to view the postsocialist economies as complex adaptive systems (CAS). The premise is that postsocialist Eastern Europe is a genuine social laboratory, not simply because researchers can use it to test competing theories but because people there are actively experimenting with new organizational forms. In and with these new forms, they are testing competing worldviews and beliefs. Unlike those of scientists, the localized experiments in Eastern Europe are not by design, nor should they be. The attempt to create and manage an entire economy by design was the colossal Leninist failure, and efforts to create capitalism by design would do well to learn from those mistakes. (See also Chapter Two; and "Path Dependence and Privatization Strategies" in Stark and Bruszt, 1998.) Instead, their experimentation is more like bricolage: making do with what is available. But if they use the existing institutional materials that are close at hand, they are not for that reason condemned to mimic the old. As John Holland (1995) shows in very different contexts, combining old building blocks is one way to innovate—innovation through recombination (see also Chapter Five).

In analyzing organizational innovation as recombination, this chapter adopts an appropriately combinatory strategy, drawing on key concepts from the CAS repertoire. The opening section introduces a core problem of the postsocialist transformation through the concept of "lock-in," the process whereby early successes can pave a path for further investments of new resources that eventually lock in to suboptimal outcomes. Current adaptation, in this view, can pose obstacles to future adaptability. But must organizations and systems accept this fate? Are there organizational forms that are better configured to learn from the environment? Such organizations would need cognitive tools that recognize (re-cognize) new resources in an ongoing reconfiguration of organizational assets.

These challenges are hardly unique to the postsocialist transformations. Therefore, the subsequent section of the chapter makes explicit the assumption that the term "transforming economies" applies no less to the societies of North America and Western Europe than to those of Eastern Europe and the former Soviet Union. Firms in both types of economies now face extraordinary uncertainties—caused by the rapidity of technological change or the extreme volatility of markets in the former and shaped by political and institutional uncertainties in the latter. The response to these uncertainties is an emergent, self-organizing form referred to here as "heterarchy," whose features are elaborated along with other CAS concepts. In pointing to processes of lateral or "distributed" authority, this chapter develops a rough analogy to the concept of "distributed cognition" in the work of Andy Clark (1997), and similarly draws on Clark's and John Henry Clippinger's notions (Chapters Three and Four respectively) of overlapping "tags" in exploring how organizations can benefit from the active rivalry of competing belief systems.

Having outlined the features of heterarchical forms, the chapter then focuses on the specific challenges facing the postsocialist firm. Once we break with the all-too-prevalent design imperative of a single model of capitalism (and its attendant notion of different stages on a progression toward it), we are able to think about diverse types of capitalism. The collapse of communism and the end of the dichotomous comparison of capitalism versus socialism make us alert to the possibilities of comparing *capitalisms* (plural). As we shall see, that collapse did not leave a tabula rasa. Eastern Europeans are not so much building *on* the ruins of communism as *with* the ruins. With these distinctive building blocks, they are constructing a distinctively Eastern European capitalism.

Lessons from Labrador

We begin with the problem of adaptation versus adaptability, and for a lesson on avoiding the problem of lock-in, we turn to an unlikely source: the Naskapi Indians of the Labrador Peninsula. Each evening during their hunting season, the Naskapi determined where they would look for game on the next day's hunt by holding the shoulder bone of a caribou over the fire (Weick, 1977, p. 45). Examining the smoke deposits on the caribou bone, a shaman read for the hunting party the points of orientation of the next day's search. In this way the Naskapi introduced a randomizing element to confound a short-term rationality that would have dictated that the one best way to find game would be to look again tomorrow where they had found game today. By following the divergent daily maps of smoke on the caribou bone, they avoided locking into early successes that, while taking them to game in the short run, would in the long run have depleted the caribou stock in that area and reduced the likelihood of successful hunting. By breaking the link between future courses and past successes, the tradition of shoulder bone reading was an antidote to path dependence in the hunt.

Mainstream notions of the postsocialist "transition" as the replacement of one set of economic institutions by another set of institutions of proven efficiency are plagued by problems of short-term rationality similar to those the Naskapi practices mitigated. As the policy variant of "hunt tomorrow where we found game today," some economic advisers recommend the adoption of a highly stylized version of the institutions of prices and property that have "worked well in the West." Economic efficiency will be maximized, they argue, only through the rapid and all-encompassing implementation of privatization and marketization. This chapter argues, by contrast, that although such institutional homogenization might foster *adaptation* in the short run, the consequent loss of institutional diversity will impede *adaptability* in the long run. Limiting the search for effective institutions and organizational forms to the familiar Western hunting ground of tried and proven arrangements locks the postsocialist economies into exploiting known territory at the cost of forgetting (or never learning) the skills of exploring for new solutions.

Recent studies in evolutionary economics and organizational analysis suggest that organizations that learn too quickly sacrifice efficiency. Allen and McGlade (1987), for example, use the behavior of Nova Scotia fishermen to illustrate the possible trade-offs of exploiting old certainties and exploring new possibilities. Their model of these fishing fleets divides the fishermen into two classes: the rationalist "Cartesians," who drop their nets only where the fish are known to be biting, and the risk-taking "Stochasts," who discover the new schools of fish. In simulations where all the skippers are Stochasts, the fleet is relatively unproductive because knowledge of where the fish are biting is not used; but a purely Cartesian fleet locks into the most likely spot and quickly fishes it out. More efficient are the models that, like the actual behavior of the Nova Scotia fishing fleets, mix Cartesian exploiters and Stochast explorers.

James March's simulation in "Exploration and Exploitation in Organizational Learning" (1991) yields similar results: he finds that interacting collections of smart learners frequently do not perform as well as collections of smart and dumb. Organizations that learn too quickly *exploit* at the expense of *exploration*, thereby locking into suboptimal routines and strategies. The purely Cartesian fleet in Allen and McGlade's study, like the organizations of homogeneously smart learners in March's simulations, illustrates the potential dangers of positive feedback and the pitfalls of tight coupling. Like infantry officers who instructed drummers to disrupt the cadence of marching soldiers while they were crossing bridges, lest the resonance of uniformly marching feet cause potentially destructive tremors, this chapter draws the lesson that dissonance contributes to organizational learning and economic evolution.

Restated in the language of the new economics of adaptive systems (Arthur, 1994, and Chapter Two in this volume), the problem for any transforming economy is that the very mechanisms that foster allocative efficiency might eventually lock development into a path that is inefficient. From this point of view, our attention turns from a preoccupation with adaptation to a concern about adaptability, shifting from the problem of how to improve the immediate "fit" with a new economic environment to the problem of how to reshape the organizational structure to enhance its ability to respond to unpredictable future changes in the environment.

Sociologists in the tradition of organizational ecology have a ready answer to this problem. At the level of the economic system, adaptability is promoted by the diversity of organizations: a system with a greater variety of organizational forms (a more diverse organizational "gene pool") has a higher probability of having in hand some solution that is satisfactory under changed environmental conditions (Hannan, 1986). From that viewpoint, the problem of socialism was not only that it lacked a selection mechanism (firms were not allowed to fail) but also that almost all economic resources were locked into one organizational form, the large state-owned enterprise. That form was formidable in achieving industrialization; but lacking capacity for innovation, it failed woefully in the subsequent competition with the West. Similarly, the problem in the current period of transformation is that "success" that is achieved during the transition through forced homogenization toward the privately held corporation might suppress organizational diversity, thereby impeding adaptability in the next round of global competition.

But where do new organizational forms come from? Understanding organizational change as taking place almost exclusively through the deaths and births of organizations, the organizational ecology perspective neglects the possibility of organizational learning and fails to address the emergence of new organizational forms. The point of view put forth in this chapter is that, in addition to the diversity of organizations within a population, *organization* of diversity within an enterprise promotes adaptability. Organized diversity is most likely to yield its fullest evolutionary potential when different organizational principles coexist in an active rivalry. "Rivalry" in this sense refers not to competing camps and factions but to coexisting logics and frames of action. The organization of diversity is an active and sustained engagement in which there is more than one way to organize, label, interpret, and evaluate the same or similar activities. It increases the possibilities of long-term adaptability by better search—better not because it is more consistent or elegant or coherent but precisely because the complexity that it promotes and the lack of simple coherence that it tolerates increase the diversity of options. The challenge of the organization of diversity is to find solutions that promote constructive organizational reflexivity, or the ability to redefine and recombine resources. The emergent organizational forms with these properties are here termed "heterarchies."

Heterarchy

Heterarchy represents a new logic of organizing based on neither the market nor hierarchy. Whereas hierarchies involve relations of *dependence* and markets involve relations of *independence*, heterarchies involve relations of *interdependence*. As the term suggests, heterarchies are characterized by minimal hierarchy and by organizational heterogeneity.

Heterarchical features are a response to the increasing complexity of the firm's strategy horizons (Lane and Maxfield, 1996), or "fitness landscape." In relentlessly changing organizations where, in extreme cases, there is uncertainty even about what product the firm will be producing in the near future, the strategy horizon of the firm is unpredictable and its fitness landscape is rugged. To cope with these uncertainties, instead of concentrating its resources for strategic planning among a narrow set of senior executives or delegating that function to a specialized department, firms may undergo a radical decentralization in which virtually every unit becomes engaged in innovation. That is, in place of specialized search routines in which some departments are dedicated to exploration while others are confined to exploiting existing knowledge, the functions of exploration are generalized throughout the organization. The search for new markets, for example, is no longer the sole province of the marketing department if units responsible for purchase and supply are also scouting the possibilities for qualitatively new inputs that can open up new product lines.

These developments increase interdependencies between divisions, departments, and work teams within the firm. But because of the greater complexity of these feedback loops, coordination cannot be engineered, controlled, or managed hierarchically. The result of interdependence is to increase the autonomy of work units. Yet at the same time, more complex interdependence heightens the need for fine-grained coordination between the increasingly autonomous units.

These pressures are magnified by dramatic changes in the sequencing of activities in production relations. As product cycles shorten from years to months, the race to new markets calls into question the strict sequencing of design and execution. Because of strong first-mover advantages, in which the first actor to introduce a new product (especially one that establishes a new industry standard) captures inordinate market share, firms that wait to begin production until design is completed will be penalized in competition. Like the production of "B" movies, in which filming begins before the script is completed, successful strategies integrate conception and execution, with significant aspects of the production process beginning even before design is finalized.

Production relations are even more radically altered in the simultaneous engineering processes analyzed by Sabel and Dorf (1998). Conventional design is sequential, with subsystems that are presumed to be central designed in detail first, setting the boundary conditions for the design of lower-ranking components. But in simultaneous engineering, separate project teams develop all the subsystems concurrently. In such concurrent design, the various project teams engage in ongoing mutual monitoring, as innovations produce multiple, sometimes competing, proposals for improving the overall design.

Thus, increasingly rugged fitness landscapes yield increasingly complex interdependencies that in turn yield increasingly complex coordination challenges. Where search is no longer departmentalized but is instead generalized and distributed throughout the organization, and where design is no longer compartmentalized but deliberated and distributed throughout the production process, the solution is distributed authority.

Under circumstances of simultaneous engineering, where the very parameters of a project are subject to deliberation and change across units, authority is no longer delegated vertically; it emerges laterally. As one symptom of these changes, managers socialized in an earlier regime frequently express their puzzlement to researchers: "There's one thing I can't figure out. Who's my boss?" Under conditions of distributed authority, managers might still "report to" their superiors; but increasingly, they are accountable to other work teams. Success at simultaneous engineering thus depends on learning by mutual monitoring.

The interdependencies that result from attempts to cope with rugged fitness landscapes are only inadequately captured in concepts of "matrix organizations" or in fads such as treating the firm as a set of "internal markets" according to which every unit should regard every other unit in the firm as its "customer." These conceptions are inadequate because they take the boundaries of the firm and the boundaries of its internal units as given parameters. In fact, the reorganization of the modern firm is more radical. As it shifts from search routines to a situation in which search is generalized, the modern firm is perpetually reinventing itself. Under circumstances of rapid technological change and volatility of products and markets, it seems there is no one best solution. If one could be rationally chosen and resources devoted to it alone, the benefits of its fleeting superiority would not compensate for the costs of subsequent missed opportunities. Because managers hedge against these uncertainties, the outcomes are hybrid forms (Sabel, 1990). Good managers do not simply commit themselves to the array that keeps the most options open; instead, they create an organizational space open to the perpetual redefinition of what might constitute an option. Rather than a rational choice among a set of known options, we find practical action fluidly redefining what the options might be. Management becomes the art of facilitating organizations that can reorganize themselves.

The challenge of the modern firm, whether it be a postsocialist firm coping with the uncertainties of system change or a digital technologies firm coping with unpredictable strategy horizons, is the challenge of building organizations that are capable of learning. Flexibility requires an ability to redefine and recombine assets—in short, a pragmatic reflexivity.

This capacity for self-redefinition is grounded in the organizational heterogeneity that characterizes heterarchies. Heterarchies are *complex* adaptive systems because they interweave a multiplicity of organizing principles. The new organizational forms are heterarchical not only because they have flattened hierarchy but also because they are the sites of competing and coexisting value systems. The greater interdependence of increasingly autonomous work teams results in a proliferation of performance criteria. Distributed authority not only implies that units will be accountable to each other but also that each will be held to accountings in multiple registers. Heterarchies create wealth by inviting more than one way of evaluating worth.

In the terms of the CAS thinking explored in *The Biology of Business* (see especially Chapters One, Three, and Four), heterarchies are organizations with multiple worldviews and belief systems, just as products, processes, and properties carry multiple "tags" or interpretations. Success in rugged fitness landscapes requires an extended organizational reflexivity that sustains rather than stifles this complexity. Because resources are not fixed in one system of interpretation but can exist in several, heterarchies make assets of ambiguity.

Making the Best of One's Resources

While managers in advanced sectors are coping with volatile markets, rapid technological change, and the challenges of simultaneous engineering, policymakers in the postsocialist world must cope with a set of different, but equally complex, strategy horizons: the uncertainties of international competition, of reading unfamiliar market signals in place of familiar bureaucratic signals, and of the simultaneous extension of citizenship rights and property rights (that is, of democratization and property transformation). How should they reorganize their economies and restructure their firms in the face of these extraordinary uncertainties?

For many Western policy advisers who flew into the region (often with little knowledge of its peculiarities), the answers were straightforward, and two positions quickly dominated the debate. On the one side was the message of the neoliberals: the best way to restructure is to use strong markets. Markets, they argued, were not only the goals but also the means. Rapid privatization, trade and price liberalization, strict bankruptcy laws, and an end to government subsidies were key elements of their policy prescriptions. But the depth and rapidity of economic recession in the aftermath of 1989 dampened enthusiasm for the neoliberal agenda, and an alternative, neostatist position entered the debate, arguing that the neoliberal strategy confused goals and means. To create markets, one cannot simply rely on markets. Strengthening the market requires strong states.

The choice seemed clear: strong markets versus strong states. The problem, however, was that the societies of the postsocialist world historically lack both developed markets and coherent states. The nonexistent starting points of the neoliberals and the neostatists recall the joke in which an Irishman in the far countryside is asked, "What's the best way to get to Dublin?" He thinks for a minute, then responds, "I wouldn't start from here."

The irony of the answer would not be lost on Eastern Europeans, for they are all too acutely aware that the best ways to get to capitalism started somewhere else. But those options are not available to our contemporary traveling companions. Accordingly, this chapter adopts a different analytical starting point—the pragmatic, self-organizing starting point of the Eastern Europeans themselves, who in place of the question "What is the best way to get to capitalism?" must ask, "How do we get there from here?" In place of the therapies, recipes, formulas, and blueprints of designer capitalism, postsocialist firms have had to adopt a different strategy. Precluded from the best ways to get to capitalism, they are making the best of what they have.

With what institutional resources have they embarked? Postsocialist societies lack strong markets and strong states, but they have decades of experience with strong networks under socialism. These associative ties of reciprocity were unintended consequences of the attempt to "scientifically" manage an entire national economy. At the shop-floor level, shortages and supply bottlenecks led to bargaining between supervisors and informal groups; at the level of the gray market, the distortions of central planning produced the conditions to create networks of predominantly part-time entrepreneurs; and at the managerial level, the task of meeting plan targets produced dense networks of informal ties that cut across enterprises and local organizations.

Some of these network ties have dissipated in the transforming postsocialist economic environment. Others have been strengthened as firms, individuals, banks, local governments, and other economic actors have adopted coping strategies to survive (not all of them legal and, in some countries, many of them corrupt). Still others have emerged anew as these same actors have searched for new customers and suppliers, new sources of credit and revenues, and new strategic allies. The existence of parallel structures in the informal and interfirm networks that "got the job done" under socialism means that instead of an institutional vacuum, we find routines and practices that can become assets, resources, and the basis for credible commitments and coordinated actions. In short, associative ties build new forms of association as the "ties that bind" shape binding agreements.

But network ties are only part of the way postsocialist firms are attempting to restructure under difficult circumstances and with few new resources. Aid, credit, and direct investment have been paltry when compared to the magnitude of the economic and political transformation in the region. In this situation, one of the principal resources of the postsocialist firm is resourcefulness. Less design than improvisation, restructuring is often a process of bricolage: making do with what is available, redeploying assets for new uses, recombining resources within and across organizational boundaries. From the aggregation and recombination of existing building blocks emerge genuinely new structures and processes.

These recombinant practices have a special character in post-socialist societies, where economies are undergoing a profound transformation in property regimes. Conventionally addressed under the rubric of "privatization" and understood as a straightforward transfer of property from public to private hands, the property transformation in postsocialist firms is in fact often neither a simple transition from public to private hands nor a clarification of property rights. Instead, the emerging new property forms blur the boundaries of public and private, erode the organizational boundaries of the firms, and multiply the operative evaluating principles with which the firm justifies access to resources. Property that has this ensemble of characteristics may be referred to as "recombinant" property.

Recombinant property involves a form of organizational hedging in which actors respond to uncertainty in the organizational environment by diversifying their assets and redefining and recombining resources. In its extreme form, it is an attempt to hold and label resources that can be justified or assessed by more than one standard of evaluation (multiple tags). The overlap of a multiplicity of property regimes in the postsocialist circumstances does not simply mean that multiple owners are making different claims on the resources of the firm. Rather, it means that the multiple regimes provide multiple opportunities for the firm to make claims for resources. "Asset diversification" in such cases differs markedly from that of the mutual fund portfolio manager, whose strategy can be captured in the algorithm that expresses optimizing preferences across risk functions, short-term revenues, long-term growth, and the like. By contrast, the recombinant strategies in the postsocialist cases are practices that seek to manage asset ambiguity. Under circumstances of asset interdependence, some assets are most valuable precisely where property claims are least clarified; thus, under circumstances where multiple legitimating principles are at play, actors gain advantage if they can exploit the ambiguity of justifications for claims. In this highly uncertain environment, therefore, enterprise survival can depend on skills that make assets of ambiguity.

Recombinant Processes in Hungary

Immediately following the first free elections in spring 1990, the new democratic government of Hungary announced an ambitious program of privatization. Because this was intended to be a state-directed course of property transformation, the government created a large bureaucratic agency, the State Property Agency (SPA), responsible for every aspect of privatizing the productive assets of the Hungarian economy—some 90 percent of which had been held by the state. From its inception, the SPA adopted the official policy that privatization would be conducted on a strictly case-by-case, firm-by-firm basis. SPA policy never treated assets as interdependent across firms or considered that firms might be broken up and their assets regrouped by economic agents with local knowledge of constraints and opportunities. Instead, it adopted the role of Big Broker, attempting to match buyers to firms, and it sought to legitimate its activities externally by emphasizing the bottom line: revenues brought into the state treasury from the eventual sale of individual firms.

Enterprise directors thought otherwise. While bureaucratic administrators in the SPA debated the merits of auctions versus public offerings and transaction officers in the agency scrambled to acquire some familiarity with the dozens of firms assigned to their supervision, enterprise management took advantage of several pieces of legislation to launch its own strategies of property transformation.

Although we typically think about owners acquiring firms, the peculiar circumstances of the economic transformation in Eastern Europe has placed extraordinary political and economic pressure on postsocialist firms to acquire owners. They do so, moreover, under circumstances in which the demand for owners greatly exceeds the supply. On one hand, the demand for owners is high: the postsocialist firm is searching for new owners at precisely the same time that thousands of other firms are doing the same. On the other hand, the supply of owners with adequate capital and interest is relatively low: the domestic population has savings that equal only a fraction of the value of the assets of the state-owned enterprises, and there are only a limited number of interested foreign buyers. Politically compelled to find owners in order to adjust to the new political setting, and organizationally compelled to find owner-allies in order to address the challenges of the new economic environment, the postsocialist firms find each other. That is, they acquire shares in other firms, and they make arrangements for other enterprises to become their new shareholders. The results are dense networks of interlocking ownership ties that extend through and across branches and sectors of the economy, especially among the very largest enterprises and banks.

Network Properties

To assess the prevalence of such interenterprise ownership, I compiled a data set on the ownership structure of the two hundred largest Hungarian corporations (ranked by sales). These firms compose the "Top 200" on the listing of *Figyelö*, a leading Hungarian business weekly. Like their Fortune 500 counterparts in the United States, the "*Figyelö* 200" firms are major players in the Hungarian economy, employing an estimated 21 percent of the labor force and accounting for 37 percent of total net sales and 42 percent of export revenues. The data also include the top twenty-five Hungarian banks (ranked by assets). Ownership data were obtained in the spring of 1994 and updated in the spring of 1996; they were gathered directly from the Hungarian courts of registry, where corporate files contain complete lists of the company's owners as of the most recent shareholders' meeting. Following the convention in the literature of East Asian business groups, analysis is restricted to the top twenty owners of each corporation. However, in the Hungarian economy, where only thirty-seven firms are traded on the Budapest stock exchange and where corporate shareholding is not widely dispersed among hundreds of small investors, the twenty-owner restriction allows us to account for at least 90 percent of the shares held in virtually every company.

Who holds the shares of these largest enterprises and banks? Through its property holding agencies, the state remains the most prominent owner. It was the sole and exclusive owner of 16.4 percent of these firms and kept its hand in as one of the top twenty owners in 44.4 percent of the largest corporations and banks in 1996. The state, although whittled down, is not withering away. Only five companies (2.0 percent) in this population were owned exclusively by private individuals in 1996. Even by the least restrictive criterion—the presence of even one individual private investor among a company's major owners—individual private ownership cannot be seen as ascendant: in 1994, 102 individuals in the data set held ownership stakes in 8.5 percent of these largest enterprises and banks. In 1996, these figures actually declined, with only 61 individuals appearing among the twenty major owners of only 7.3 percent of the units in the population.

Intercorporate ownership, on the other hand, is increasing. The percentage of units with at least one corporate owner rose from 66.3

percent to 77.6 percent in 1996. Most notably, the number of units in which all the top twenty owners are other corporations increased from 35.6 percent to 40.2 percent. Many of these owners are themselves the largest enterprises and banks, the very firms for which I gathered the ownership data.

Property with Emergent Properties

Beyond confirming the prevalence of such interenterprise ownership, the data also allow us to identify the links among these large enterprises. These ties are dense and extensive, and they yield numerous networks of interconnected holdings.

Direct ties among the largest firms, however, are only the most immediate way to identify relational properties in the field of interacting strategies. For in addition to knowing the direct ties between two firms (for example, Company A is a major shareholder of Bank B), we can also identify the patterns formed by their mutual shareholdings even when two firms are not themselves directly tied (for example, Enterprises C, D, E, and F share a relation by virtue of their tie to Bank X, which is a major shareholder in each; or Bank X and Bank Z are linked by their mutual ownership of Enterprise M).

Incorporating this more complete ensemble of ties allows us to probe a concept that network analysts refer to as structural similarity. To take a simple example, if all your friends are my friends, we are structurally similar even if we do not know each other. The notion of structural similarity gives a more robust view of the overall properties of the field because it provides a richer interpretation of proximity in a structural space: we might be indifferent to knowing precisely who is friends with whom if our question is to ask who runs in the same social circles. The strategist for a biotechnology firm who is trying to anticipate the next moves of the competition might well want to know which firms tend to license identical patents, even when the competitors do not directly license patents from each other (for example, A's competitors, B and C, do not license each other's patents but both tend to license patents from D, E, and F).

For my data set, two companies are structurally similar if their overall sets of relations, compared to all the other members of the data set (that is, to all the possible owners as well as to all the units that can be owned), are nearly alike. I use a clustering algorithm to identify the major business groupings of the Hungarian economy formed through interenterprise ties.

The results take a broader view to show the various "teams" in the whole field. To understand such a representation, as a first approximation, think of each firm as having a portfolio of holdings (the other companies in which it holds shares) and as having a port-folio of owners (its shareholders). Then instead of taking the indi-vidual firm as the unit of analysis, take the relatively discrete network of firms as the unit. Also, think of property (ownership or holdings) as having properties (characteristics or features). That is, think about property as the network properties of a group of firms and about a portfolio not as a feature of a single firm but as the prop-erty of a network.

Once we think of each network as a distinctive portfolio, the very unit of strategic action changes. Firms do not disappear in the story, for it is their individual actions of shareholding, of making and breaking ties, that drive the process. But the whole is more than the sum of the parts. Or, more accurately, simply summing the indi-vidual portfolios yields the descriptive statistics of percentages held by this or that type of owner whereas aggregating their relational properties yields new orders of phenomena above the constituent units. Restated in the language of complex adaptive systems: prop-erty has emergent properties. A Hungarian business network is not a megafirm, it has no single decision-making center, and unlike the Japanese *keiretsu*, it has no distinctive emblem or flag through which affiliate members signal their collective identity. Too extensive to be called a single strategic alliance, it is a complex network of inter-secting alliances.

More detailed analysis of the discrete networks indicates that their strategies of portfolio management are distinctive (for details, see Stark, Kemeny, and Breiger, 1998). In some, structure derives from the role of key banks that own shares in manufacturing enterprises. In others, banks are also prominent, not as owners but by being mutually owned by the affiliated enterprises. Some of the networks span branches and sectors. Others group firms in particular sectors. Network 3, for example, contains the major bus, railroad, trucking, and airline firms, linked with three banks and six foreign trade companies. The elongated configuration of Network 7 corresponds to its character as an integrated commodity chain that links firms in petroleum, petrochemicals, chemicals, and pharmaceuticals.

But despite the distinctive shapes of their network properties, all of these major business groupings share an important feature of heterarchies: common to each is a strategy of combining heterogeneous resources. Each business network attempts a strategy of portfolio management that diversifies across the resources (and constraints) that derive from ownership by state agencies as well as from the new resources of multinational enterprises and other foreign investors. None is exclusively public or predominantly private. Each regroups assets that allow it to operate across the playing field. All are poised to take advantage of continuing subsidies, exemptions from tariff restrictions, and state largesse in forgiving inherited debt, while benefiting from new sources of capital, access to markets, and technology transfers. In the postsocialist context, networked property is recombinant property.

Similarly recombinant strategies take place inside the postsocialist firm. Consider Heavy Metal, one of Hungary's largest metallurgy companies, which remains predominantly state owned. At the same time that it was participating in one of the interenterprise business networks described above, Heavy Metal was spinning off its assets into limited liability companies (*korlátotl felelöségü társaság,* or KFT). Limited liability companies are the fastest growing business form in the Hungarian economy, having increased from 450 at the end of 1988 to 158,000 by the end of 1998. Some of these KFTs are genuinely private ventures. But many are the corporate satellites of large enterprises. These satellites have ambiguous property status.

Like Saturn's rings, Heavy Metal's satellites revolve around the giant corporate planet in concentric orbits. Near the center are the core metallurgy units, hot-rolling mills, and energy, maintenance, and strategic planning units—all held in a kind of synchronous orbit by 100 percent ownership. In the next ring, where the corporate headquarters holds roughly 50 to 99 percent of the shares, are the cold-rolling mills, wire and cable production, the oxygen facility, galvanizing and other finishing treatments, specialized castings, quality control, and marketing units. The satellites of the outer ring are involved in construction, industrial services, computing, ceramics, machining, and similar activities, and are usually of lower levels of capitalization. Relations between the company center and the outer- and middle-ring satellites are marked by the center's recurrent efforts to introduce stricter accounting procedures and tighter financial controls. These attempts are countered by the units' efforts to increase their autonomy, coordinated through personal ties and formalized in the biweekly meetings of the Club of KFT Managing Directors.

These corporate satellites are far from unambiguously "private" ventures, yet neither are they simply state-linked residue of the socialist past. Property shares in most corporate satellites are not limited to the founding enterprise. Top and mid-level managers, professionals, and other staff can be found on the lists of founding partners and current owners. Such private persons rarely acquire complete ownership of the corporate satellite, preferring to use their insider knowledge to exploit the ambiguities of institutional co-ownership. The corporate satellites are thus partially a result of the hedging and risk-sharing strategies of individual managers. We might ask why a given manager would not want to acquire 100 percent ownership in order to obtain 100 of the profit. But from the perspective of a given manager, the question instead is "Why acquire 100 percent of the risk if some can be shared with the corporate center?" With ambiguous interests and divided loyalties, these risk-sharing owner-managers are organizationally hedging. These managers are joined to one another by ownership stakes in the part of other limited liability companies spinning around yet other large enterprises. The new property forms thus find horizontal ties of cross-ownership intertwined with vertical ties of nested holdings.

Risk Spreading and Risk Taking

These interenterprise networks are an important means of spreading risk in an uncertain environment. Firms in the postsocialist transformational crisis are like mountain climbers assaulting a treacherous slope, and interorganizational networks are the safety ropes latching them together. Such risk spreading, moreover, can be a basis for risk taking. Extraordinarily high uncertainties of the kind we see now in the postsocialist economies can lead to low levels of investment with perverse strategic complementarities (as when firms forgo investments because they expect a sluggish economy based on the lack of investments by others). By mitigating the reluctance to invest, risk spreading within affiliated networks might be one means to break out of otherwise low-level equilibrium traps.

This relationship between risk spreading and risk taking suggests that it would be premature in the postsocialist context to impose a rigid dichotomy between strategies of survival and strategies of innovation. Above all, we should not assume that firms will necessarily innovate even when survival seems to demand it, as if necessity in itself created the conditions for innovation. Recent studies (Miner, Amburgey, and Stearns, 1990; Grabher and Stark, 1997) provide strong theoretical arguments that firms are more likely to undertake the risky business of innovation (exposing themselves to the "liabilities of newness" by engaging in unfamiliar routines) not when they are pushed to the wall but when they are buffered from the immediate effects of selection mechanisms. They further demonstrate that interorganizational networks provide this buffering by producing the requisite organizational slack through which enterprises can find the available resources that make it possible to innovate. Thus, these studies suggest circumstances in which the simple imperative "Innovate in order to survive" is reasonably reversed: "Survive in order to innovate."

These insights have been independently confirmed in a recent study by Ickes, Ryterman, and Tenev (1995), who demonstrate, on the basis of rich survey data on Russian firms, that enterprises that are linked in interenterprise networks are more likely to engage in various forms of economic restructuring than similar firms that are not so linked. That finding, moreover, is robust: purely private enterprises are not more likely to undertake restructuring than firms in state ownership or in mixed property arrangements embedded in interenterprise networks. A related study on innovation in the Hungarian economy (Tamas, 1993) found that firms with the organizational hedging strategy of mixed (public and private) ownership were more likely than purely private or purely state-owned firms to have innovated by introducing new technologies or bringing out new products. In short, when we abandon the forced dichotomy of survival versus innovation, we can see that there are circumstances in which survival strategies can be the prelude to strategies of innovation.

Accounts

In the highly uncertain organizational environment that is the post-socialist economy, relatively few actors (apart from institutional designers such as International Monetary Fund advisers or local policymakers in finance ministries) set out with the aim of creating a market economy. Many would indeed welcome such an outcome, but their immediate goals are more pragmatic: at best to thrive, at least to survive. And so they strive to use whatever resources are available. As they do so, they maneuver not only through an ecology of organizations but also through a complex ecology of ordering principles.

To analyze this process, I exploit a notion of "accounts." Etymologically rich, the term simultaneously connotes bookkeeping and narration. Both dimensions entail evaluative judgments, and each implies the other: accountants prepare story lines according to established formulas, and in the accountings of a good storyteller we know what counts. In everyday life, we are all bookkeepers and storytellers; we keep accounts and we give accounts. Most important, we can be called to account for our actions. It is always within accounts that we "size up the situation," for not every form of worth can be made to apply, and not every asset can be mobilized, in a given situation. We evaluate the situation by maneuvering to use scales that measure some types of worth and not others, thereby acting to validate some accounts and discredit others.

The multiple accounts voiced in Hungarian heterarchies respond to and exploit the fundamental, though diffused, uncertainty about the organizational environment. In transforming economies, firms have to worry not simply about whether there is demand for their products, or about the rate of return on their investment, or about the level of profitability, but also about the very principle of selection itself. Thus, the question is not only "Will I survive the market test?" but also "Under what conditions is proof of worth on market principles neither sufficient nor necessary for survival?" Because there are multiply operative, simultaneously existing principles of justification according to which you may be called to give an account of your actions, you cannot be sure what counts. By what proof and according to which principles of justification are you worthy to steward a given set of resources? Because of this uncertainty, actors will seek to diversify their assets: to hold resources in multiple accounts.

This ability to glide among principles and to produce multiple accountings is an organizational hedging. It differs, however, from the kind of hedging used to minimize risk exposure that we would

find in a purely market-based logic as, for example, when the shop-
keeper who sells swimwear and sun lotion also devotes some floor
space to umbrellas. Instead of acting within a single regime of evaluation, this is organizational hedging that crosses and combines disparate evaluative principles. Recombinant property is a particular
kind of portfolio management. It is an attempt to have a resource
that can be justified or assessed by more than one standard (analogous to the rabbit breeder whose roadside stand advertises "Pets and
Meat" in the documentary film *Roger and Me*). In managing one's
portfolio of justifications, one starts from the axiom "Diversify your
accounts."

The adroit agent in the transforming economies of Eastern
Europe diversifies holdings in response to fundamental uncertainties about what can constitute a resource. Under conditions not
simply of market uncertainty but of organizational uncertainty, there
can be multiple (and intertwined) strategies for survival, based in
some cases on profitability but in others on eligibility. Your success
is judged, and the resources placed at your disposal determined,
sometimes by your market share and sometimes by the number of
workers you employ in a region; sometimes by your price-earnings
ratio and sometimes by your "strategic importance." When even the
absolute size of your losses can be transformed into an asset yielding an income stream, you might be wise to diversify your portfolio;
to be able to shift your accounts; to be equally skilled in applying
for loans as in applying for job creation subsidies; to have a multi-
lingual command of the grammar of creditworthiness and the syntax
of debt forgiveness. To hold recombinant property is to have such
a diversified portfolio.

To gain room to maneuver, actors court and even create ambiguity. They measure in multiple units; they speak in many tongues.
In so doing, they produce the heterarchical discourse of worth that
is postsocialism. We can hear that polyphonic chorus in the diverse
ways Hungarian firms have justified their claims for participation in
a debt relief program established by the government after its earlier

programs had precipitated a near collapse of the financial system (Stark, 1996). The following litany of justifications for why a firm should be included in the debt relief program is a stylized version of claims encountered in discussions with bankers, property agency officials, and enterprise directors (Stark, 1996):

Because we will forgive our debtors.

Because we are truly creditworthy.

Because we employ thousands.

Because our suppliers depend on us for a market.

Because we are in your election district.

Because our customers depend on our product inputs.

Because we can then be privatized.

Because we can never be privatized.

Because we took big risks.

Because we were prudent and did not take risks.

Because we were subject to planning in the past.

Because we have a plan for the future.

Because we export to the West.

Because we export to the East.

Because our product has been awarded an International Standards Quality Control Certificate.

Because our product is part of the Hungarian national heritage.

Because we are an employee buy-out.

Because we are a management buy-in.

Because we are partly state owned.

Because we are partly privately held.

Because our creditors drove us into bankruptcy when they loaned to us at higher than market rates to artificially raise bank profits in order to pay dividends into a state treasury whose coffers had dwindled when corporations like ourselves effectively stopped paying taxes.

And so we must ask, into whose account and by which account will debt forgiveness flow? Or, in such a situation, is anyone accountable? By making assets of ambiguity, Hungarian managers gain flexibility. But this flexibility is not an entirely unmixed blessing. When spreading risk becomes shedding risk to the public coffers, flexibility occurs at the cost of accountability. The Eastern European road to capitalism is not the most desirable road. And whether it will be a viable road at all remains open to question. But it is not too early to conclude that this social experiment and its organizational mutations are giving rise to a new species of capitalism.

Conclusion

Our Hungarian chorus sounds strange and exotic only upon first encounter. For although that litany expresses multiple accounting principles in an especially acute form, the notion of coexisting evaluative frameworks is far from foreign in the highly uncertain environments of advanced sectors in our own society. If the successful Hungarian manager must be as skilled in the language of debt forgiveness as in the language of negotiating with a prospective multinational partner, the CEO of a start-up firm in biotechnology might well survive only with a talent for writing grant proposals to federal agencies as well as a knack for making the pitch to prospective venture capitalists. We need not travel to Eastern Europe to encounter difficulties in assessing the value of firms, when stories of the difficulties of evaluating Internet stocks fill the front pages of our newspapers. We are not strangers to the problems of distinguishing public and private, for we need look no further than the complex proprietary arrangements between private firms and public universities in the fields of computer science, biotechnology, new media, and engineering. (Consider, for example, the biotech industry collaborations mentioned in Chapter Three.) And the search for a mutually comprehensible language across the cultures of science, politics, and business in the Human Genome Project offers no less acute problems of public and private accountability.

To write of "problems" is not to denounce the creative organizational solutions that are evolving in all of the areas mentioned above. On the contrary, it calls attention to the fact that the most sophisticated, dynamic, and groundbreaking sectors are likely to be arenas where public and private are closely intertwined.

Complexity, in the field of organizations, is the interweaving of diverse evaluative principles. These principles can be those of public and private accountings, but they can also be the diverse worldviews of different professional identities, each with its own distinctive ways of measuring value and selecting what counts. The challenge of a new media firm, for example, is to create enough of a common culture to facilitate communication among the designers, business strategists, and technologists that make up interdisciplinary teams, without suppressing the distinctive identity of each. The assets of the firm are objectively increased when there are multiple measures of what constitutes an asset. Value is amplified precisely because values are not shared. The heterarchical organization of diversity is sometimes discordant. But to still that noisy clash by the ascendancy of only one accounting would be to destroy the diversity of organizing principles that is the basis of adaptability.

8

Adaptive Operations
Creating Business Processes That Evolve

William G. Macready and Christopher Meyer

We take for granted that over generations the "design" of a bird—its plumage, song, nesting behavior—evolves to increase its likelihood of getting a mate. What if an automobile could do the same, the "mate" being a customer, and could do its evolving in a simulation, much faster and cheaper than in the real world?

Sound impossible? Well, consider this: a major auto company is developing adaptive modeling techniques by which designers offer their opinions of how attractive a car design is to a particular marketplace, and the design *evolves* features, shapes, and characteristics that make it more so. This is a far cry from the days when a team of engineers would explicitly trade off weight coefficients of drag, manufacturability of body panels, and aesthetics. It is an example of "adaptive operations," an evolutionary approach to managing the traditional tasks of running the guts of a business, whether product design, parts manufacturing, fleet scheduling, or quality control. These approaches borrow techniques used by nature for coping with complex problems in an unpredictable world and are already yielding some results superior to those obtained using techniques that

---

Note: The authors would like to thank Johanna Woll for her research and editorial contributions to this chapter.

assume linear trade-offs, predictability, and an ever higher degree of control.

This chapter summarizes the evolution of industrial-era practices in managing operations, then describes some of the new methods that are being explored to cope with the rapidly changing information economy. These methods are not merely novel algorithms or calculations. Instead, they constitute a new mindset with different attitudes toward control, variability, and prediction; new approaches to problem solving suitable for nonlinear, highly connected systems; and the new tools required to execute these approaches. This mindset is discussed in the section on the history of operations management. Three fundamental processes of natural evolution are defined—recombination, coevolution, and self-organization—that are needed to conceptualize and create business processes as adaptive systems. The discussion details the tools, including agent-based modeling and "genetic" algorithms, that make adaptive operations possible. Throughout, examples are drawn from both nature and the business world.

New Challenges in a Connected Economy

The volatility of the late twentieth-century economy creates steep challenges, especially for companies that are slow to react to market shifts. Businesses must be willing to change to keep up, and most often the changes must be made with little warning and at a rapid pace. To survive today, an organization or system must adapt to a high degree of external variability.

In the past, the influence of external forces on businesses was less significant. The model industrial factory was in one sense a simple, somewhat isolated, machine. Designed around a narrow, constant product mix to ensure long production runs and to minimize expensive setups and tooling changes, insulated from shortages and stock-outs by parts and finished goods inventories, and rewarded for maximizing utilization regardless of effects on margins downstream, the factory stood alone. Because mass production was the dominant value-creating technique of the industrial economy, the rest of the system was organized around it, making factory management as simple as possible. The customer accepted "any color . . . as long as it's black" and the workers accepted conditions like those in Fritz Lang's *Metropolis*.

But today it is customization, rapid delivery, and instant response to the ever changing landscape of customers' desires that allow a business to prevail in the market, and it is tight supply-chain integration that creates efficient use of resources. These new challenges are neither simple nor static; they are too complex to visualize, and they have too many variables to be modeled effectively using traditional programming methods. Above all, many of the variables change daily or, as in the case of the newly deregulated power industry, minute to minute. Solutions must be flexible and must be implemented to ensure real-time adaptation to machine failures, design changes, and market shifts. In operations today, robust flexibility in the face of change is paramount.

Biology, of course, has been in the business of creating robust, adaptive "production" solutions for four billion years. But biology has no production quotas, no order books, no direction set by a market. How can techniques learned from observing nature apply to business situations that require the same devices but implemented at a greater-than-glacial pace?

A few industry leaders have begun to realize benefits from imitating nature and are applying complex adaptive systems (CAS) theory to become smarter than their competitors, better equipped, and, most important, more flexible. Thanks to computers, managers now possess the means to speed up what nature proposes and to look at the economy through the lens of complexity science. With powerful technology, managers are able to visualize, simulate, evaluate, and control complex business processes. These approaches provide them with new views of potential obstacles, views that also reveal what John Holland (1995) calls the hidden order in their operations.

The First and Second Waves

It was Frederick Taylor ([1947] 1993) who systematized the study of efficiency in manufacturing. In the 1920s large-scale industrial factories were a new phenomenon. Although they reduced labor costs, they required unprecedented amounts of capital to construct and maintain. To earn a return on this investment, managers struggled to maximize the throughput of these facilities. Taylor began applying rigorous experimental techniques of observation and measurement to the essential task of organizing work in factories for maximum efficiency.

He thus set into motion the first wave of operations studies, which came to be known as "scientific management." With a strong bias toward deterministic, quantitative problem solving and characterized by an efficiency mindset, scientific management focused on labor expenses and the application of time-study concepts to lowering labor costs. The goal was to keep the factory busy. By timing each operation and experimenting with alternative ways of performing it, Taylor reduced the time and effort needed to complete each task. This, in turn, maximized the number of units produced per period and minimized the fixed cost of the factory allocated to each unit produced. It also maximized the productivity of each worker.

One unexpected and far-reaching effect of Taylor's approach was its impact on the view of labor and the role of the worker. Although he was often vilified as an oppressor of workers, Taylor actually strove to raise their standard of living. But his studies were part of an efficiency mindset that brought with it standard cost systems and a "we don't pay them to think" attitude toward labor. Taylor's work also set the stage for an ongoing search for parallels between science and business. The scientific approach to management emulated the methods used in scientific research, where a subject was measured under controlled conditions, a salient variable adjusted, the results studied, and the process repeated.

By the 1950s, business as a topic of study had gained legitimacy in academia, and economists had begun to apply techniques borrowed from mathematics and physics to business operations. For example, William Baumol used differential calculus to determine the theoretically optimal reorder point for inventories; queuing theory was used to prove that five bank tellers were more productive serving a single queue of customers than five separate ones; and decision trees were developed to sort out complex sequences of choices and events.

Then the computer came on the scene. Suddenly the options for resolving complicated problems were vastly expanded. In time, computers were able to handle the sophisticated linear and quadratic mathematical machinery used in areas like job-shop scheduling, refinery yield maximization, and financial asset allocation. These advances were the avant-garde of the second wave of operations studies in the 1950s and 1960s, characterized by an optimization mindset. It was called "operations research."

Methods of optimization first applied in operations research still prevail in industry today and continue to improve certain kinds of operations processes. In fact, they have been institutionalized in systems such as manufacturing requirements planning (MRP) that are well entrenched in the industrial infrastructure.

But the fundamental assumptions of earlier scientific methods are often ill suited to today's business environment. Old maxims, such as "Reduce the number of options," "Minimize setup costs," or "Maximize throughput," do not always maximize profits today. To understand why, consider the movement toward mass customization. This is a new imperative in the market and thus in production. Speed of delivery has become more important to the customer than unit cost, and there is a constant demand for new gizmos and the latest upgrades. As a result, the half-life of product design has shortened dramatically. As businesses strive to meet the new imperatives, they are forced to adapt their production goals. Long production runs, a reduced number of product variations, and infrequent tooling changes are no longer the best economic decisions, even though these techniques may still minimize factory costs. In contrast to the industrial era, when value was added primarily in manufacturing and when factory economics were dominant, today manufacturers expect 80 percent of a product's value to be added elsewhere—in time and place utility, in configuration downstream, or in customization, service, and upgrades (Ernst & Young, 1998).

The Third Wave

The most challenging operations problems of today, which arise from these new production imperatives, are marked by a large number of conflicting constraints; variables that shift rapidly relative to the time available to reach a decision; and value-chain relationships that change from time to time. The computationally intensive linear methods of operations research are not effective in such cases because they take too long to reach an answer and are not easily respecified when the situation changes.

Techniques drawing on the ideas of complexity theory, however, are specifically designed to meet these challenges. Thanks to several high-profile success stories, these techniques are beginning to gain acceptance in the business world. As successes accumulate, the optimization mindset will give way to an adaptive mindset and a new set of tools. Adaptive techniques explicitly

- Accept that solutions will not be globally optimal
- Reject predictability as a criterion of effective management
- Understand that variability of process performance is a reflection of the environment, not a management flaw

The adaptive mindset manifests a definitive shift toward a more nonlinear, multiobjective, integrative, decentralized approach. We are now riding the third wave of the twentieth century, and adaptive operations are gaining force.

The Trinity of Adaptation

Biologists and geneticists who study how nature adapts describe three fundamental concepts that drive its success: recombination, coevolution, and self-organization. These are the keystone ideas in complexity science. Those in the business world who wish to perform as well as nature does must begin the mindset shift by understanding these three essential notions. Companies that have succeeded with complexity-based operational approaches do so by observing these principles and by building their operations around them.

Recombination

Nature approaches the notion of efficiency not by designing solutions from scratch but by recombining successful elements to create new versions, some of which thrive. The very first nucleated cells (eukaryotes) developed as a result of a collaboration of ancient bacteria, which combined because their biochemical efficiency together was greater than that of any bacterium alone. Such combinations of bacteria eventually evolved a new structure because a compartmentalized cell with individual organelles, such as the mitochondria and chloroplasts, performing specific functions is able to convert resources into energy better and is thus more likely to survive. A more fit organism has a better chance of being able to colonize a new, more hostile niche in the environment and will be less vulnerable to the intense competition for less-demanding habitats (Rothschild, 1990). The eukaryotic cell thus made possible multicellular organisms, and the process continued from there. In much the same way, businesses form strategic alliances to create new capabilities and inhabit new market niches.

The recent alliance of Electronic Data Systems (EDS), Hewlett-Packard, and Hewlett-Packard's VeriFone unit demonstrates the same collaborative approach. In this case, competing vendors pool their technologies in an effort to make the development of electronic commerce capabilities easier. The group, called the First Global Commerce Initiative, proposes an open architecture that will support all types of electronic payments. Each of the members contributes a particular expertise or enabling technology. For EDS this is access to smaller financial institutions through its experience as a service integrator. VeriFone provides its integrated payment system for Internet commerce and point-of-sale electronic payments, and the use of smart cards. Hewlett-Packard brings its significant hardware capabilities and market clout to the mix.

Another recent trend in the corporate community illustrates a similar means of achieving mutual profitability: interoperability. Nature here provides both the metaphor and the example, which is not surprising; after all, nature built the prototype. In response to the increasingly complex process of integrated circuit design, Cadence and Synopsys, the two major vendors of electronic design automation (EDA), created an open architecture from the two companies' most commonly used design tools. Called Spine99, this "backbone" offers a way for smaller third-party vendors to plug "ribs" (their own tools) into the EDA technology, recombining, in effect, the suite of software features and creating many different versions. The market will decide which are the most successful, just as nature filters genetic variations, selecting for suitability.

Coevolution

The successful recombination of genes depends on the survival of the beast bearing them. The environment selects for fitness, and only surviving genes are available for reexpression. But once selection occurs, the phenotypes produced by the surviving genes set about selecting others in their environment. Thus the environment will change in response to the evolution of each species, causing the next round of selection to reward different genes. The species and its environment endlessly affect one another in a process called coevolution. This is also true in today's business culture, where, for example, the cost of memory and the size of software products have clear, direct effects on one another.

Stuart Kauffman (1995) describes how sticky-tongued frogs cause slippery-footed flies to come into being. Flies evolve clever defenses against their sticky-tongued predators, such as slippery feet, a foul taste, "sticky-stuff dissolver," and faster flying speeds. Frogs meet these countermeasures by evolving clever tricks themselves; they might develop a faster-flicking tongue, a farther-reaching tongue, or sticky stuff that is less stinky and therefore less likely to drive the flies away. Each species adapts to its environment, which in turn coevolves with it.

Consider a business example that is at this point so familiar that it is nearly invisible. More transistors on a chip means more processing power, which in turn allows for more complex and feature-laden software applications. Such applications in turn place greater demands on processing power. The continual advances of computer hardware and software represent a coevolutionary cycle.

Once a new combination of genetic material is embodied in a phenotype, it can begin to change its environment or cohabitants. As Winston Churchill once said, "First we shape our buildings, then they shape us." The same can be said of businesses and their factories. Coevolution, this cycle of action and reaction, is a continuous shaping and selecting in the search for stability and fitness.

Alaska Airlines is taking this notion and actively pursuing the advantages it offers, deliberately reshaping the physical space for one of its busiest processes. In response to today's huge volume of air travelers, the company streamlined its check-in operations by replacing many of its counter staff with self-service alternatives. Already an innovator in the airline industry as one of the first companies to sell and issue tickets on-line, Alaska Airlines now plans to redesign its terminal in the Anchorage airport to minimize long lines at ticket counters. Its state-of-the-art facility will feature roving agents with handheld computers and miniature printers, as well as self-service kiosks with sensors that detect frequent fliers' "smart" key fobs, which identify their users and automatically access their accounts (Carey, 1999).

Self-Organization

When left to their own devices, the flora, fauna, and mineral elements of nature continuously rearrange themselves, adapting to one another and to their surroundings in a delicately balanced ecosystem. Yet no one "designed" the millions of compounds into which all chemical elements formed themselves. Rather, as one element encountered another (such as hydrogen and oxygen), new compounds (such as water) were formed because the elements' atomic structures led them to bond. Once water was formed, a whole new set of possibilities emerged, for water participates in several kinds of bonding and interactions. It is an excellent solvent and a powerful reactant. It not only transports other compounds but also serves as a sort of vessel or holding tank for them: the ocean, for example, "holds" great quantities of carbon dioxide. When carbon dioxide combines with calcium hydroxide (ash plus rainwater, washed into the ocean via rivers), it makes calcium carbonate, a basic component of seashells. Each one of these chemical compounds is an "agent"; each possesses the capacity to link to others. As a group, they create a self-organizing system, an entire ecology.

The World Wide Web is perhaps the quintessential modern example of a self-organizing system. A multitude of geographically dispersed individuals—from the creators of the Linux operating system to book reviewers at Amazon.com, from information seekers at Motley Fool's financial markets site to members of theglobe.com's beer-making forum—have assembled a vast virtual network.

This approach has been applied by Champion Sporting Goods, where management organized its garment workers into "bucket brigades," which functioned as a self-organizing system and spontaneously achieved an optimum configuration. This global coordination arose, unplanned, from the local, adaptive interaction of the workers. A more traditional approach to assembling garments requires each worker to assume responsibility for a specific stage in the production sequence; partially completed work piles up between stations. The bucket brigade model calls for workers to move from station to station, going to where the work is, rather than waiting for the work to come to them. This system accommodates workers of varying speeds and keeps the line running smoothly and without interruption. Workers follow a few very simple rules, such as lining up initially from slowest to fastest and moving always downstream in search of more work (Eisenstein, 1997).

Self-organization takes place on a larger scale as well: John Holland (1995) has pointed out that New York City always maintains a two-week supply of food, a process "managed" by tens of thousands of businesses coordinated only in that they are responding to the same overall set of market signals. Each has its own decision rules, yet the emergent behavior is a relatively stable inventory-to-sales ratio.

A Mindset Shift at Mohawk Industries

The shift to an adaptive mindset is as important as the implementation of new tools. A new mindset opens the door for new approaches to problems. Although it is often the most difficult aspect of redesigning a system, this mindset shift is pivotal, and it alone can elicit greatly enhanced performance.

In the past three years, several of the world's leading companies have used these three relatively abstract principles—recombination, coevolution, and self-organization—and have seen great improvements in the performance of their business processes as a result.

In one example, Mohawk Industries, a major manufacturer of commercial carpeting, recently revamped its production scheduling in an effort to respond to unexpected and rush orders. With more than four thousand different products and a complicated sequence of processes, forecasting orders and scheduling production runs had been an enormous challenge, one that managers had long been unable to optimize. The old system, based on actual order queries, was proving too rigid, and the factory was fulfilling only 80 percent of its orders on time. With the help of a quantum chemist and some advanced modeling techniques, Mohawk Industries tried a new approach. Its production schedules are now designed to meet an expected flow of queries, and today the factory is able to fulfill 95 percent of its orders on time. To achieve such an improvement, managers had to adopt an entirely different mindset and cede significant explicit control of the planning. Less than half of the carpet produced each day has been specifically ordered by customers whereas that number had been 80 to 90 percent in the past. The new system now runs smoothly; it is adaptive, robust, and responsive to a volatile market (Petzinger, 1998).

Tools for Adaptation

It is new tools that enable the execution of these new approaches. Great advances in communications technology, computational power, and software standards, like SAP, have fueled the high level of connectivity in today's economy, the rise of multifirm networks and integrated supply chains, and new, information-intensive forms of planning. The exponential growth of computer processing power has, in particular, spawned the development of simulations and other modeling techniques essential to the adaptive enterprise.

Analytic tools that rely on calculations of averages and differential equations can no longer rise to the challenge of today's highly complex problems, but new tools like agent-based models, genetic algorithms, and simulated annealing now can. They can improve operations on the factory floor, speed up new product design, and minimize some of the guesswork and risk inherent in resource allocation and pricing. These techniques are most useful in situations where the number of variables and connections among variables is small enough to remain manageable yet large enough to defy traditional linear mathematical analysis (Flake, 1998).

Agent-Based Modeling

The most effective agent-based simulations offer one feature that is especially well suited to the complexity of today's business problems: graphical representations. The graphical user interface of a simulation allows managers to visualize processes and to grasp the interplay of multiple components that might otherwise be impossible to analyze. This is especially true for nonlinear phenomena, which give rise to systems whose output is nearly always by some measure greater than the sum of the system's parts (Holland, 1995). Computer simulations are used to study agents and their interactions with their environment and with other agents; they invite what-if questions and are thus an invaluable and extremely versatile tool (Epstein and Axtell, 1996; Axelrod, 1997).

Recombination and Coevolution: The Central Japan Railway

The Central Japan Railway Company looked to agent-based technology for help scheduling its one thousand bullet trains, which travel at speeds of 130 to 170 miles per hour and carry more than 1 million passengers per day on seven hundred miles of track. The existing control and monitoring system was not capable of handling unexpected events such as snowstorms, earthquakes, or breakdowns. To prevent cascading backups and overloads on the power supply, Central Japan Railway needed a more agile system that could adapt, recover, and coevolve with each new situation: one that could, in effect, recombine past solutions and schedule segments, for almost instantaneous updates.

Central Japan Railway chose an agent-based simulator composed of more than 130 train agents and 20,000 track-segment agents. Logic elements and sensors embedded in the railroad tracks monitor speed and operate switches; they are in constant communication with the central information station in Tokyo. Dispatchers are still responsible for scheduling, but now, because they can run the simulations faster than in real-time, they are able to predict situations in advance. In emergency situations, this capability is crucial.

Simulating such a complex system with conventional programming would be extremely lengthy and costly: sequential processing cannot keep pace with so many factors interacting at once. But the new agent-based software tool is modular and designed to handle many agents running in parallel. Adding agents, such as faster trains or new lines, or adjusting parameters, such as safe spacing intervals, is relatively simple. In addition, the new tool captures the experience and knowledge of dispatchers because they are its users. They input the data to test changes and evolve the system on their own, even with no programming skills (Ernst & Young, 1996).

Visualizing Emergent Behavior in "Boids"

Agent-based models have not always been perceived as tools. Some of the earliest versions of these types of simulations were built for fun, and they illustrated how complex adaptive systems work in nature. In an effort to explain the sources of group behavior in flocks of birds, schools of fish, or herds of sheep, computer animator Craig Reynolds created "Boids," a simulation that displayed the realistic-looking flight of flocks of cyberbirds. Reynolds's novel approach to programming a group dynamic revealed how valuable the features of computer modeling are for adaptive operations.

In "Boids," Reynolds endowed each agent with a few simple characteristics. Four basic goals directed the actions of each boid:

- Alignment: steering toward the average heading of nearby flockmates

- Separation: steering to avoid crowding nearby flockmates

- Cohesion: trying to match velocity of nearby flock-mates

- Avoidance: veering away from obstacles.

Reynolds could not control or predict exactly where any particular boid would be at any particular time. At the beginning of the simulation, the boids were positioned randomly. Not one of the rules instructed the boids to flock, but incredibly, they did. The boids gradually formed a flock that wheeled and turned, behaving much like a real flock of birds.

The simulation space, visible on the screen, was full of obstacles, and sometimes an unlucky boid would collide with an object. Such occasional clumsiness was perhaps to be expected from cyber-birds. Far more surprising was the flock's consistent agility. When confronted with an obstacle, the flock would split apart, fly around the object, and reconverge with striking fluidity. In the language of complex adaptive systems, the birds self-organized. And Reynolds produced a simulation that illustrated convincingly what is called emergent behavior, in this case flocking.

An agent-based model provides a framework for decision-making components (agents), such as animated birds, molecules in a gas, employees in a firm, machines in a factory—autonomous entities whose behavior is determined by their current circumstances and a set of internal rules. The rules govern how agents make choices. Rules may be simple if-then clauses or sophisticated machine-learning algorithms such as neural networks or Bayesian networks (algorithms that mimic the way people think), which can describe more complex behavior. "Genetic" algorithms, which select, mutate, and recombine, can be used to evolve the rules.

Once parameters are set to represent a situation of interest, agents are placed in the simulation space and the model is run for a given number of iterations. At the end of the runs, the internal dynamics and external output of the simulation give a good idea of how the real system would behave under the conditions portrayed in the model.

The remarkable thing about these models is that they evolve continuously as new information becomes available, and they often come up with unexpected results. Once they have been validated through a cross-check of their results against outcomes observed in the real world, they can be used to test and study in advance the potential effects of changes in a business process that would be too time consuming and complicated to test mathematically, too complex to be studied analytically, and most likely too costly or dangerous to be tested in a real physical system.

Self-Organizing Agents at General Motors

An agent-based model lends itself beautifully to a complex production line with its tangle of interacting processes. "Factories are havens of erratic behavior," declares Dick Morley, one of the creators of the floppy disk and father of the programmable logic controller (personal conversation, date n. a.). Factories are composed of very large numbers of highly interconnected parts. When any one part falters, a cascade effect disrupts the sequence, often throwing off everything downstream as well.

By contrast, biological systems, which are also composed of very large numbers of highly interconnected parts, generally do not grind to a halt when one part breaks down. They have an amazing ability to adapt. For example, when a tree is exposed to light on only one side, it preferentially grows branches on that side; if an animal is not getting enough carbohydrates, it makes them out of proteins.

Morley believed that it would be possible to build this kind of adaptive behavior into factory operations. He felt that, instead of building a system that explicitly dictates the behavior of every part and traces errors to their source when something goes wrong, factories could be designed with a built-in assumption that parts will break from time to time. Based on such a framework, the factory system could figure out for itself the best way to accomplish a task given current conditions. This kind of system is sometimes called fault tolerant: when something goes wrong, it responds adaptively.

In 1992, Morley's ideas were put to the test in the paint shop of a General Motors assembly plant in Fort Wayne, Indiana. In the past, when an unpainted truck body rolled off the assembly line, a centralized controller routed it to one of ten paint booths to which it had been preassigned. However, it was almost impossible to predict the exact order in which trucks would come off the line, and at any time, several paint booths might be out of service. Paint booths break down frequently, and they require frequent routine maintenance to clean out clogged nozzles or to adjust temperature or pressure settings. The schedule was rigid, and delays due to paint changeovers were common; so deciding in advance which booth would paint which truck was something of a nightmare.

Morley reprogrammed the booths to act as free agents, each pursuing two simple goals: keep busy (minimize wasted time) and do not waste paint (minimize costly color changeovers). The emergent property that he hoped to achieve was threefold: (1) a robust schedule that allowed painting (2) as many trucks as possible using (3) as little paint as possible.

With Morley's system in place, when a truck rolled off the assembly line, each booth would electronically "bid" for the right to paint it. Bids were based on a booth's ability to do the job efficiently and were measured by the relative weight of three factors: easy job (same color), important job (rush), any job (space available). Bidding was subject to certain conditions, such as the color the booth was set up to paint, how many other trucks it was already committed to painting, and whether or not the booth was currently operational.

From the scheduler's perspective, the scenario would start at a decision point for a truck. For example, the program might have told the booths, "I have a truck that needs to be black." A booth already loaded with black paint and near the end of its current job would bid very high for the black truck. A booth with another color but almost empty would bid slightly lower. A booth that is farther away, filled with red paint, broken down, or otherwise less suited for the job would bid lower still. Based on the outcome of this virtual auction, the scheduler assigned the truck to the highest-bidding paint booth.

The system was self-organizing; the schedule, emergent. The bottom-up process flow was far smoother than one controlled by top-down authority. The system was able to respond in real time to unexpected events like equipment failures and delays. The procedure by which booths collectively "decided" which one would paint each truck was similar to the way ants collectively construct an anthill or immune cells attack an invader.

The impact of the new system was remarkable. It saved GM more than $1 million per plant annually in paint alone. Major paint changeovers decreased by 50 percent, which in turn cut down on equipment wear and tear, a primary cause of breakdowns. The number of lines of computer code needed to run the booths dropped tenfold from the old command-and-control model, further emphasizing the superior efficiency of this adaptive operations approach. The system was able to direct itself spontaneously, matching each truck to the booth best suited to paint it. Unpainted trucks no longer built up in bottlenecks in front of broken booths, and functioning booths were less likely to sit idle. What was gained through the increased responsiveness at the local level inherent in this approach was a more flexible, scalable, and robust solution. In return, two things were "lost": the system was no longer deterministic, that is, no one could predict exactly how a given truck would be painted; and although overall output was higher, the variability of output also increased. While neither of these results created logistical or economic problems, they were nonetheless unpopular among GM's process control engineers.

Assessing whether an agent-based model can be helpful begins with a qualitative look at what is actually going on in the environment that it represents. Often, even if a model is not quantitatively correct in its details, it may nevertheless reveal some robust features that correspond to reality. These can easily be identified by running many iterations using different inputs: robust features stand out as those outputs that are not sensitive to initial changes (Axelrod, 1997). This might be, for example, a process that involves more paint changeovers than expected but that is still able to adapt with a minimum of disruptions and wasted time.

Agent-Guided Strategies in the Electric Power Marketplace

Adam Smith argued that if people were acting on their own behalf individually, a collectively optimal solution would naturally emerge. This simple statement evokes the elegance of agent-based optimization, which suits so well the complexity of today's world. Its potential applications span a wide range and could address many kinds of operations problems, from resource allocation to supply-chain management or the pricing of airline seats in competitive markets. Imagine being able to explore through simulation the pros and cons of different realizations of an operation in the retail market without bearing the usual risks associated with change. The electric power industry is doing just that. In this newly deregulated market, the pressure to understand the interaction of forces influencing profitability is great, and predicting demand in a competitive environment is a real challenge.

Power industry players have a great deal of practice sorting out all of the different factors influencing their business: customer demand, generating capacity, operating efficiency, marketplace dynamics, and so on. But deregulation threw a wrench into their well-greased machine.

The Electric Power Research Institute in Palo Alto, California, has been helping member companies of its research consortium cope with the changes. Last year, they appealed to the Bios Group, because they knew of cofounder Dr. Stuart Kauffman's studies of "economic webs." They had the right mindset, asking, "What if we modeled the power industry as a web?" The challenges they faced, exacerbated by deregulation, seemed right for an agent-based modeling approach, with agents representing brokers, producers, generators, and consumers, and their interactions driving the simulation dynamics. Getting a complete view of the picture would be very difficult by any other method. The result of this collaboration became a simulation with great potential for helping managers at electric power companies (Wildberger, 1997).

Designed to determine the most cost-effective and efficient configurations for allocating demand among generating units, the simulation's adaptive optimization tools allow users to test pricing and marketing strategies through what-if scenarios. With this model, companies can look at the distribution of power requirements among generating stations based on demand, then calculate, from moment to moment, the potential cost of selling an additional block of power to a new consumer or compare the results of locking in profits with forward contracts to those achieved through short-lead-time "spot market" sales.

The simulation prototype is set up to run using either historical data from a company's database or using a "live" data feed. The model incorporates costs and time delays associated with adjusting the power output of each generation unit. Graphically displayed agents follow rules set by the user before the simulation is run, each emulating the real-world behavior for that kind of agent. A broker, for instance, is chiefly interested in maximizing profit; a hospital or factory consumer is more concerned with the reliability of the power supply.

Power companies cannot afford to wait until a real disaster strikes to find out what their needs are. If one of five generators in a grid is down, a company needs to know ahead of time what is required of the other four, so that it can adapt quickly. This knowledge will be essential in a dynamic environment.

Genetic Algorithms

A genetic algorithm (GA) is a computational method used to search for solutions to difficult problems. It is derived by analogy from the process of evolution through natural selection, which it mimics. GAs will only function as evolution does in nature under certain conditions. They are a good match for problems whose components can be broken down into bits and arranged in patterns. For a GA to work, there must be a detectable pattern in a set of information, such as a sequence of tasks in a job shop, and a way of varying that pattern. In addition, there must be at least one criterion for fitness—that is, some rationale for selecting certain patterns, such as flexibility, cost, or timing, over others. Finally, there must be a way to amplify or replicate selected patterns, which in computing means a programming routine (Mitchell, 1996; Vose, 1998; Goldberg, 1989).

In nature, an organism's patterns are encoded in genes. Mutation introduces variation from one generation to the next. Sexual reproduction (recombination) introduces yet more variation by mixing the genetic material of two individuals and generating unique offspring. Selective pressure comes from the constraints of the environment, such as the need to find food.

The parallels to business arise in several ways. Many business tools, such as data mining, work because they sort through large amounts of information to find answers. But in many cases they do not go far enough or explore deep enough. A GA, however, takes business data and treats it like genetic material. Patterns are encoded as process guidelines and corporate culture, and mutational variation is introduced when the guidelines or culture change, such as in response to some shift in the market. Recombination-like effects occur when companies merge, share processes, or form strategic alliances.

When GAs are embedded in business tools, nature's genetic code becomes a computer's binary code. The usual information pattern of a GA is a bit string: a vector of 1s and 0s. This bit string codes for a possible solution to some problem. New patterns form when bit strings are artificially mutated, by changing a 1 to a 0, for example. Two strings can be artificially mated by combining, say, the bottom half of one with the top half of another. Successive iterations breed generation after generation of these bit strings, and each generation is tested on the problem at hand until one that works is found.

Trying to maintain or improve operations in a constantly changing environment is a very tricky task. But recombination is a powerful adaptive tool, and the iterative process of a GA is uniquely suited to exploit its advantages. If both a and b are good, then maybe the combination of a plus b will be even better. If not, a little local tweaking, or mutation, can probably get things back on track. Successful applications of this technique cover a range of practical problems, from VLSI circuit layout and gas pipeline control to trade-offs in the design of aircraft, the architecture of neural networks, and management of international security (Fogel, 1995).

Recombination and Self-Organization at John Deere

At the John Deere and Co. factory in Moline, Illinois, staff analyst Bill Fulkerson looked to GAs to address the daunting task of production scheduling. As customers increasingly demand products built to their specifications, the manufacturing facility finds itself faced with an overwhelming number of model configurations. For seed planters alone, this means over a million possible combinations: differences in soils, seeds, tractors, and climates all demand different planter characteristics. Some tractors require four-row planters, others twenty-four-row planters, others something in between. Some farmers want planters that apply liquid fertilizer, others want dry fertilizer, others no fertilizer at all.

Producing such a diverse product line put a severe strain on the factory scheduling process and customer delivery dates. Unanticipated problems would cause serious backups. For example, if two wide planters—say a four-row and an eight-row planter—were scheduled too close to each other, they would be unable to pass by each other in the aisle of the factory and would choke production.

The process flow on the line is affected by more than fifty major constraints concerning timing, space, and capacity. Each day the order book is different, so it is not sufficient to find one scheduling solution to be run repeatedly. Orders used to be filled by shipping planters in pieces for assembly by local dealers, but in 1992, John Deere began assembling planters at the factory in order to enhance quality and decrease inventory. Workers were organized into self-directed teams, each devoted to a particular system of planter.

However, problems soon arose. Half-assembled machines were bunching up at one station, while another station remained idle. Neither linear optimization techniques nor any amount of intuition or experience could handle the complexity of this production scheduling problem. Throughput at the facility was managed by spreadsheets that organized orders into production patterns for specific models to be pursued in succession. But in the face of mass customization, this method was both inflexible and inefficient. Fulkerson said, "[W]e've got to be able to produce any volume, any time, any model, any option, anywhere, anything. Implicit in that is, we still want to make money. And so the question is, how can we do that?" (Ernst & Young, 1996).

The answer was a GA. Now, every night before the factory closes, a GA program running on a PC generates a population of random factory schedules, each consisting of a sequence of instructions for assembling planters. Individual schedules are then "bred," and the program evaluates each new generation of schedules, rating them based on their ability to cope with the current backlog of demand. The best schedules are selected to participate in the next round of "breeding."

This process produces more than six hundred thousand possible schedules each night. The one adopted in the morning is not necessarily optimal in the usual sense, but it is the best that the program could find overnight within the bounds of certain constraints. It is optimal in the way that a resistant bacterial strain is optimal: it is well adapted to the selective pressure exerted by its environment.

Planters now flow smoothly through the production line. Monthly output has increased substantially. Significant improvements in resource allocation and supply-chain management have made the facility more efficient. But most important, the schedule has proved both reliable and flexible.

Eugenics for Cars: Coevolution at an Automobile Manufacturer

GA-based techniques are also being tested for use in product design processes. For a major auto manufacturer, Bios Group is developing a user-guided evolutionary search tool allowing designers to streamline what is normally a lengthy trial-and-error design process. Automobile designers must balance aesthetic considerations with technical specifications, an often frustrating juggling act.

In a traditional process, designers have no way of tracking the history of a shape or of reverting to an earlier version. Because the final step in the design process involves building a life-sized clay model, last-minute revisions are extremely costly.

In the Bios system, the designer will begin with a stock profile of a pleasing shape. Working within general parameters that represent technological constraints (such as wheelbase length, windshield angle, and size of engine compartment), the program will evolve a group of designs. A designer will then be able to select one shape, modify it, and evolve it further—or even use two designs as "parents" for a new generation of shapes.

Because the user is always able to view both the current state of the design and all earlier mutations, any shape can be easily compared with its predecessors at every stage of the process. The option of going back to a previous version is always available. The program also studies and learns the user's behavior and preferences. For example, if it notes that the designer often chooses a particular slant for a line, it will begin to generate more possibilities in that direction. With this tool, designers can create and compare a vast number of designs in a short time, greatly accelerating the design process.

Other Tools

One of the primary advantages of an agent-based model is its capacity to extend a manager's vision beyond a few moves. Thus, these models have a valuable place at the heart of strategic planning. GAs are especially good for searching very large solution spaces, beginning from random starting points. They are the powerful engines that tackle challenges too vast and too formidable for linear methods. No one would argue that business problems are becoming any less complex, and thus GAs will be in high demand.

While these are broad, useful tools, they cannot unlock every kind of business problem. There are other methods that are much more effective at searching for solutions within smaller, more restricted regions.

A Hybrid Technique for Nasdaq

Sometimes GAs are used to "breed" the rules for agents in an agent-based model. This would be, for example, an excellent way to introduce novel trading strategies. In a joint venture with Nasdaq, Bios Group has developed a robust simulation of the trading mechanics at Nasdaq that can be used to study how the market performs under varying rules and regulations with different market conditions.

This model of the dealer-mediated securities market can be used to investigate various questions pertaining to the market rules that encourage a fair process of price discovery. In the simulation, dealer and investor agents buy and sell shares using various strategies. The agents' access to price and volume information approximates that available in the real-world market. Agent behaviors range from very simple user-driven strategies to more complicated evolutionary strategies, and the results of all types are easily graphed and compared for effectiveness.

The simulation can be managed and run with an easy-to-use graphical interface, or it can be run in batch mode to produce larger amounts of data more quickly. The model has already produced some highly suggestive and unexpected results, with potential implications for real-world issues at Nasdaq.

Solutions and the Fitness Landscape

A business seeking solutions to a problem must scan the search space—the set of all possible solutions to the problem. Obviously, some solutions will be more effective than others; a fitness function measures the relative value, or fitness, of each potential solution with respect to a set of criteria.

In a given fitness landscape, each potential solution is mapped according to its fitness ranking; thus, all relationships between neighboring solutions in the search space are defined. If there are multiple objectives described by different fitness values, it is called a multiscape. A business can study the fitness landscape or multiscape of its operations process to identify practical improvements. Finding the best solution boils down to maximizing the fitness function. Think, for example, of the paint booths bidding for trucks, where each bid is ranked according to various criteria of readiness.

Fitness landscapes were traditionally understood through the use of mathematical models. Unfortunately, these must often be based on simplifying assumptions that limit their applicability to real-world situations. Now, more detailed, flexible, and true-to-life agent-based models and simulations can be used to define the landscape of operations.

To construct an agent-based model, first identify the factors, whether a handful or many thousands, that affect operations. Each factor represents an agent, such as a train agent or track-segment agent. Then, assign to each agent the decision rules that dictate its behavior. These programmed instructions are like genetic code. In fact, they are often embodied in genetic algorithms, the key to what Jim Dowe (1997) has called "solution by evolution." More than one agent might come up with a good solution to a problem; if so, successful solutions should be "bred" to arrive at even more robust descendants. After running the simulation at one setting of variables and recording the outcome, "mutate" some of the variables and record the new outcome. This will generate a detailed image of the topography of the entire fitness landscape. (In some cases the method outlined here might be slow even on a fast computer. In such cases, sophisticated techniques from machine learning can be used to infer the landscape from a much smaller sampling of fitness values.)

In a fitness landscape, breeding the best solutions amounts to exploring the high-fitness or hilltop regions more thoroughly than the valleys. This method, known as the population approach, is particularly useful for simultaneously reviewing a whole "population" of solution candidates drawn from different regions of a search space.

A solution in isolation does not convey very much about its desirability relative to other possibilities. By mapping all solutions on a landscape, with solutions represented as peaks, the relative fitness of each becomes more evident. A jagged and bumpy terrain with lots of starts and stops—a "rugged" landscape—is more analogous to most real-life challenges than a smooth curve is.

Adapting in a Rugged Landscape

The difficulty with a rugged landscape, however, is that it is easy to get trapped on what is merely the highest peak in the immediate vicinity. Another optimization tool, called simulated annealing, avoids this trap by making the solution itself an active agent in the rugged fitness landscape. A simulated annealer wanders around the problem space in search of a premium solution, much the way a taxi driver searches for expensive fares. This is a very effective method for searching complex problem spaces because the annealer can jump to regions where the best results reside, like a taxi cruising the train stations, shopping districts, and hotels.

The techniques of operations research often assume that a fitness landscape is highly regular and single peaked, meaning it has a single optimal solution possessing a higher fitness value than any other potential solution; it might, for example, be lower unit cost through economies of scale. This is the case in linear programming, in which the more a solution differs from the optimal solution, the lower its fitness.

Sometimes these assumptions of regularity hold true; but more often fitness landscapes represent the practical reality of many different optimal solutions, such as multiple unit costs corresponding to a diverse line of products. The "you can't get there from here" phenomenon causes many landscapes to be rugged—that is, irregular, with multiple peaks. Using simple optimization techniques, solution queries start off from a point on the landscape and "hill-climb" until they stop improving; they thus often get stuck on a local optimum. It is like blindly expending all of your energy climbing to the top of a mountain, only to realize that the "mountain" you are on is merely the highest point in a valley and is surrounded by yet higher peaks.

Adaptation in a rugged landscape is not about reaching the highest peak. Your best bet is to make local changes that gain you the greatest improvement. Biology and physics offer some very useful hints for adapting in rugged landscapes. GAs and simulated annealing are two of nature's clever devices.

Simulated Annealing

Simulated annealing is very often used with other search techniques as an intermediate step in the overall search process. It is especially useful for searching within a smaller region that has been identified as promising by a GA search. This method emulates the physical process of annealing, during which a material is first heated, then slowly cooled, to remove defects. During annealing, the component atoms of a material are allowed to settle gradually into a lower energy state throughout the cooling process in order to attain a very stable arrangement (van Laarhoven, 1987; Vidal, 1993). Annealing makes a material stronger, more flexible, and less brittle, like the well-tempered swords of the Japanese samurai.

In simulated annealing, an individual step toward a solution does not always have to be favorable; sometimes exploring an initially unpromising path yields greater, if more distant, discoveries. A simulated annealer functions as an accept-or-reject tool seeking a single solution rather than as a select-and-recombine tool searching among a population of solutions. Once the annealer has found a promising path, it is often combined with additional search instruments, such as random walk, hill-climbing, or steepest gradient algorithms.

The computer simulation of annealing is somewhat counterintuitive, for it favors change and encourages searching farther afield, even if a locally optimal solution has already been found. Every rise in "temperature," or in orientation within the solution space, if that is easier to imagine, is like a request to climb a neighboring hill with the hope of finding better solutions. Permission is most likely to be granted when there is already a high degree of volatility, represented in simulated annealing as high temperature. The distance to optimality depends on the temperature: the closer the temperature is to zero, the closer the optimal solutions will be. The logic behind these simulation rules is that something in a high energy state is less likely to get stuck on a local peak than something that is relatively static and in a low energy state.

At high temperatures almost any proposed change is accepted regardless of whether or not it improves things (that is, whether or not it increases or decreases fitness). In this high energy state, the system is fairly robust. However, as the temperature is lowered, the proportion of changes accepted becomes increasingly linked to the degree of potential improvement offered by such changes. So, as the temperature is lowered toward the optimum, a change will be accepted only if it promises to improve fitness.

A simulated annealer self-adjusts in order to reach a solution within an allotted time. As a deadline approaches, the annealer synchronizes the decision-making process to the time remaining by decreasing the temperature, which in turn lowers the acceptance level. Within a given time constraint, there is a gradual settling toward a final solution.

In the end, the behavior at high temperatures—knowingly accepting changes that might temporarily worsen things—allows the system to explore more options and therefore to find better compromises. It is a controllable trade-off between a solution's optimality and its robustness. In the virtual tug-of-war between current local optimality and potential but as yet unrealized global optimality, a change is a long shot only when it is the only option.

Less Than Perfect Is Sometimes Best

Adaptive operations focus on finding a solution that is robust, that can be implemented quickly, and that is good enough to get the job done. In a complex process like GM's truck-painting lines, the optimal solution can, in practice, be almost impossible to determine, or it might be too expensive or too disruptive to current operations to be implemented. Better to find a solution that works fairly well in almost any situation than to find one that works perfectly but only under ideal conditions. It might be more practical to choose the best of "nearby" solutions—the best solution given multiple conflicting constraints.

This same kind of trade-off has been studied by biologists because organisms in the natural world also face such constraints. In biology if changes in the system (mutations) are too severe, an organism is unlikely to survive. Similarly, a business needs to know whether or not it can migrate to a solution from its current position. The optimal solution is useless if "you can't get there from here."

In contrast to traditional operations theory, in which optimization focuses on a single global objective, adaptive operations call for a Pareto optimal solution, whereby a number of criteria are optimized simultaneously (Statnikov and Matusov, 1995; Steuer, 1986). Finding the best possible compromise that satisfies immediate requirements is vastly different from aiming at long-term production goals. Multiobjective optimization is responsive to variability, flexible, and robust; it is usually rapid and often less expensive than pursuing the single best solution. In the long term, it creates a win-win situation.

We learn from these new approaches to optimization that the use of mutation and recombination can result in a host of robust solutions. We find that lessons learned from errors might end up being more valuable than any amount of improvement. We understand that in a real-world context it may be best to find an operating regime that is less than perfect but adaptive to the constant perturbations of a business environment.

Equipping for the Future

These flexible CAS approaches hold great promise for making operations more adaptive. They can help businesses cope with the variability of the marketplace and meet changing demands—something that linear trade-off analysis does poorly. They can reduce uncertainty by allowing a company to test in advance the outcome of a proposed change rather than rely on predictions based mostly on guesswork. They can reduce capital costs by more efficiently employing production facilities. They can simplify the management of interconnected and highly complex operations in a volatile environment by relieving managers of time-consuming and sometimes impossible tasks, which also means "relieving" them of a certain degree of control. Perhaps these methods will even limit disruptions caused by unwelcome surprises, by pointing out in advance some imminent nonlinear catastrophes.

The first step for anyone seeking to benefit from adaptive operations is to adopt the mindset. Not only must a business know its environment; it must understand its ability to evolve and must choose an appropriate problem-solving approach. The potential of a business to evolve depends on the structure of its fitness landscape. How can a business structure and position itself to maximize that potential?

We are just beginning to see how we can move from the metaphors of complex adaptive systems to concrete applications in business. Complexity science does not tell you about business; it tells you about science. To apply it to business, you have to interpret the science by bringing together scientists and businesspeople to conceive the creative solutions needed.

Evidence of the third wave in operations is all around us, growing from a desire to solve new kinds of problems brought on by speed and customization. At GM, at John Deere, at Nasdaq, all it took to initiate change was one person looking at problems through the powerful lens of complexity theory and asking, What are the agents in this system? What emergent property should we pursue? How could we make the process more flexible and more robust?

Operations research told managers that a schedule and production system or a factory could be optimized. Total quality management proposed continuous, incremental improvements from small, bottom-up changes. But managers who have adopted the adaptive mindset realize that continuous improvement can now be built into an operation, that learning can be automated and embedded within a production line. A factory can eventually find its own design and its own flexible, optimal space plan.

Thus, complexity approaches hold the promise of automating a third level of human work. In the first level, we replaced muscle power, initially with animals and then with engines. In the second, only begun, we are replacing human intelligence applied to reasonably standard tasks with now familiar combinations of hardware, software, and networks. The science of complex adaptive systems holds the promise of augmenting human creativity, and perhaps even accelerating the economy's capacity to learn, by finding innovative solutions and by paying untiring attention to the question of how new solutions may be found.

9

Buying and Selling in the Digital Age

An Ever-Increasing Bandwidth of Desire

John Julius Sviokla

What is the world's largest *man-made* complex adaptive system? There is nothing bigger than our global markets. Over thousands of years, they have grown from the tiniest beginnings—perhaps a sack of grain in exchange for some woodworking—into countless commercial mediums of ever increasing sophistication, diversity, and cohesion.

Consider an itinerant scissors grinder in Pinsk, a village square in Costa Rica, Wall Street, the L. L. Bean catalog, the eBay Web site, the black market in Moscow, a pygmy trading monkeys for metal pots on the banks of the Congo: all these and countless other people, places, and processes are connecting with each other a little more tightly every day as new capillaries appear in the market system and novel types of exchange begin to flow.

As a man-made complex adaptive system, what rivals in size does the global market have? Not government, not language: governments and languages partition more than they unify activity. In the case of governments especially, it is in their nature to exclude in order to protect the interests of a core group. Markets, on the other hand, tend toward universal inclusiveness, for an equally natural reason. Markets maximize the realm of possibility by encouraging specialization and trade. The result has been a trend toward greater economic good worldwide, despite recurrent crop failure, endemic disease, persistent warfare, and other inescapable catastrophes.

Like other complex adaptive systems, markets do not self-aggregate in any uniform fashion. The gains have been unevenly distributed, and connections are imperfectly shared. Some regions are assimilated quickly; others are bypassed. Whole cultures, even whole continents, languish for generations, mostly untouched by modern commerce and technology. Nevertheless, almost everyone on the planet today contributes, directly or indirectly, to the world market.

The ball bearings on which all markets spin are prices: prices are the basis for all market transactions. Price may be expressed in the form of barter (I trade my pig for two of your pots) or in the form of money (I sell my pig for $82). In both cases price is a quantity, but only in the second case is it readily comparable to most other transactions, which is why money is so useful and such a universal tagging mechanism.

Although the importance of price is self-evident, the concept of price is elusive. Price is a tag among many other tags in the complex adaptive system of the market. However, it also performs a unique function. It is a translator, the common denominator of commercial description. That is why price is ubiquitous in commerce. Probably it is indispensable. Money, on the other hand, may not be indispensable to a modern market. It may be that money is simply the best technology known for expressing price. Someday we may be able to forget money and move on to some superior way of expressing price. The challenge is that we need an entire grammar of value that is as exchangeable as price: a semantics that allows people from all over the globe to discover locally, nationally, or globally what the value is of some "thing" in time and place. This kind of new semantics, largely defined by the customer, is beginning to appear in the capital markets and on the World Wide Web.

This chapter explores how price functions as the driver behind mankind's largest complex adaptive system, the world market (see

Crane, 1995, for a set of interesting and useful perspectives). It contains some speculations about how barter and money may be intermediate technologies for establishing price. It argues that a richer description of reality in a digital setting will set the stage for direct transactions and new fitness criteria, in which desire will find satisfaction directly and in a self-organized manner. Such a global "pricing" mechanism may or may not contain money. We may just be starting to see the emergence of new grammars for price that could allow a Technicolor description of desire, instead of the black-and-white world of money we know today. What would that look like and how would it work?

Pricing in the Past

Throughout history, improvements in information access and standardization have led to booms in pricing. Development of a coherent accounting system enabled the Egyptians to keep track of the tributes they extracted, which allowed them to extract more. Classified advertisements in the early *Boston Globe* created a whole new category of "want ads" by publishing information to facilitate buying and selling. Edison's ticker tape spread information rapidly around the world, inviting people to contribute to the already vast pool of capital driving the expansion of railroads and heavy industries. This was a big mental shift for most investors because they almost always had to accept the transactions sight unseen. The growing sophistication of these and other forms of description have greatly increased the ability to track, price, and buy or sell just about any asset or service.

Pricing allowed more uniform trade across the world by giving local pools of capital a scaffold from which to work with large risks. Bonds and stocks, embodying complex descriptions of price, were and are important building blocks of the channels that enable free flow of price. Fluid prices in turn sped the flow of trade globally, in part by permitting people to buy and sell both locally and globally at the same time. England took the lead by sanctioning creation of the Royal Stock Exchange (Morgan and Thomas, 1971). The Exchange proved to be a model of self-organization, using direct trading of equities to aggregate demand and supply from widely dispersed sources into a single active market. For England it was a spectacular success. State-of-the-art pricing at the Exchange did much to fund and energize the nation's drive to empire.

Equities and other price-denominated devices could be combined in novel ways to create new social and economic capabilities. For example, in the 1970s when Salomon Brothers created the mortgage-backed security, the aggregation of financing for single-family homes into a single $250–500 million security created a vehicle whose characteristics differed vastly from those of the individual home mortgages from which it was constructed. The composite security was more predictable in behavior, and this caused billions of dollars to flow into the home mortgage market as institutional investors began to appreciate that the interesting financial characteristics of this type of "paper" were far preferable to the individual encapsulated entities. Today we have a rich ecology of complex financial instruments, all built through creative variations on the simple concept of price.

However, in this aggregation (as in any aggregation) the identity of the subsumed item, in this case the houses, becomes obscured. In addition, the new flow of funds available to the aggregate (that is, to the mortgage-backed security) does not reach far down: funding flow to the individual mortgage is little improved. A house loan may become a bit more liquid than it was but never attains anything like the flexibility or power enjoyed by the aggregate. This lack of flow (or lack of liquidity) is due to many factors, central among them the steep costs of search and transaction.

The advent of cheap, decentralized information technology is quickly changing that. The marvels of digital calculation and communication not only allow fast data aggregation and corresponding self-organization in the market but also make it possible to trade the

whole instrument while keeping an eye on key particulars of its constituent parts. That is, the current buyer of a mortgage-backed security can view the paperwork on the different properties in real time.
That is only the beginning of improved "visibility." Soon a prospective investor will be able to "tour" the homes on-screen by opening
a financial Web page. From there, the investor may have the lati-
tude to trade the entity, its constituent parts, or some of both. This
form of heightened flexibility improves performance of the complex
asset class overall, creating new value. As the grammar of description becomes more robust, we may not be limited to trading simply
the aggregate; this opens up a world of possibilities.

The Virtual Value Chain

This type of increasingly granular description is happening in financial and nonfinancial markets. The depth and precision of description of just about every product and service is increasing. In
medicine we see the advent of outcome measures and standard
prices in the form of diagnostic related groups (DRGs). In retail
stock brokerages, transaction costs and commissions have never
been more clear and pertinent to the consumer. Cheap commissions
have been a driving force in getting customers to switch from their
traditional broker interactions to Internet-based interactions. We
see the creation of consumer guides for cars, insurance, loans, and
other products and services. These guides provide detailed price
information to the consumer.

This trend toward fuller description of everything will continue.
The trend is linked to the appearance of what may be called the
"virtual value chain" (Rayport and Sviokla, 1994, 1995). Like a
conventional value chain (Porter, 1985), a virtual value chain
injects new and different forms of value as a product or service travels down the metaphorical assembly line. However, in a virtual
value chain, the injected value has nothing to do with physical
processes like raw materials mining, metal stamping, or trucking; it

has to do with the injection, channeling, and recombination of information so that things can be done in a more intelligent, efficient, speedy, timely, or precise way than before.

The recent technological strides underlying the virtual value chain are almost unimaginable. In the manufacturing realm, products now carry enough computer memory that they can tell the potential buyer what their condition is; an Indy race car's instrumentation tells engineers how it is performing. In like manner, the used car of the future will provide potential buyers with a profile of how the car has been driven (how many times it went over one hundred miles per hour, when its oil was changed, if it crashed, where it has been damaged, and so forth). This increasingly complete record will allow even nontechnical people to evaluate the car's quality and reliability. Analogous profiling methods are already being developed for evaluating services: doctors have standard ratings, as do hospitals; insurers are rated by the consumers; and restaurant ratings are more consistent and available.

From a complex adaptive systems standpoint, increasingly precise, detailed, and updateable descriptions will enable more things to be tagged more accurately with a price (Holland, 1995, 1998). Systemwide, the result will be greater pricing granularity. Early examples include reservation systems that allow airlines to price each and every seat on an airplane at a different fare in order to maximize the flight's overall profitability (Copeland and McKenney, 1988). These days, it is not at all uncommon for a single aircraft to be carrying passengers who have, among them, paid fifty different fares. Such variety would not be possible without cheap and reliable descriptions of the seat inventory in terms of time until departure, alternate routes, competitor pricing, and much more. As more and more virtual value chains become more robust in information, pricing will gain microscopic accuracy.

The question will be, To whose benefit? For the moment, instantaneously adaptable reservations systems primarily benefit the airlines rather than their customers. The airlines retain most of the information. But the balance of power is already shifting in the direction of buyers, and that shift is bound to continue (Mui and Downes, 1998; Mui, 1999).

These new technologies should make it easier to start and grow companies. Freely available price information makes it much easier to gather resources and build a plan to address a market. Yet full impact and efficiency from the virtual value chain will require more efficient means of discovering the "correct" price in real time and across many markets (Sviokla, 1998).

Fuller descriptions of goods and services have begun to have some very interesting impacts on price. First, customers can now search much more efficiently, and they are doing so. In 1998, a large percentage of the millions of Americans on-line were using the Web to search for information about purchases. But the more interesting phenomenon is that we have begun to see a much more robust set of buyer-side listings of desires, information, and prices—some take-it-or-leave it, some negotiable, and in the case of giant corporations like General Electric, more of it via buyer-initiated auctions (in which the low-price supplier wins the bid). The Web site www.priceline.com enables consumers to list what they want to pay for an airline seat or a vacation. Priceline is much more than a simple buyers' club that aggregates group demand to negotiate a more favorable price or benefit package for its customers. (Sites such as www.netmarket.com perform this type of service.) Priceline enables customers to state the price they expect to pay. As obvious as this sort of price setting may seem, very few mechanisms are able to perform the function for consumers on a large scale and across a broad range of supply.

The arrival of organizations like Priceline marks the beginning of a very interesting trend toward customers self-organizing—millions of them, all acting individually on their own account, around price. That is, the customers now have the ability to drive the pricing. The outcome is vastly more granularity and variety in transacted value. No longer is the supplier necessarily the price setter.

So-called standard price is under attack. From now on there will be a systemic tension. Who organizes the price and how many prices there are will be in doubt. That means it will be difficult to keep price changes stable. Indeed, the very notion of a fixed price could very well disappear.

In the business-to-business market, emerging champions of the buyer-set price are headed by Ariba, a service that helps corporations of the world list their preferred prices in the $300 billion market for maintenance, repair, and operations. When a big corporation like GE needs a new water cooler, its representative can go on-line and say what the company is willing to pay, then let suppliers bid on the demand (Farrell, 1999). Likewise, in the consumer spaces portals such as Yahoo!, Excite, and Lycos are gearing up to give shoppers greater efficiency, range of options, and convenience.

However, even with these advances, suppliers and buyers will still "play" the system. Buyers will list a price lower than the real price they are willing to pay to find out if they can get the airline seat at an even lower price. Sellers will list a few items on-line to lead customers into a relationship and hope to get them to buy a higher-priced product or service package. Indeed, the current stage of revolution in demand articulation has changed the contour of the micromarket. Gaming remains but alters its tactics. That is because a good distance continues to separate buyer-set prices from "true" value. Discovering true value requires true flexibility on all sides, by multiple buyers and multiple sellers throughout the market.

Changing the Micromarket Structure

Even in electronic markets, there are at least two key deficiencies in any current mechanism of price discovery. First, the incentives to express true demand are too weak. The vulnerabilities associated with full disclosure overwhelm them. Second, the semantics of pricing are still too simple for the task at hand. For example, an equities buyer can enter either a "limit" order or a "market" order. A market order requires the buyer to take whatever the market offers. This is often a poor price. More frequently, buyers give limit orders, which state the buyer's preference in three dimensions: size of trade, price of equity, and duration of order. For example, a limit order might be two thousand shares at $50.00 per share good for one day. Even a limit order is discrete and binary. It states that the buyer is 100 percent interested in the stock at $50.00 and 0 percent interested in the stock at $50.25. It also states that if the stock goes to $40.00 the next day, the buyer is totally uninterested in the security (Clemons and Weber, 1998; Sviokla and Dailey, 1998).

This is not necessarily a perfect reflection of the buyer's desire. An antiquated, simplistic mechanism for price expression governs complex purchases like futures or stock. A visit to the Chicago Board of Exchange, where traders in a pit yell out to signal price and volume purchases and sales, reminds us of the bazaars and livestock auctions that have existed for thousands of years. It is almost dumbfounding that trillions of dollars in futures contracts are traded daily by hollering and hand waving. Even at the more staid New York Stock Exchange, the sequence of broker to trader to specialist creates significant costs. The inefficiencies of processes like these, even in "sophisticated" industries, cost the market dearly.

What we would really like is a system that enables the expression of preferences along a continuum rather than as a single point: "I would be willing to pay up to an eighth of a point more to fill my entire order and will pay an eighth of a point less if the order is merely 90 percent of my target." The same flexibility across time is also desirable and potentially expressible: "I'm interested in buying one hundred shares of Acme if it drops more than 10 percent within forty-eight hours, or 8 percent in twenty-four hours." Buyers would also like to be able to tie their preference for one financial product to the fortunes of others: "If oil futures move down by 10 percent, I'd like to buy American Airlines stock at fifty and an eighth."

The mechanism to "price" in this flexible way, either as a seller or as a buyer, is needed, inevitable, and on its way. For the sophisticated buyer, it is already here in the form of brokers and traders who act within discretionary limits (for example: "Buy ten thousand shares at my price, plus or minus an eighth"). However, reliance on agents introduces significant costs into the transaction.

The emerging information economy will eventually give us better tags for pricing, and these days "eventually" tends not to be too far away. At least two components will be needed. One of these can be thought of almost literally as a black box where all potential participants, both buyers and sellers, express the full range of their desires for something without being identified. The second necessary component is a richer language to describe the multidimensional thing we call "preference to trade." The dimensions are essentially the same in any market, from cars to candy bars, from surgery to shoe shines: price, quantity, quality, timing. Imagine a world in which you could list your honest selling price preference and be assured that you would get linked to the buyer with the highest price ceiling in the market for your product or service. That ceiling might be considerably higher than you had dared hope. We are so accustomed to thinking about commerce from supply-side givens that it takes considerable imagination to conceive of a world in which we could enter a "confessional" of desire and privately name what we would sell or buy, and on what parameters of terms. Further, imagine that this confessed desire could then be efficiently and discreetly compared with the true desires of every other participant in the market and that this process of potential matching could take place within moments.

The speed, precision, range, and anonymity of such a system would radically increase the ability of markets to self-organize. Technology is beginning to make this possible. Not long from now it will be possible, and at significantly lower cost than that of any conventional alternative. Think what this would mean for the entire market system. Many prices for goods and services could exist simultaneously.

This is not an easy possibility to imagine, but it is real. An analogy might be what it must have been like thousands of years ago when someone handed you a little piece of shiny metal when you had been used to thinking in terms of cattle. The mental leap here is at least as great. The mapping of multidimensional desire to a grammar of transaction would allow pure supply to meet pure demand, boosting self-organization in commercial markets to a new and utterly unexplored level.

1999: Watershed Year for Pricing

An innovative start-up company in the securities market is building the first generation of such a system. Called OptiMark, the system creates an anonymous, real-time, robust price discovery mechanism for equities (Petruno, 1998). Using advanced computer algorithms adapted from defense industry technologies, OptiMark precisely matches supply and demand on a global scale. At the same time, OptiMark removes the limitations inherent in the conventional market's need for a single price at a single moment. OptiMark does this by capturing what might be called the "overtones" of price: fainter and fainter willingness to buy or sell at prices farther and farther above or below market. This richer recording is a giant step toward ideal liquidity and fairer trading.

If the OptiMark system of price discovery indeed works, it could be used to trade not just equities (a market now at 1.5 billion shares a day worldwide and climbing fast) but a wide variety of products and services. Rapid growth in electronic products and services magnifies the opportunity still further. OptiMark could turn out to be the culmination of "old" pricing and the birth of "new" pricing.

OptiMark was founded by Bill Lupien, a former specialist and securities trader, and Terry Rickard, a mathematician and former military analyst who had worked in naval intelligence. Lupien and Rickard believed that current market structures, especially the New York Stock Exchange, were not meeting the needs of institutional investors. As the world's largest equity market, the New York Stock Exchange represents companies with a cumulative market capitalization of well over $10 trillion. In that huge pool of value, selling a small amount of stock, such as one thousand shares, presents no problem to either buyer or seller. However, those wishing to acquire or divest a large position must pay a significant "liquidity premium." Such transaction costs are one of the reasons that 75 to 80 percent of all money managers underperform a simple index of the stock market. For nearly all investors this is a thorny issue because money managers manage 55 percent of all money held in stocks and make 85 percent of all trades.

The liquidity premium arises because information about an order often precedes the order itself into the marketplace. Say that a fund manager wants to sell a million shares of Sears, Roebuck, & Company stock. The fund manager usually begins by calling a trader. To minimize the seller's cost to trade, the trader most often breaks up the order into smaller trades, attempting to hide its size from potential counterparties. The smaller trades are jobbed out to a number of "block desks," which specialize in trading large blocks of stock. Even with such "unwinding" tactics, however, the chunks of stock remain fairly bulky, and the cost of liquidity is relatively high. Research by the Plexus Group estimates the all-in transaction cost of a large trade to be as high as 1.36 percent of the trade's value (Clemons and Weber, 1998, p. 301). The 1.36 percent figure may be at the low end of the range because it represents trading cost for stocks capitalized at over a billion dollars. For small-capitalization stocks the liquidity premium is estimated to be as high as 3 to 4 percent per trade because the smaller float of stock makes the relative impact of a large trade even greater.

The magnitude of this premium is significant when set against the long-term expected return on the equities of roughly 10 percent per annum. If a portfolio manager completely turns over his investment (for example, sells Sears and with the proceeds buys IBM), the transaction cost is 1.36 percent times two, or 2.72 percent. So with each stock turnover, performance must exceed "normal" by the equivalent of 2.72 percent for a year to match the long-term expected return of a simple buy-and-hold strategy for the market index. When the trades involve small-capitalization stocks, the hurdles to acceptable performance become nearly insurmountable.

With OptiMark, the semantics of price are greatly enhanced. The buyer or seller can create a multidimensional set of preferences that can be optimized for the market as it is expressed at that moment. The current implementation of OptiMark allows the equity trader to describe a preference curve of price and volume, and duration with a weighting of value. This function is then matched against all other profiles and returns an optimal solution every three minutes. The matched trade clears at the exchange in the world that has a price that creates the greatest preference for all buyers and sellers in the market for that three-minute global window. It then clears the trade on the most efficient market (Sviokla and Dailey, 1998; Rickard and Lupien, 1996a, 1996b).

OptiMark lowers the costs of search and trade significantly. The company began its trading operations (in one stock only, that of the 3M Corporation) on January 29, 1999, just days before this chapter was completed. If the OptiMark system works as planned, it will provide a much richer system of tagging of desire. It is a multidimensional pricing mechanism that retains the variety of a band of price preference and time validity. The variety of monetary transactions often relies on derivative financial instruments to provide semantic richness, but a system like OptiMark will allow such trading strategies to be embedded in the underlying trade itself. For example, in future implementations it will be possible to enter a trade that is relative to other stocks. That is, I may wish to sell Coke and buy General Electric, but I only want to do it if the effect on my portfolio is neutral. Therefore, if I own Coke at $50 and GE at $100 when I make the trading decision, I could enter an order that says, "Sell Coke and buy GE as long as the difference is $50." In a large pool of orders, I could swap my shares for those of someone else, either in constituent parts or as a matching total order. Thus, the market has increased in its variety of combinations and kept the granularity that allows for the trading of the underlying constituent parts.

OptiMark should be able to add many different dimensions of desire to the trading activity. It will allow users to embed their preferences and trading strategies right into their transaction order rather than leaving these considerations outside the trade itself. OptiMark's designers believe this will deprive intermediaries of the information asymmetry that today enables them to make such a huge margin on the current inefficient micromarket structure. The result will be a low-cost, low-gaming environment and a significant lowering of liquidity premiums.

The tagging mechanisms OptiMark introduces should increase in semantic richness and open the way for a much more efficient set of trading capabilities in the global market. It becomes realistic to start planning for continuous, twenty-four-hour-a-day global stock trading, with a concomitant surge in liquidity and flow.

Expanding the Expression of Desire

The OptiMark type of innovation is possible in the financial markets and comparatively easy to envision because in those markets there is already considerable tagging sophistication and information technology penetration. With the coming of global computer networking and an increasingly deep model of reality embedded in information systems (Quinn, 1992; Nolan and Croson, 1995), the ability to express object and desire in many nonfinancial markets also increases.

Informationalized Objects of Desire

Acute descriptive capability, naturally enough, developed earliest on the seller side. Organizations have for some time been able to express what they have, what they have had, and what they expect to have, precisely, instantaneously, and globally. Modern distributors can tell you what is in stock, what is on back order, and the likely time of arrival of your delivery at any place on the face of the earth. This increasing virtualization of their value chain has enabled much superior control of their business capabilities. A tangible example of such a system is Dell's ability to take a customer order and customize it to the individual in three days or less: this is post-demand production (Narayandas and Rangan, 1996). By having a business system with a superior virtual value chain, Dell can take expressed desire and deliver it as an experience faster than any of their competition at only a slight premium over mass manufactured computers.

Amazon.com is remaking the market-identification model for the book retailing industry. Industry economics have dictated pushing the masses toward a mass product. The essence of publishing is therefore the blockbuster title that sells millions of copies, such as a sequel by a well-known author who can more or less guarantee a minimum volume of sales. By contrast, Amazon is starting to articulate market preference for titles, authors, and story lines at a level of fine detail that book publishers could not have dreamed of even five years ago. As a vast range of customer preferences is expressed by individual customers' actual purchases, Amazon can afford to market new titles for known audiences, with much less market risk. The longer it holds on to these customers, tracks their purchases, and succeeds in enticing them to participate actively in its reader community by commenting, recommending, or even searching (which can be tracked and analyzed), the lower the risk becomes. In this way, Amazon creates new predictive capability based on a robust description of the swirls and eddies in the fluid demand of real people who remain distinct and unique buyers in the company's database.

Think about residential real estate from the seller side. Soon people will have the ability to put their family house discreetly "on the market" not merely as soon as they want but continuously, all the time. True, most people do not really want to sell their house. But on the theory that everything has its price, it may be worthwhile for each homeowner to establish a "reservation price" at which they would be willing to endure the pain of moving and the loss of neighborhood. Perhaps it is double or triple what nearly all potential buyers would think it is "worth." But what is true worth? Is it the mean value, higher than half the people's appraisals and lower than that of the other half? Or is true worth equal to the highest bid, if the person willing to make that bid could only see that house? If there is little cost to posting a price in the "digital plate-glass window," the homeowner has nothing to lose by listing an extremely high holdout price for the property, in case someone really wants that house and is willing to pay that price. In such an information-rich setting, price becomes more robust, and far more decentralized, than it is today. It will become perfectly rational and efficient to offer any and all assets that you have on a global basis, with complete anonymity and at an extremely low price. This is a kind of direct "postmoney" barter system that could create an entirely different relationship between things, desires, and trading.

Informationalized Desire

Money is, and always has been, an intermediate object of desire, a form of potential experience. As reality becomes better and better described and reflected in a broadband virtual value chain, people will gain the ability to put prices on their desires more clearly and inspect possible experiences more fully. In order to trade directly in experiences, we will need mechanisms of expression that are richer than simple monetary denomination as well as a mechanism to aggregate and transact this pool of desire. As the inhabitants of "communities of value" such as GeoCities self-aggregate in the virtual world, we can already detect mounting pressure for mass insurrection against the selling classes. Customers will then turn around and price their design needs back to those capable of production and fulfillment. Before long, consumer buying cartels will have coalesced sufficiently to make serious price-related demands. The more members of the community who participate, the more value will shift toward the allied customers. They will also create a much more liquid market in goods and services among themselves with such a scaffolding.

As this shift occurs, a secondary effect will also arise, the likes of which few people expect. What customers self-design will less and less take the form of products and services. More and more, customers will design—and price—the highly intangible, profoundly personal experiences they desire. As B. Joseph Pine and Jim Gilmore have written in *The Experience Economy* (1999), people and companies alike will cease to think of "customer satisfaction," where the starting point is a predesigned, prefabricated product. Instead, it will become normal for buyers and sellers to think in terms of "customer sacrifice," which comes with an assessment of value from the customer's perspective.

This process will involve ever better methods of mass customization as well as richer descriptions. If we are to trade on such a set of experiences, we need a better tagging system for desire that enables complex trade-offs to be fed into a market mechanism. Imagine, for instance, that some people would be just as happy to have a Porsche as they would a thirty-five-foot motor yacht. If there were a slight change in the relative desire, however, the owner of one might give it up to obtain the other. At present, the costs of putting together such a transaction are so great that few people even conceive of such a trade-off. However, these costs are falling rapidly.

Virtual documentation is one reason among many: a digital camera might record the yacht's voyages, compress the transcript down to a few minutes of view time, and finish with an up-to-the-minute inspection of the boat inside and out, augmented by historical read-outs of its onboard instrumentation. At this point, we are no longer talking about just any thirty-five-foot yacht of this make and model; we are talking about this very boat.

As communities begin to discover what is of value to their members, the decentralized nature of the Web will empower them to find new ways to price. Scaffolding such as the OptiMark system is a preliminary example of the type of wide-bandwidth pricing mechanisms that can allow people to begin to describe their desires more directly.

At the same time, the tools of design are becoming more available to consumers through increasingly revealing models of reality. Kitchen designs, houses, and cars are all becoming described not only by pictures but by kinesthetically detailed models that reflect a potential design and the constraints of performance demanded by materials of manufacture. Thus, the customer can specify the demand by simulation before purchase to a much higher degree of fidelity than was ever possible before. Both of these trends—toward more revealing description and toward ways to virtually experience what will potentially be really experienced—create a new tagging architecture of possibility for consumers.

The missing dimension has been a tagging architecture to allow the direct translation of capabilities with all the richness of the experiences being modeled. Right now we have the very thin mechanism of price. But we are well on the way to developing an effective multidimensional expression of transactable desire. Figure 9.1 illustrates this idea. Over time we will develop more and more robust descriptions along the dimensions of demand, supply, and "price." Markets will self-organize with a vast new capability to fill out all three dimensions of this desire space.

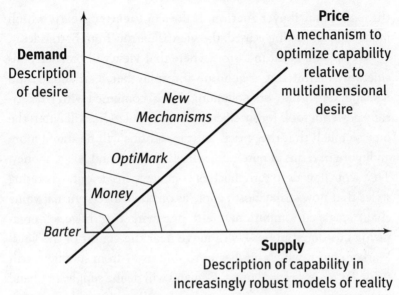

Figure 9.1. The Evolution of Pricing.

Conclusion and Implications

Until now we have seen only part of the evolutionary pattern. The expression of price has advanced from crude physical correlates (pigs for pottery) to precise but nondescriptive financial representations (a pig for $82). We are now, I believe, on the cusp of two qualitative changes in commercial transactions that will remake the way market activity self-aggregates.

First, the bandwidth of expression of desire will widen. These days, even when buyer and seller are face to face (an increasingly rare luxury), their dialogue is subject to severe limits of time, motivation, vocabulary, and prior experience, to name a few. Moreover, even after a rich conversation, their understanding has to be funneled down and squeezed through the thin pipe called price. Sometimes price is set by the seller, sometimes set by the buyer, sometimes negotiated between the two, and sometimes determined through a multibuyer auction. It does not matter greatly which mode of price setting is used; the view is narrow from both sides.

We are at a point in history where that view will broaden considerably, permitting a genuine interplay between supply and demand. Open-network communications, combined with fantastically powerful tools for specification and calculation, will fatten the pipe so much that the "price" of transactions will be stated more and more in terms of pure information, and less and less as money. That will allow us to turn much of commerce inside out. Operating styles that now strike most people as on the fringe—virtual value chains, mass customization, one-to-one marketing, huge self-organizing customer groups—will move near the center of the field. Market power, which has begun to shift away from suppliers, will swing far more toward buyers. Demand will define supply, not bend to accommodate it, because most supply will only be produced after the demand has been registered. Customers will be promoted to become initiators of their own personal microsupply; they will become, in a Hollywood-like sense, the producers of their own desires.

Second, high-speed, massive-scale information technologies will redefine commercial transactions. We have gotten a taste of this already in the financial services arena and on the Web. As yet, however, most business still works much as it did before. The calculation of value has been mostly a subjective exercise, but it will become so well automated that matching its quality will be simply beyond the capability of human beings. Most of us will largely give up trying and will pay less and less attention to "the numbers." Instead we will concentrate primarily on the resulting matchup between what is wanted and what is obtained. Invisible pricing mechanisms will help us make smooth adjustments accordingly.

At its core, the purpose of business is to harvest desire at a margin. With the coming of better and better descriptions of supply and demand, consumers will expect that companies show their wares virtually and in real time. Moreover, the tags of price will include the desires of people; attributes such as reviews, time to availability, and location; and other dimensions of preference yet to be discovered. Companies that cannot capture and express their offerings will not be able to compete because the expectation of such capabilities will be as common as the expectation that water will be pure and that the car will start on a cold day.

There will be an increasing premium on the seller's ability to tell a story, for technology will continue to increase the efficiency of the physical world, making for more competition. Therefore, differentiation will come in the realms where individuals can begin to link desires to price. Movies will be grand merchandising events, and many more companies will operate like Disney by taking icons of desire and pricing them in the physical world, on movies, books, tapes, and every mode of icon available for margin extraction.

We will also see the birth of a large "barter" economy as people become able to share information experiences at a fraction of the cost of current distribution and as other tangible goods are brought into such trades. Price will be much more personalized in such an environment and will have as much personality as the products of wineries in Italy or boutiques in France. People will have the opportunity to trade in ways never before imagined.

Perhaps most important, better pricing will help to create a low-cost barter method to trade creative output. The coming century will have a means and a method of transacting for goods and services that will be globally efficient and locally accessible. A return to creativity should flourish as people self-organize their tags and their markets, taking money or other tribute in return. The result—market "prices" that substitute rich descriptions for simple numbers—will be manifestly better for all concerned.

10

Emergent Law and Order

Lessons in Regulation, Dispute Resolution, and Lawmaking for Electronic Commerce and Community

David R. Johnson

Law and political philosophy have always drawn on the science of the day for analogies and for insights into the human condition. So it should come as no surprise that new findings by scientists regarding the operation of self-organizing systems may lead to new forms of lawmaking and to new ideas about the relationship between citizens and the state.

The science of complex adaptive systems (CAS) gives us a new way to understand legal phenomena that are well established. The complex structure of the "common law" evolved over time from the differential survival of competing doctrines, woven together in the course of complex flows of information among courts and litigants (Katsh, 1989). Nation-states, objects of our collective imaginations, organized themselves on the basis of many complex interactions among local customs, distinct languages, boundary-changing territorial conquests, and the continual information processing of markets.

What is different now, and what calls for a reevaluation of our legal doctrines and institutions, is the recent appearance of a fast, low-cost, jurisdiction-crossing communications technology: the Internet. This new technology accelerates the rate of change, ignores the geographic boundaries around which much of the existing legal system has been organized, and facilitates the creation of new types of imagined collectivities (organizations that either make and administer law or are recognized by sovereigns as legal persons entitled to create and enforce their own internal order) (Johnson and Post, 1996). The rise of the Internet has not just posed novel legal questions—for example, should "spamming" (unsolicited commercial bulk e-mail), "framing" (incorporating another's Web page in your own), and on-line anonymity be prohibited? It has also provided a completely new, legally significant, persistent social "space" in which a new form of law may grow (Lessig, 1996).

On-line communities have been experimenting for years with new ways to create a "virtual social order." But the newly recognized potential for electronic commerce, which involves substantial financial stakes for existing companies and new potential for social problems that will affect large numbers of the constituents of traditional governments, has recently brought the problem of electronic collective action and protection of the on-line commons into sharper focus. Who will police fraud on the Web? What regulations regarding the practice of professions should apply when the doctor's office or the lawyer's office is in cyberspace? Who decides whether the "thread" collectively authored by contributors to a usenet newsgroup, from all around the world, is a collective work owned as a piece of intellectual property and who owns it? When can electronic fences be established to keep out unwelcome guests or search engines? What form of virtual vigilante action to "flame" or "mailbomb" or to filter out a social outcast should be permitted? What "clickwrap" adhesion contracts, setting the terms and conditions for any given on-line space or resource, should be enforceable, and which should be unenforceable as violations of public policy? Who exactly is the public that sets that policy? What protection extends to the right to control a particular on-line space (is it virtual property?) or identifier (is this virtual personhood?), and by what means? All of these questions will take on new urgency as more and more companies, customers, and communities take their business and other activities on-line.

This chapter draws lessons from the science of complex adaptive systems—especially the concepts of "tags" and "flows"—that elucidate the nature of law and its development. The chapter explores the ways in which global networking will change the sources and the nature of law, describes what we can expect the developing law of the Internet to look like, and considers questions of new forms of legal personhood. Drawing on the notion of a "sweet spot" between excessive order and chaos, the discussion points out the lessons of CAS theory for regulators in this new environment. The nature of civic virtue and citizenship, or "netizenship," in the global electronic economy is examined, as are new forms of dispute resolution that may arise. The conclusion of this chapter is that this new view of the law, informed by CAS theories, gives reason for optimism that we can better understand and contribute to, if not manage, the growth of a healthy, complex legal system.

Lessons from CAS Science

The lessons of self-organizing systems for dispute resolution and lawmaking can best be understood against the background of the outmoded doctrines that developed long before we began to see the world in terms of complexity theory. If you think of the world in hierarchical, theological terms, as did our medieval forebears, then law is merely an expression of God's will—a set of rules promulgated from above (albeit through an increasingly secular state) and beyond question by mere reason. If you begin to think of the world as a simple rational machine, such as the Enlightenment's metaphor of the clock, you then aspire to a law that is "discovered" like the laws of physics and that possesses a coherent rational consistency. Influenced by the disillusionments of the early twentieth century, some legal scholars began to see law as stemming solely from physical and cultural power and providing a top-down order in which the top represented nothing more than the accidental identity of those who had prevailed in conquest or who had control of mainstream culture. The pleasant new lesson drawn from the study of complex systems is that the legal order, although no longer defensible as "God given" or even wholly rational and although still based in large measure on historical accident, may nonetheless be a product of a mechanism by which order emerges naturally from the bottom up and through which individuals and groups may continuously find new forms of freedom, community, and empowerment.

Complex self-organizing systems prosper under, and help to create, circumstances characterized by an intermediate degree of order, a sweet spot between randomness and rigidity (Kauffman, 1995; see also Chapter One). How can such an intermediate dynamic state be achieved when laws take the form of authoritative statutory texts and legal precedents? One answer is that most laws and many mechanisms for dispute resolution are far from rigid. Statutes are interpreted by prosecutors and judges, who react to specific circumstance and adapt their decisions to find an acceptable rate of change. Many rules are established by private contract, which is itself influenced by, and interpreted in light of, evolving trade custom. Thus, contrary to some popular imagining, the law is anything but a static set of rules. It has been neither rigid nor random but seeks a flexible middle point.

However, the transactions and legal entities governed by law now occur and form on-line at a historically unprecedented pace. The study of complex systems suggests new ways to address resulting social problems. For example, we may have to allow the more flexible tools of private contractual ordering to become more dominant, as compared with statutes and litigation, in order to preserve a desirably intermediate state between order and chaos in the new, rapidly evolving context of the Internet. Fortunately, the faster "cycle time" of interactions on-line means that decentralized law creation will probably work well to find better solutions to public policy problems, allowing ample opportunity for decentralized choices to evolve the best-nuanced compromises among conflict-ing goals.

Our established legal traditions are rooted in processes and insti-tutions whose rates of change are radically slower than now required by the pace of commerce and social interaction on the new global Internet. The common law, as we have known it, is based on print: standardized case reports in a physical library that legal profession-als mastered, resulting in arguments based on precedent before courts that issued new decisions at a leisurely pace (Katsh, 1995). This worked well in the context of business deals that took months to form and that remained unchanged for years. Statutes provided an adequately orderly means of defining and punishing wrongful conduct when the nature and impact of wrongdoing, in a world dominated by physical actions and geographical proximity, remained stable over long periods of time. By contrast, a self-orga-nizing legal system that develops doctrine for the new global elec-tronic commerce will have to adapt much more rapidly.

Law as a System of Tags and Flows

Before turning to the novel processes that may develop to create a new law of electronic commerce, it will be useful to review current processes and concepts of law through the lens of complex adaptive systems analysis. This involves a look at the "tags" that differenti-ate one legal artifact from another, the "flows" by means of which tagged elements interact, the internal models available to and cre-ated by legally significant agents, and the building blocks that cre-ate aggregations of legal meaning (Holland, 1995). Such a review makes clear that the current legal institutions have emerged in rel-atively unpredictable ways from complex interaction among basic legal ideas. It suggests that it is possible to influence the flexibility of future doctrine by operating on the types of legal tags available to a diverse set of private and public actors whose interactions cre-ate legal doctrine, contractual relationships, and institutions.

The participants in a modern legal system start with certain tags—citizen or alien, adult or child, lawyer or client, sheriff or suspect—that differentiate their relationships to the state and their abilities to assume various roles or take various actions. The objects they deal with may be labeled "private property" or "public domain." Their businesses may be in specially designated regulated industries, such as "common carriers" or "public utilities." Their actions may then be labeled "torts" or "crimes" or "breaches of contract." Their collaborations—their actions in groups—may be labeled "conspiracies" or "cults" or "corporations." All these tags divert the flow of disputes and claims and related counseling through various alternative procedures and substantive pathways. These tags also determine what roles individuals can play and what kinds of composite legal sentences may meaningfully be composed in the articulation and development of legal doctrine. If we are approached by an "employee" of a "licensed company," offering to enter into a "contract," we instantly know (and incorporate into our decisions) a vast amount of information about the likely authority of this person to make promises that will have a particular degree of reliability over time. If we are deciding whether to impose liability on one party for having caused a harm to others, we sort the world out into "rights" and "duties" and "roles" that imply various types of "breaches" and "powers" and "justifications" and "remedies" and "immunities." You can bring a court case in your capacity as a "consumer," but not in your role as a lover of poetry (Vining, 1978). A public official has immunity for actions taken "in his official capacity," yet a company has no liability for actions of employees on a "frolic and detour." Every person, action, and thing, and all their roles, relations, and interactions, can be evaluated by the legal system only by means of attaching or recognizing labels that, implicitly, invoke large bodies of social grammar and legal doctrine. The lawyer's and regulator's trade involves manipulation of these labels and their relationships at the margin or in the context of surprising new collisions. But the overall progress of the legal system toward a more complex and sophisticated order is based on the gradual growth of the vast territory of coevolving meanings and interconnections that can be taken for granted. This is the mostly orderly "autocatalytic" base (see Kauffman, 1993) on which new doctrine may grow: a substructure of mostly well-accepted ideas about "intent" and "cause" and "value" and "property" and "citizen" and countless other legally significant concepts that, like a coral reef, become useful substructure long after the day when they presented vital new social, political, and philosophical challenges.

In general outline, it is easy to see that the legal system has achieved increasing complexity over time, not just in the sense of becoming difficult for laypeople to understand but also in the special, valuable sense of allowing more sophisticated differentiation of legal relationships. Simple ownership of land by one family became transformed into the widespread distribution of partial and contingent interests (such as real estate investment trust shares) held by numerous unrelated parties, all subject to various regulatory claims that might be made by the state on behalf of a still larger group, such as environmental cleanup duties designed to benefit the public at large. The simple contract for joint investment in a ship has evolved into a flexible corporate charter allocating rights and duties to numerous classes of shareholders, managers, employees, and other stakeholders (Fuller, 1967). The simple concept of a ruler's duty to subjects drifts toward more subtle and complex notions whereby treaties among sovereigns can delegate roles to transnational nongovernmental organizations, such as the International Environmental Standard Setting Organization or the Internet Corporation for Assigned Names and Numbers, that aspire to represent particular interests in negotiating the terms of codes for self-regulation by global corporate bodies. In all of these processes, simple doctrines that once governed the relationships among individuals, families, or small groups have mutated into a rich conceptual tapestry, the ever more complex legal scaffolding with which we build the internal models that constitute our social, economic, and civic selves.

Global Networking and Law

The impact of the new global electronic network on this process is to increase the pace of change and reduce the costs of communication and transactions. The resulting speedup in evolution makes the contingent character of legal institutions and doctrines more visible and deflates any pretentious claim by legal "authorities" to be propounding timeless truths. The global character of the new electronic commerce makes clear that certain parts of our previous scaffolding—especially the tendency to tie the source of authoritative texts to geographically defined sovereigns—will have to change. And the new speed and flexibility of information and money flows suggest that the Internet will produce new kinds of aggregations and many surprising, emergent legal phenomena. We will see an increase in specialized legal doctrines that apply to particular types of global electronic commerce rather than to particular geographical areas. We may see the creation of new corporate forms, facilitated by the ability to create and interweave new workplace roles via Web sites that support collaboration. We will very likely see the growth of new kinds of tags attached to particular messages or online spaces, the flow and interaction of which will create still more complex sets of legal relationships. None of this can be predicted with specificity, but we can explore some concrete possibilities and then assess the significance of all this new, growing complexity for decisions by real-world lawyers, legal administrators, and private parties seeking legal advantage or the resolution of their disputes.

By creating a new forum for trade and by disregarding the geographical boundaries that limit the jurisdiction of existing sovereigns, the Internet has created a need for new doctrines that apply to on-line interactions and that can be enforced on a global basis (Johnson and Post, 1996). This new legal niche is already being filled by private contracts that specify international arbitration as the required means for resolving disputes. Indeed, there are already calls for the development of on-line alternative dispute resolution systems, such as a proposed World Intellectual Property Organization system for on-line arbitration of domain name disputes, to provide a suitably speedy and geographically unconstrained mechanism for bringing order to Internet commerce. Private actions, by means of "choice of law" clauses in contracts, have eliminated a prior rigidity that stemmed from local citizenship and geographically limited jurisdiction of particular judges and courts. These actions have also created optional status for signatories to an agreement that provides for resolution of disputes with reference to laws, and at the hands of arbitrators, of the parties' own choosing.

Another important new "legal" mechanism emerging in the context of the Internet is the provision by the owner of any given on-line space of a set of "terms and conditions" under which these services will be offered. Because the system operator ("sysop"), who controls the server that distributes Web pages or issues on-line identities for those engaged in electronic conferencing, enjoys a legitimate monopoly on what amounts to force on the Internet—the power of exclusion or banishment—it is up to this local authority (whether it is AOL, the local Internet service provider that issues your e-mail account, or the moderator of a closed listserv) to set the rules in the first instance. If you do not agree with the rules, you can decline to visit the on-line space in question or get your Internet identity from someone else who offers what you consider to be better terms and conditions. This new form of lawmaking, which has elements of both contract and real estate law, and which implicates both commerce and personal identity, relies on and creates tags (identifiers) that flow through the Internet to create newly and privately demarcated, but legally significant, territories. All electrons flowing through the Internet behave the same way at the physical level. But meaningful messages go only to those participants who have agreed to be bound by (or are forced to comply with) codes of conduct associated with such tags. As a result, particular messages or users are filtered out of, or welcomed into, particular on-line locations. Out of the complex interaction of diverse private parties—not the top-down decrees of a sovereign—will emerge, somewhat unpredictably, a new on-line legal order (Lessig, 1997).

A Concrete Example

One striking example of the new tagging mechanisms at work is the P3P protocol, developed to facilitate exchanges of personal information and the protection of privacy. The protocol establishes, in effect, a language used by a Web browser and a Web server to negotiate an "agreement" regarding what types of personal information will be submitted to facilitate a transaction and what policies will thereafter be applied to protect the user's interests in privacy. The user first sets some preferences, using this privately developed but legally significant vocabulary. Each Web site also selects the privacy policies it will undertake to respect. If there is a mismatch, the parties are remitted to normal discussions, but in other cases something very much like a binding contract will have been entered into by semiautonomous software code. Obviously, the choice of nouns for this new language (that is, the different types of data that might be treated differently) and the choice of verbs (the different types of uses of the data that the Web site may or may not promise to avoid) will determine what kinds of deals are entered into. This new legal language will evolve over time in response to the demands of users to be spared the painful and time-consuming task of full-blown negotiations. Many users may never bother to read the underlying categories, but they will be able to follow the practices of trusted others, setting their Web browsers to a popular default. In consequence, replication of default settings, based on the reputations of opinion leaders (another tag), will over time allow increasingly complex and nuanced relationships to evolve, on a stable base, at low cost.

The New Law of the Internet

The law of the Internet, considered as the aggregate effect of the rules applicable to particular on-line spaces, is not likely to be simple or homogeneous. Everyone who can establish a Web page or issue e-mail addresses can establish distinct and conflicting rules. Yet a new form of order is already emerging from this on-line chaos. Purely arbitrary (random) rules are avoided because there are ample incentives for sysops to attract and retain users who prefer on-line spaces with stable characteristics. The possibility of rigid, tyrannical order is also kept at bay because sysop power is constrained by user mobility. Unlike sovereign power over territory, which must be constrained by legal rights and duties because it is so difficult for citizens to leave their physical locations, this new kind of sysop "sovereignty" can lose citizens readily if the "local law" becomes oppressive (Froomkin, 1997). Some sysops are expressly delegating their authority to users, as AOL does when it establishes an "e-rule" system enabling users to file complaints that can, if a certain number accumulate, lead to banishment of a bad actor. Others, like GeoCities and certain multi-user domains, establish procedures for civic order through which participants can enact new rules and, in effect, sit as on-line juries. The new on-line form of order is thus likely to evolve toward those sets of rules that "netizens" find most empowering (Post, 1996).

The science of complex adaptive systems gives us reason to hope that, insofar as the Internet develops as a patchwork of interacting on-line areas with diverse rules, the result will not be chaos but a better kind of order that emerges from multiple interdependent, decentralized decisions. Each user will be free to invest various amounts of time and energy in on-line spaces that have the mix of rules and dispute resolution mechanisms that seem most appealing. Sysops will establish filters and connections that make their areas more desirable to local users. The pull and tug among contending rule sets will, over time, create a better overall solution to the problem of collective action—the search for the greater good in a context of conflicting goals—than could otherwise have been achieved by any centralized regulatory state, even a democratic one. (See Johnson and Post, 1998.)

There will be no way to argue that the results of this new legal order arise from theological command or even pure reason. The very notion of sovereignty may become incoherent—insofar as order does not come from above (from a legitimated king or president) or even from below (from a sovereign people choosing elected officials as their representatives) but from the continuous evolution fueled by decentralized interactions that cycle around the Möbius strip of self-referential social discourse. There will be no guaranteed "equality" of the "rights" of netizens subject to this new form of law. But there will be an orderly set of rules pursuant to which netizens can plan and organize their own affairs. And there will be previously unknown degrees of freedom to choose which laws should apply to which aspects of your individual (or your collective or corporate) activities. The continuous discussion and migration between diverse on-line spaces with differing local laws will produce an upward spiral, generally moving toward better and better means of reconciling the conflicting goals of individuals and groups (Johnson and Post, 1996; Perritt, 1995).

New Forms of Legal Personhood

Perhaps the single most important phenomenon of self-organizing law in the context of the Internet may be the rise of a new form of "corporate" organization. Corporations and other forms of social organization (churches, clubs, and so on) are themselves examples of self-organizing systems. These systems result from the decisions of individuals who act as founders, employees, investors, or agents. The organizations take on a life of their own because the parties that deal with them, including the law-making and dispute-resolving institutions of the state, treat them as legal persons with rights and duties of their own (Fuller, 1967). This kind of shared internal model is

more than a mere legal fiction because an organization that can possess a bank account or hire and fire a lawyer of its own really does
have power. Consider, then, the implications of the ability of any
arbitrarily located group of individuals, communicating through the
Internet, to form a new "corporate" entity. They decide to pool their
work or their intellectual capital and insist that third parties with
whom they deal respect the resulting tags that identify the roles
played by collaborators, the terms and conditions governing use or
access to their materials or services, and the personhood of this new
virtual entity.

Some traditional authorities may view some Internet-based col-
lectives as conspiracies and treat them as threats rather than as
engines of financial and social productivity. But the geographical
state's instinctive fear of organizations that it has not chartered or
registered is merely an indirect confirmation that collectively imagined institutions have real power. These self-organizing systems now
have a new medium in which to form, and they can operate on-line
independently of any piece of paper filed, for instance, in Delaware.
They might instead choose a new "Delaware" of the Internet, say
Ireland (now a transfer pricing tax haven and encryption-friendly
zone) or a Caribbean island whose laws and courts are friendly to the
kind of electronic commerce in question (Romano, 1993). Those
virtual organizations that make their peace with local sovereigns
whose citizens they affect, by acting responsibly and paying taxes,
will in all likelihood get the respect they deserve. The doctrine of
comity and established doctrines of choice of law in international
settings will suggest that they be allowed to govern their own affairs,
at least with respect to matters that more significantly affect the
interests of their members than those of outsiders (Wriston, 1997).

Migration Toward the Sweet Spot

The science of complex adaptive systems suggests that, if unim-
peded, an interconnected system that is sufficiently complex tends
to move toward and maintain an optimal type of order. This place

of optimal order—the "sweet spot"—is a mixture of stability and chaos that provides both consistent form on the basis of which new order can evolve and sufficient flexibility to adapt to changes in the surrounding environment (see Chapter One; and Kelly, 1995). There is reason to expect that this natural tendency toward a sweet spot will govern the evolution of new types of aggregations in the social and commercial spheres (Kauffman, 1995). Activities that live comfortably together or that reinforce one another will cluster into on-line spaces that allow stable relationships to form. The healthiest on-line spaces and virtual organizations will be those that admit occasional disruptive and diverse messages so as to promote adaptation to changing external circumstances. We may say that the company or the marketplace is becoming "virtual," but what we are describing is the growth of a new level of stable, collective identities. We may see the evolution of intermediate levels of social and commercial organization—a structure like that of medieval guilds—that allows individuals to create their identities in collaboration with others along both economic and social lines. Whatever new social structures evolve, it is a good bet that those that prosper will be the ones that adjust their information flows and tags so as to preserve an intermediate mix of stable self-conscious identity and unpredictable interaction with the outside (Ford, 1996).

The desirable nature of this new emergent form of legal ordering has implications for all types of social engineers. It creates, in effect, a new agenda for local and national policymakers. The optimal self-organizing qualities of lawmaking on the Internet, and the benefits to participants in such private lawmaking, can only be achieved if each netizen is as free as possible to exit (or decline to enter) any on-line space that develops rules that the individual deems suboptimal. Real choice regarding which on-line spaces to use requires education and low-cost access. The best public policy will be made by the decentralized choices of individuals with conflicting goals who can and do migrate to on-line areas that best serve their own aspirations. This suggests that the highest priority of any local government that wants to enhance the well-being of its territorial subjects, with reference to the on-line world, should be the provision of education, access, and the other social goods that allow everyone to exercise maximum freedom in choosing for themselves when to join, leave, and migrate among on-line spaces.

The Need for Congruence

Participants in electronic commerce will need to bring the external impact of their activities into balance with the opportunities for those thus affected to have a say in making applicable rules. It is possible to foist costs—and fraud—on defenseless victims in cyberspace, and local governments are right to attack such activities. The best (intermediate) level of interconnection is found in systems that only impose minor costs on outsiders and that give most of the people significantly affected by on-line activities a say in setting policy. In other words, the highest hills in the public policy fitness landscapes are occupied by systems that divide rule making into subsidiary "patches." These "federal" systems do best if they interconnect spillover effects and "voting" in such a way that most, but not all, of the impact of any local constituency's decisions is felt by the same group whose welfare is considered when the rules are made (Post and Johnson, 1997). It is unlikely that we can achieve this healthy congruence between affected parties and rule-making parties (the governed and the governors) if we tie the governance of the Internet to rules made by geographically local sovereignties (Johnson and Post, 1998). So it appears likely that we will need to develop new institutions for involving netizens in rule making that are more closely fitted to the practically significant, but physically intangible, boundaries separating one on-line space from another.

Law as an Emergent Protocol Stack

The regulators who would normally expect to make laws governing electronic commerce would do well to study the behavior of complex adaptive systems for still another reason: such study would demonstrate the futility of attempting to impose a single set of rules from the top down. Any regulation of electronic commerce that bans, for instance, gambling or sex will not eliminate the behavior but only drive most of it "offshore," to the territory of a sovereign that will harbor it. By contrast, a bottom-up solution, such as a software system that lets Internet users rely on third-party ratings to filter out unwanted, distrusted, or obnoxious sources, will do much more to build an area of the Internet where good order (by any given user's definition) prevails.

The order that emerges from complex adaptive systems is built in many layers. Languages give rise to currencies (at first as marks on a clay tablet signifying grain held in reserve), which facilitate trade, which in turn supports companies. Operating systems support protocols, which allow software applications, which in turn permit formation of new social groups. To maximize the potential adaptive quality of any particular layer, we need to maximize freedom of choice based on the established characteristics of the layer just below. But if the order established at a lower layer is allowed to constrain choices at a higher layer, the benefits of emergent aggregation are lost. The implications for antitrust theory are obvious: we should prohibit the use of market power or intellectual property claims to reduce the competitive or adaptive potential of any given layer or marketplace by means of conditions that cross layers in the protocol stack. In other words, we should not allow the winner of the evolutionary competition at any one level (say, that of the operating system), no matter how virtuous or deserving of its victory, to use that power to prevent or stifle a competitive struggle at the level of the new layers that are supported by the underlying order its victory has created.

Finding the Sweet Spot

A final and perhaps most significant lesson for regulators may be that they should keep their eye on the degree to which the overall system of laws and dispute resolution mechanisms is drifting too far in the direction of either chaos or order. Does litigation threaten to become a lottery, with random results that prohibit planning and demoralize all but the lucky winner? If so, the appropriate response may be to constrain that diversity, either by reducing available types of claims (thereby limiting awards) or by allowing the self-organizing process of mediation and contract-based arbitration to draw disputes back into a more orderly realm. Do outmoded statutory and regulatory commands (for example, FCC regulations based on out-of-date categories) prevent needed change and flexibility, stifling the lively growth of new business entities? If so, look for ways to push the overall system back toward more disorder by placing more decisions into diverse private hands. In either case, the appropriate response is to look for ways to allow appropriate amounts of order and chaos to develop, rather than simply imposing new rules from above.

The best methods available to a regulator or judge seeking to foster the growth of commerce, on-line or off, become more obvious when attention is paid to the key characteristics of complex adaptive systems. If aggregation into large firms threatens to stultify flexibility and creativity in a particular line of business, breaking up the aggregations may be the answer. If existing tags, such as legal labels we attach to organizations and people, get in the way of change, then do some untagging—if only by allowing interactions in which full identifiers need not be used. If insufficient tagging makes it difficult to distinguish an honorable merchant from an on-line fraud, facilitate the creation of new labeling that allows orderly reputation building. If increasing the flows across previously meaningful boundaries causes unwelcome randomness, keep the flows going but allow good tagging to help users avoid unwanted content. Think filters, not "rights." Learn to expect that order created by private initiatives will accumulate into building blocks (as transactions create firms and firms create markets) so that commerce will get steadily more intertwined as it goes "out of control" (Kelly, 1995).

Private actors seeking personal advantage in this complex new electronic world must also pay attention to the same CAS phenomena. Their primary levers will be decisions to enter or exit particular information flows and their ability to read, create, and disperse new tags. For example, if established employment law is too constraining and costly, firms will contract with independent consultants or outsource various functions, choosing among the tags that label particular functions as inside or outside their enterprise and achieving a level of flexibility appropriate for their economic environment. If intellectual property law is too rigid to allow (or prevent) newly desired (or feared) flows of copies, then new types of electronic tags (encrypted "watermarks" or access controls) and licenses (electronically self-destructing copies of movies) will be invented to permit those flows. If the very newness of the Internet creates an unacceptable level of randomness, chaos, or uncertainty (such as unacceptably low assurance regarding the rights to exclusive use of a company trademark as a domain name), then private initiatives will likely create new forms of order (such as new domain name registration systems and associated contracts and enforcement mechanisms). If new practices, like hypertext linking, create new questions about risks and liability, then private conversations will create new terms, like "framing" (compilation of others' on-line works into a single Web page) and "caching" (storing downloaded Web pages locally for use by other customers), around which new "trade practices" and general community standards (codes of conduct and operating norms, software protocols, and form contracts) can evolve.

The key lesson for both the participants in electronic commerce and their would-be regulators is to focus continuously on one all-important variable: the degree to which the systems they are concerned with have drifted too far toward either randomness or order. Good things—self-organizing processes that lead to adaptive and productive structures—happen automatically in any part of the system that is poised at a midway point, on the "edge of chaos" as described by Clippinger (Chapter One). The means by which order arises in economic institutions—the tags that classify people and products, and the flows that allow such tags to interact to create new aggregated units—provide both the key indicators of system "health" and the levers that can be used by social engineers to achieve an optimal degree of order and disorder. If chaos is winning, add more reliable, honest tags and encourage their use to develop new internal models and building blocks, perhaps by encouraging standards bodies or creating common baseline expectations regarding terms of trade. If an excessively rigid legal order has a choke hold, then do the opposite: use newly created tags to promote diversity and flexibility, new relationships and new roles.

Civic Virtue and Netizenship

As we reconceive the legal world in terms of tags and flows that produce emergent aggregates composed of diverse building blocks (as opposed to rules imposed from above by some authority), we necessarily rethink the state's relationship to individuals, organizations, and markets. Insofar as the laws for on-line commerce will arise from complex interactions among private contracting parties who select applicable rules by entering on-line spaces or attaching commonly recognized labels to their messages, we will begin to see law as a constantly adapting language of social discourse rather than as a repository of authoritative, top-down, timeless truths. Yet this temporal and social contingency does not necessarily degenerate into chaos or mere contention among selfish interests. The widely accepted norms of electronic trade tend to serve the needs of participating communities, and the core values of such communities generally change only as fast as the underlying economic and social ecologies in which those communities operate. This kind of complex, bottom-up system self-adjusts to its external environment, answering complexity with complexity, change with change.

What does it mean to be a "good citizen"—or a responsible lawyer or a creative government official—in the context of this new private-sector-driven, rule-making, dispute-resolving system? First, it means exercising self-restraint with respect to those older forms of legal order: rules imposed from the top down, on the assumption that applicable categories and flows of information and goods would not change. We must accept that we cannot constrain the development of complex adaptive systems. So we must recognize that we should not, in this new realm, claim or attempt to create new "inalienable rights" or "entitlements," which tend only to rigidify relationships between citizens and particular states rather than freeing up and empowering a new complex set of interactions. We should not pass new laws that can only be changed by means of slow and expensive litigation or amendment. We should not try too hard to "harmonize" global legal doctrine but should instead learn to live with and welcome diversity, as long as it is coupled with voluntary choice.

More positively, this new view of the law as a living, complex adaptive system allows any individual or organization to reconceive its aspirations in terms of contributing to the enrichment of the legal terrain, for the benefit of the new structures that will certainly arise on the scaffolding created by prior generations. Do create a new, short model contract or set of terms and conditions for an empowering on-line space because you can expect those who come after you to make some surprising and valuable use of it. Do coin a new term for a productive social or economic relationship that does not seem to be fully captured by "employee" or "owner." Do imagine new forms of on-line cooperation with goals more subtle than maximizing economic return and figure out how to allow such organizations to grow and prosper in the richest sense. Do invent a new marketplace, not just a new product, so that many different parties besides you can enter into new types of value-creating transactions. Do remain on the lookout for those sources of once useful social order that have become stultified "roles" or "rights" or "property" and that now need to be reenlivened by the introduction of new flows of ideas and new roles. Such a result can often be accomplished simply through calling these phenomena by a different name—through attaching a different tag. We have opened up previously rigid control structures for corporations by calling for "corporate responsibility." We have avoided the constraints of overly rigid regulatory or bureaucratic structures by calling for "self-regulation" and "privatization." We have avoided the costs and delays of litigation by inventing "alternative dispute resolution." And we can create new life for markets by tagging ownership and employment roles, and customers and services, in new ways.

Tagging, Again

Markets, organizations, and individuals all operate as both tag readers and tag originators. All three enter or exit various flows—areas or types of communication that expose them to particular sets of other tags and that give their own tags differing types of circulation or context. If an organization cannot recognize certain individuals as potential customers, then its tag recognition system has made it blind to some opportunities. By contrast, if it reads every interested approach as a potential opportunity, it will lose focus and disperse its resources unduly. Analogous states of blindness or indiscriminate receptivity can cripple individuals (withdrawal or information overload) and markets (monopoly or excessive and socially costly product proliferation). Even states have serious problems if they recognize too few tags (ignoring significant constituencies and interests) or undertag (for example, by failing to create a shared sense of citizenship and community), or if they recognize too many tags (becoming surveillance states) or overtag (for example, by labeling too many types of socially tolerated behavior as criminal).

Thus, every system must strive for an appropriate balance between input and output and an appropriately moderate level of tag literacy and tag origination. But how can any system monitor its own blind spots or excesses? How can you know what you do not know, or recognize your own lack of judgment? This has been a central problem for management consulting (and education of all types) for many years. The science of complex adaptive systems may suggest an answer, in the form of a second-order effect corresponding to the amount of order or chaos in the system in question. If a system has not changed at the pace required to remain "fit" in the context of its evolving ecosystem, then it will have become recognizably "too orderly" and will need an infusion of new flows or tags or the elimination of some previously stabilizing flows or tags. Correspondingly, if its behavior is too disorderly or random, relative to the degree of stability in a surrounding system, then it may have too many incoming signals or a tendency to recognize and attempt to act on too many incoming tags for its own processing capability. In this case it needs instead to narrow its focus. Anyone concerned with the health of a particular system (at any level, whether individual or group) can watch the degree of order and chaos evidenced by the system and seek to nudge the system slightly toward either chaos or order, as appropriate, so as to keep it in the sweet spot. We cannot see the whole economic and social ecosystem in which we are embedded, but we can see indicia of our relationship to it—and use those as indicators for navigation.

To make this prescription concrete, consider in more detail the problems and opportunities of company and product identity. Brands are a kind of tag that, when attached to products and services flowing into commerce, creates a valuable and useful order. Customers looking for assurances of quality can pick out products that have recognizable brands. Companies that want predictable characteristics in contractual counterparts can act on the basis of reputations associated with particular company names. No one legislates or allocates such reputations. The values created by brands and company names emerge from diverse interactions and from unpredictable flows of information regarding past transactions, helping market participants build a mental model of the likely behavior of third parties and their wares.

Now consider how the law deals with conflicts regarding the property rights associated with such names. Traditionally, local, territorially based sovereigns have passed trademark and trade name statutes that allow registration of names, provide exclusive use rights to registrants, and prohibit the fraudulent or conflicting and confusing use of such names by third parties. That system worked reasonably well until the global Internet presented a new environment in which the use of certain kinds of identifiers (domain names) could not be constrained to particular local jurisdictions. In this new context, categories of products and services change rapidly: Is the Web page for Kraft food to be classified as a food product or an information service? Moreover, Internet identifiers, like domain names, can be "registered" by anyone who sets himself up as a "registry" and can be created and used by a much larger, more diverse group of actors than can actually produce jars of mayonnaise. The impact of any name or symbol uploaded to the Internet can be felt instantly, anywhere. And no single established sovereign has the ability or authority to define and constrain all confusing or wrongful uses.

Thus in one sense, the increased speed and global reach of electronic markets have created a condition of disorder with respect to the law of company, product, and service names. No one knows what the rules are. The likely outcome of litigation between an early registrant and a late-coming claimant is, unfortunately, too random. In another sense, the old law of trademarks has been shown to be too rigid to adapt to this new environment. It does not readily adapt to uses of marks that are physically based in one country but have an impact (at least on those who use the Internet) in many other countries. It does not readily take into account the many noncommercial uses of these new domain name identifiers. "Fair use" under trademark law allows noncommercial, nonconfusing uses of marks, but because domain names can only be registered to one party, trademark law has been forced into a binary approach, often ousting a noninfringing user of a domain name on the antiquated ground that such use "dilutes" the commercial use of the mark.

There are two ways in which the legal system might adjust to this suboptimally disorderly situation. The first would be to try to create a new, globally harmonized, international law of domain name registration and trademark and trade name use, imposed from the top down. This would require a treaty, however, which could well take a very long time to achieve. Worse, such a top-down approach would likely impose one rule on all on-line spaces rather than allow differing rules to emerge in differing on-line venues so as best to fit a new trade practice to the needs and preferences of participants.

The alternative is to allow diverse independent registries to compete to provide registration and labeling schemes that the market will find acceptable. This might take the form of directories, as is already happening with the Internet search engine sites. It might take the form of alternative domain name regimes that offer differing degrees of assurance with regard to the stability and meaningfulness of their registrations. For example, some registrars rigorously enforce rules regarding the qualifications of registrants, allowing, say, only four-year higher education institutions to register with .edu or only companies agreeing to submit to the jurisdiction of a given country to register in that country code domain. Some registrars may promise to renew registration of a domain name to the same owner indefinitely; others may reserve the right to cancel a registration without cause. There is already significant diversity in the registration policies followed by the over two hundred top-level domains of the net (such as .com, .edu, .uk, .ru, and .md).

The science of complex adaptive systems gives us reason to hope that, if we allow this decentralized and emergent process to work, it will yield sets of rules for the registration and use of company, product, and personal names that provide a better overall balance among conflicting interests and more flexibility to deal with changing circumstances than could any centralized, harmonized, top-down decree. We will see a proliferation of different types of identifiers: not just domain names but meaningful tags on e-mail addresses, identification codes used to control access to particular on-line spaces, and differing identifiers associated with differing levels of implicit or explicit promises regarding the identity or reputation of the identification holder. No treaty or statute could possibly match the richness, diversity, and sheer complexity likely to evolve if we allow decentralized action by diverse parties to create a "marketplace" in Internet identifiers and in the accompanying rules that may apply to various participants in the various roles they may choose to adopt. The first reaction of policymakers, in light of our new understanding of complex adaptive systems, should be to allow this new form of order to emerge and flourish, not to seek to anticipate all possible legal and policy issues and then attempt to impose some set of rules by legislation.

A New Form of Dispute Resolution

Consider a different example as a means of assessing a new form of dispute resolution made possible in the context of an emergent law of electronic commerce. One party may want to send bulk unsolicited commercial e-mail ("spam") to the customers of another party, an Internet service provider. They have a dispute about whether this conduct ought to be permitted. Under a traditional, top-down, geographically based sovereign legal system, they would take this dispute to a court or a legislature, either of which would purport to act on behalf of the entire polity and would establish a rule that then applies to all similarly situated parties within the jurisdiction. But insofar as this dispute arises on the Internet, it may well involve parties that are not within or subject to the physical control of any one jurisdiction or even two jurisdictions that cooperate by treaty (Perritt, 1996). Moreover, the basic circumstances surrounding the dispute will change rapidly as the technology evolves, changing such key issues as what kinds of messages (text, pictures, sound, video) are feasible and what kinds of technical defenses (filters) can be deployed. In this new, complex context, the best way to "resolve" the dispute may well be to allow both parties to make unilateral decisions regarding what tags to dispense or recognize and what flows of information to enter or leave. The spammer will try to get lists of addresses, and the antispamming party will create filters that recognize and delete messages coming from the spamming source. There will be a technical "arms race" as individual users and the system operators they choose to act on their behalf adopt defenses that coevolve with the offensive weapons of those who seek to send unsolicited messages. It is most likely that a middle ground will evolve, creating an adequate degree of "order" in the sense that the most egregious practices will be identified and stopped (if only by means of banishing those who tolerate such activities from the core facilities of the Internet) and in the sense that some unsolicited messages will get through, preventing excessively rigid filters from perfect operation. Some on-line spaces will be relatively spam free, and other spaces will tolerate unsolicited marketing messages but offer countervailing advantages. The dispute between the parties will have been resolved by a complex interplay of decentralized selections among rule sets in the marketplace—probably in a manner that better serves the overall good of a public with conflicting goals than would any decision by an authoritative judge, statute, or treaty (Johnson and Post, 1998). If traditional states did anything, perhaps they could best act to prohibit fraudulent tags rather than attempting to define and ban spam.

Bottom-Up Law and Order

Whether in your role as citizen, business manager, or individual seeking empowering roles in the evolving social order, this new view of law should, on reflection, seem both natural and easy to apply. You already know when the activities of the organizations you seek to mold have become too random, but now you have scientific support to reinforce the sense that you should use this as a key indicator of the need to seek more orderly behavior. You already know when excessively rigid structures impede organizational adaptation, and you already know you cannot change the world, your company, or even yourself by fiat. You already know that your potential for orderly, valuable growth—or that of your company—is fundamentally determined by what you pay attention to and how you identify yourself to others. What the science of complex adaptive systems does is provide a new context in which to heed these intuitively obvious truths, along with hints about what to do when the leading indicators of excessive order or chaos call for a move back toward the sweet spot. There is no reason to doubt that value will be increased by introducing diversity to the stultified or by providing order-supplying tags to reduce chaos. We can't predict precise outcomes; the new science shows us this is theoretically impossible. But we can get reaffirmation of our instinct that what we do matters and illumination of the mechanisms by which we are most likely to make a difference for the better.

Some areas of the law and trade practice of on-line communications have already begun, intuitively, to adopt this new model. The Electronic Communications Privacy Act of 1986 protects private communications but deliberately and expressly allows every system operator to define what types of posting will be "private" and what will be made "readily accessible to the public," allowing users to control their actions and expectations accordingly. The U.S. government encourages Web sites to post "privacy policies" but has not said what these must provide. Regulations of the Securities and Exchange Commission have begun to allow on-line securities businesses to decide whether to classify themselves under one category ("exchanges") or another ("broker-dealers"). Insurance companies will charge differing rates to cover the risks of on-line businesses, depending on what trade practices are followed and verified, but leave it up to the insured to pick its own practices and resulting rates. Users are beginning to use different accounts or identifiers to signify the differing roles they play when they go on-line. There is no one right answer to questions about roles and relationships, based in legal authority. Rather, there is a continuous pull and tug among contending choices made by parties with differing goals, who use their ability to send and receive increasingly compact and meaningful tags to negotiate ever better compromises.

The history of the law is one of continuous attempts to replace the use of force with some form of civil discussion, thereby diminishing the arbitrary domination of one person over another. Early forms of "reasoned discussion" cited various apparent sources of authority, such as tradition, religion, charisma, or reason itself, for the proposition that mere force should not win the day. But it has been very difficult, until now, to argue for a form of law that does not, at least ultimately, reintroduce force into the equation, albeit in a more "legitimate" way. Hobbes is explicit and pessimistic about the need for this trade-off. Even the more optimistic social contract theories of Locke, Mill, Rousseau, and Jefferson serve to justify a democratic system for selecting officeholders who control force on behalf of the state as the basic means of creating socially valuable order.

What the science of complex adaptive systems tells us is that much of the current order in the world has emerged from complex interactions among the tags that define social roles, property rights, and legal concepts. It also tells us that, at least with respect to the new intangible area of on-line commerce—where "force" can take the form of decentralized decisions to grant or deny access to, or to use or discard, the tags that select among various information flows—a socially valuable order can arise without our granting a monopoly on the use of "force" (no matter how rationalized or legitimated) to any person or group. Political and legal theorists have been asking for centuries how we can achieve a just social order and what sort of collective action will produce legitimate, efficient, and optimal governance. We can now begin to see a new answer to these questions: such an order can arise naturally from the sustained interaction among diverse netizens, whose decentralized decisions create an evolving, complex, and emergent form of "law" that both empowers individual choice and best serves the overall public interest in this new global, intangible sphere. (See articles produced by the Cyberspace Law Institute at http://www.cli.org.)

One who looks to law for certainty—for stable rules that define the place of an individual or a company in the social order—will be disappointed, if not dismayed, by this vision. But one who thinks of law as a continuing group conversation about core values may be inspired by a renewed conviction that everyone can make a contribution to that conversation. Everyone can enrich the legal discourse by creating new words, and indeed whole new sentences, that will thereafter be used and reused by many others to discover and discuss the path toward optimal collective action and the sweet spot between social order and disorder. Worthy is the ancestor who leaves his successors a more complex world with more scaffolding on which to grow a form of order that the ancestor could not have prescribed or even predicted. The lawmaker and dispute resolver of today must be more gardener than sovereign, building a trellis, grafting new plants, fertilizing open ground. The wise ones, who know they can only water and weed, not manufacture or command, will be rewarded with the knowledge that their actions will lead to a richer social and economic harvest.

References

Chapter One

Arthur, W. B., and Arrow, K. *Increasing Returns and Path Dependence in the Economy*. Ann Arbor: University of Michigan Press, 1994.

Arthur, W. B., Derlauf, S. N., and Lane, D. (eds.). *The Economy as an Evolving Complex System*. Santa Fe Institute Studies in the Sciences of Complexity, vol. XXVII. Reading, Mass.: Addison-Wesley, 1997.

Ashby, W. R. *An Introduction to Cybernetics*. New York: Wiley, 1963.

Bateson, G. *Mind and Nature: A Necessary Unity*. New York: Bantam Books, 1979.

Chandler, A. *The Visible Hand: The Managerial Revolution in American Business*. Cambridge, Mass.: Belknap Press, 1977.

Clark, A. *Being There: Putting Brain, Body, and World Together Again*. Cambridge, Mass.: MIT Press, 1997.

Holland, J. H. *Adaptation in Natural and Artificial Systems*. Cambridge, Mass.: MIT Press, 1992.

Holland, J. H. *Hidden Order: How Adaptations Build Complexity*. Reading, Mass.: Addison-Wesley, 1995.

Kafka, F. *The Castle*. New York: Schocken Books, 1995. (Originally published 1922.)

Kauffman, S. A. *The Origin of Order: Self-Organization and Selection in Evolution*. New York: Oxford University Press, 1993.

Langton, C. G., Taylor, C., Farmer, J. D., and Rasmussen, S. (eds.). *Artificial Life II: Proceedings of the Santa Fe Institute Studies in the Sciences of Complexity*. Vol. 10. Reading, Mass.: Addison-Wesley, 1992.

Pustejovsky, J. *The Generative Lexicon*. Cambridge, Mass.: MIT Press, 1995.

Smith, A. *An Inquiry into the Nature and Causes of the Wealth of Nations.* 2 vols. (R. H. Campbell and A. S. Skinner, eds. W. B. Todd, textual ed.). Indianapolis: Liberty Classics, 1981.

Sober, E. *The Nature of Selection: Evolutionary Theory in Philosophical Focus.* Chicago: University of Chicago Press, 1984.

Chapter Three

Ashworth, J., and Dee, J. *The Biology of Slime Molds.* London: Arnold, 1975.

Beach, K. "The Role of External Mnemonic Symbols in Acquiring an Occupation." In M. Gruneberg and R. Sykes (eds.), *Practical Aspects of Memory,* Vol. 1. New York: Wiley, 1988.

Calow, P. *Biological Machines.* London: Arnold, 1976.

Clark, A. "Magic Words: How Language Augments Human Computation." In P. Carruthers and J. Boucher (eds.), *Language and Thought: Interdisciplinary Essays.* Cambridge: Cambridge University Press, 1998a.

Clark, A. "Twisted Tales: Causal Complexity and Cognitive Scientific Explanation." *Minds and Machines,* 1998b, 8, 79–99.

Clark, A., and Thornton, C. "Trading Spaces: Connectionism and the Limits of Learning." *Behavioral and Brain Sciences,* 1997, 20(1), 57–90.

Clark, A., and Wheeler, M. "Genic Representation: Reconciling Content and Causal Complexity." *British Journal for the Philosophy of Science,* forthcoming.

Deacon, T. *The Symbolic Species.* New York: Norton, 1997.

Delisi, C. "The Human Genome Project." *American Scientist,* 1988, 76, 488–493.

Dennett, D. "Learning and Labeling: Commentary on A. Clark and A. Karmiloff-Smith." *Mind and Language,* 1994, 8, 540–548.

Dennett, D. *Darwin's Dangerous Idea.* New York: Simon & Schuster, 1995.

Elman, J., and others. *Re-thinking Innateness.* Cambridge, Mass.: MIT Press, 1996.

Goodwin, B. *How the Leopard Changed Its Spots.* London: Phoenix, 1994.

Johnson, M., and Bolhuis, J. "Imprinting Predispositions and Filial Preference in the Chick." In R. Andrew (ed.), *Neural and Behavioral Plasticity.* Oxford: Oxford University Press, 1991.

Jordan, M., Flash, T., and Arnon, Y. "A Model of the Learning of Arm Trajectories from Spatial Deviations." *Journal of Cognitive Neuroscience,* 1994, 6(4), 359–376.

Keijzer, F. "The Generation of Behavior." Unpublished doctoral dissertation, Leiden University, Netherlands, 1997.

Kelso, S. *Dynamic Patterns*. Cambridge, Mass.: MIT Press, 1995.

Kirlik, A. "Everyday Life Environments." In W. Bechtel and G. Graham (eds.), *A Companion to Cognitive Science*. Oxford: Blackwell, 1998.

Maturana, H., and Varela, F. *The Tree of Knowledge*. Boston: New Science Library, 1987.

Polit, A., and Bizzi, E. "Processes Controlling Arm Movements in Monkeys." *Science*, 1978, *201*, 1235–1237.

Powell, W. "Inter-organizational Collaboration in the Biotechnology Industry." *Journal of Institutional and Theoretical Economics*, 1996, *152*(1), 197–225.

Resnick, M. *Turtles, Termites and Traffic Jams: Explorations in Massively Parallel Microworlds*. Cambridge, Mass.: MIT Press, 1994.

Stark, D. "Heterarchy: Asset Ambiguity, Organizational Innovation and the Postsocialist Firm." [http://www.sociology.columbia.edu/faculty/stark/papers/heterarchy.html]. Paper presented at the annual meeting of the American Sociological Association, New York, 1996.

Thelen, E., and Smith, L. *A Dynamic Systems Approach to the Development of Cognition and Action*. Cambridge, Mass.: MIT Press, 1994.

Thompson, R., Oden, D., and Boysen, S. "Language-Naive Chimpanzees Judge Relations-Between-Relations in an Abstract Matching Task." *Journal of Experimental Psychology: Animal Behavior Processes*, forthcoming.

Vygotsky, L. *Thought and Language*. (A. Kozulin, ed.). Cambridge, Mass.: MIT Press, 1986.

Chapter Four

Beaken, M. *The Making of Language*. Edinburgh: Edinburgh University Press, 1996.

Brown, J. S. *Seeing Differently: Insights on Innovation*. Cambridge, Mass.: Harvard Business Review Press, 1997.

Deacon, T. W. *The Symbolic Species: The Co-evolution of Language and the Brain*. New York: Norton, 1997.

Durham, H. W. *Co-evolution: Genes, Culture and Human Diversity*. Stanford, Calif.: Stanford University Press, 1991.

Holland, J. H. *Hidden Order: How Adaptations Build Complexity*. Reading, Mass.: Addison-Wesley, 1995.

Holland, J. H., and others. *Induction: Processes of Inference, Learning, and Discovery*. Cambridge, Mass.: MIT Press, 1986.

Kauffman, S. A. *The Origin of Order: Self-Organization and Selection in Evolution*. New York: Oxford University Press, 1993.

Kelly, K. *Out of Control*. Reading, Mass.: Addison-Wesley, 1996.

Kelly, K. *New Rules for the New Economy*. New York: Viking, 1998.

Kelly, K., and Wolf, G. "Push." *Wired*, March 1997.

Moravcsik, J.M.E. *Meaning, Creativity, and the Inscrutability of the Human Mind*. Cambridge, Mass.: Cambridge University Press, 1998.

Pustejovsky, J. *The Generative Lexicon*. Cambridge, Mass.: MIT Press, 1995.

Ridley, M. *The Red Queen: Sex and the Evolution of Human Nature*. London: Viking, 1993.

Wilson, E. O. *Consilience: The Unity of Knowledge*. New York: Knopf, 1998.

Chapter Five

Arthur, W. B., and Arrow, K. *Increasing Returns and Path Dependence in the Economy*. Ann Arbor: University of Michigan Press, 1994.

Bartlett, C., and Ghoshal, S. *The Individualized Corporation*. New York: HarperCollins, 1997.

California Management Review. Special issue on knowledge and the firm. 1998, 40(3).

Clark, A. *Being There: Putting Brain, Body, and World Together Again*. Cambridge, Mass.: MIT Press, 1997.

Davenport, T. *Information Ecology: Mastering the Information and Knowledge Environment*. New York: Oxford University Press, 1997.

Davenport, T., and Prusak, L. *Working Knowledge: How Organizations Manage What They Know*. Boston: Harvard Business School Press, 1998.

Drucker, P. *Post-Capitalist Society*. New York: HarperCollins, 1993.

Holland, J. H. *Hidden Order: How Adaptation Builds Complexity*. Reading, Mass.: Addison-Wesley, 1995.

Kauffman, S. A. *The Origin of Order: Self-Organization and Selection in Evolution*. New York: Oxford University Press, 1993.

Kauffman, S. A. *At Home in the Universe: The Search for the Laws of Self-Organization and Complexity*. New York: Oxford University Press, 1995.

Manville, B. "What's the Management in Knowledge Management?" Paper presented at a DCI Conference on Knowledge Management, Boston, June 22, 1998.

Micklethwait, J., and Wooldridge, A. *The Witch Doctors*. New York: Times Books, 1996.

Nonanka, I., and Takeuchi, H. *The Knowledge Creating Company*. New York: Oxford University Press, 1996.

Polanyi, M. *The Tacit Dimension*. New York: Peter Smith Books, 1966.

Wenger, E. *Communities of Practice: Learning, Meaning, and Identity*. New York: Cambridge University Press, 1998.

Chapter Six

Abernathy, W. *The Productivity Dilemma*. Baltimore: Johns Hopkins University Press, 1979.

Bak, P. *How Nature Works: The Science of Self-Organized Criticality*. New York: Springer-Verlag, 1996.

Campbell, D. T. "Variation and Selective Retention in Socio-Cultural Evolution." In H. R. Barringer, G. I. Blanksten, and R. W. Mack (eds.), *Social Change in Developing Areas: A Reinterpretation of Evolutionary Theory*. Cambridge, Mass.: Schenkman, 1965.

Campbell, D. T. " 'Downward Causation' in Hierarchical Systems." In F. J. Ayala and T. Dobzhansky (eds.), *Studies in the Philosophy of Biology*. London: Macmillan, 1974.

Clark, A. *Being There: Putting Brain, Body, and World Together Again*. Cambridge, Mass.: MIT Press, 1997.

Drucker, P. "The Theory of the Business." *Harvard Business Review*, Sept.-Oct. 1994.

Gell-Mann, M. "Complex Adaptive Systems." In G. A. Cowan, D. Pines, and D. Meltzer (eds.), *Complexity: Metaphors, Models and Reality*. Reading, Mass.: Addison-Wesley, 1994.

Halberstam, D. *The Reckoning*. New York: Morrow, 1986.

Hammer, M., and Champy, J. *Re-engineering the Corporation: A Manifesto for Business Revolution*. New York: HarperBusiness, 1993.

Holland, J. H. *Hidden Order: How Adaptation Builds Complexity*. Reading, Mass.: Addison-Wesley, 1995.

Kauffman, S. A. *The Origin of Order: Self-Organization and Selection in Evolution*. New York: Oxford University Press, 1993.

Kim, D.-J., and Kogut, B. "Technological Platforms and Diversification." *Organization Science*, 1996.

May, E. R. *The Lessons of the Past: The Use and Misuse of History in American Foreign Policy*. New York: Oxford University Press, 1973.

Pfeffer, J. "Management as Symbolic Action: The Creation and Maintenance of Organizational Paradigms." In L. L. Cummings and B. Staw (eds.), *Research in Organizational Behavior*. Greenwich, Conn.: JAI Press, 1981.

Popper, K. R. *Of Clouds and Clocks: An Approach to the Problem of Rationality and the Freedom of Man*. St. Louis: Washington University Press, 1966.

Prigogine, I. *From Being to Becoming*. New York: Freeman, 1980.

Simon, H. A. *The Sciences of the Artificial*. (3rd ed.) Cambridge, Mass.: MIT Press, 1996.

Wasserman, S., and Faust, K. *Social Network Analysis: Methods and Applications*. Cambridge: Cambridge University Press, 1994.

Weick, K. E. *The Social Psychology of Organizing*. Reading, Mass.: Addison-Wesley, 1979.

Chapter Seven

Allen, P. M., and McGlade, J. M. "Modeling Complex Human Systems: A Fisheries Example." *European Journal of Operational Research*, 1987, *24*, 147–167.

Arthur, W. B. *Increasing Returns and Path Dependence in the Economy*. Ann Arbor: University of Michigan Press, 1994.

Clark, A. *Being There: Putting Brain, Body, and World Together Again*. Cambridge, Mass.: MIT Press, 1997.

Grabher, G., and Stark, D. "Organizing Diversity: Evolutionary Theory, Network Analysis, and Postsocialist Transformations." In G. Grabher and D. Stark (eds.), *Restructuring Networks: Legacies, Linkages, and Localities in Postsocialism*. London and New York: Oxford University Press, 1997.

Hannan, M. T. "Uncertainty, Diversity, and Organizational Change." In N. J. Smelser and D. R. Gerstein (eds.), *Behavioral and Social Sciences: Fifty Years of Discovery: In Commemoration of the Fiftieth Anniversary of the "Ogburn Report."* Washington, D.C.: National Academy Press, 1986.

Holland, J. H. *Hidden Order: How Adaptation Builds Complexity*. Reading, Mass.: Addison-Wesley, 1995.

Ickes, B. W., Ryterman, R., and Tenev, S. *On Your Marx, Get Set, Go: The Role of Competition in Enterprise Adjustment*. Unpublished manuscript, the World Bank, September 1995.

Lane, D., and Maxfield, R. "Strategy Under Complexity: Fostering Generative Relationships." *Long-Range Planning* 1996, *29*.

March, J. G. "Exploration and Exploitation in Organizational Learning." *Organization Science*, 1991, *2*(1), 71–87.

Miner, A., Amburgey, T. L., and Stearns, T. M. "Interorganizational Linkages and Population Dynamics: Buffering and Transformational Shields." *Administrative Science Quarterly*, 1990, *35*, 689–713.

Sabel, C. F. "Moebius-Strip Organizations and Open Labor Markets: Some Consequences of the Reintegration of Conception and Execution in a Volatile Economy." In P. Bourdieu and J. Coleman (eds.), *Social Theory for a Changing Society*. Boulder, Colo., and New York: Westview Press; Russell Sage Foundation, 1990.

Sabel, C. F., and Dorf, M. C. "A Constitution of Democratic Experimentalism." *Columbia Law Review*, 1998, 98(2), 267–529.

Stark, D. "Recombinant Property in East European Capitalism." *American Journal of Sociology*, 1996, *101*, 993–110.

Stark, D., and Bruszt, L. *Postsocialist Pathways: Transforming Politics and Property in East Central Europe*. New York and London: Cambridge University Press, 1998.

Stark, D., Kemeny, S., and Breiger, R. "Post-Socialist Portfolios: Network Strategies in the Shadow of the State." Paper presented at the annual meeting of the ASA, San Francisco, 1998.

Tamas, P. "Inovacios teljesitmenyek es vallalati strategiak" ["Achievement in Innovation and Company Strategies"]. Unpublished working paper, Institute for the Study of Social Conflicts, Budapest, 1993.

Weick, K. E. "Organization Design: Organizations as Self-Designing Systems." *Organizational Dynamics*, 1977, 6(2), 31–45.

Chapter Eight

Axelrod, R. *The Complexity of Cooperation: Agent-Based Models of Competition and Collaboration*. Princeton, N.J.: Princeton University Press, 1997.

Carey, S. "Airline Searches for Methods to Improve Check-in Gauntlet." *Wall Street Journal*, Jan. 4, 1999.

Dowe, J. Presentation at the 2nd annual Embracing Complexity conference, Boston, 1997.

Eisenstein, D. "Bucket Brigades: Self-Organizing Work." In *Embracing Complexity: A Colloquium on the Application of Complex Adaptive Systems to Business*. Proceedings of the Ernst & Young Center for Business Innovation colloquium on the business application of complexity science, 1997.

Epstein, J. M., and Axtell, R. L. *Growing Artificial Societies: Social Science from the Bottom Up*. Cambridge, Mass.: MIT Press, 1996.

Ernst & Young. *Embracing Complexity: Exploring the Application of Complex Adaptive Systems to Business*. Proceedings of the Ernst & Young Center for Business Innovation colloquium on the business application of complexity science, 1997.

Ernst & Young. "The Connected Manufacturing Enterprise." Research project report from an Ernst & Young study, summer 1998.

Flake, G. W. *The Computational Beauty of Nature: Computer Explorations of Fractals, Chaos, Complex Systems, and Adaptation.* Cambridge, Mass.: MIT Press, 1998.

Fogel, D. B. *Evolutionary Computation: Toward a New Philosophy of Machine Intelligence.* New York: IEEE Press, 1995.

Goldberg, D. E. *Genetic Algorithms in Search, Optimization, and Machine Learning.* Reading, Mass.: Addison-Wesley, 1989.

Holland, J. H. *Hidden Order: How Adaptation Builds Complexity.* Reading, Mass.: Addison-Wesley, 1995.

Kauffman, S. A. *At Home in the Universe: The Search for the Laws of Self-Organization and Complexity.* New York: Oxford University Press, 1995.

Mitchell, M. *An Introduction to Genetic Algorithms.* Cambridge, Mass.: MIT Press, 1996.

Petzinger, T. "In This Carpet Mill, the Best Laid Plans Are Rolled Out Daily." *Wall Street Journal*, Oct. 30, 1998.

Rothschild, M. *Bionomics: Economy as Ecosystem.* New York: Henry Holt, 1990.

Statnikov, R. B., and Matusov, J. B. *Multicriteria Optimization and Engineering.* New York: Chapman & Hall, 1995.

Steuer, R. E. *Multiple Criteria Optimization: Theory, Computation and Application.* New York: Wiley, 1986.

Taylor, F. W. *The Principles of Scientific Management.* London: Routledge/Thoemmes Press, 1993. (Originally published 1947.)

van Laarhoven, P. J. *Simulated Annealing: Theory and Applications.* Boston: Kluwer Academic, 1987.

Vidal, R. *Applied Simulated Annealing.* New York: Springer-Verlag, 1993.

Vose, M. D. *The Simple Genetic Algorithm: Foundations and Theory.* Cambridge, Mass.: MIT Press, 1998.

Wildberger, M. A. "Independent Adaptive Agents for Distributed Control of the Electric Power Grid." Unpublished paper, Electric Power Research Institute, Palo Alto, Calif., January 15, 1997.

Chapter Nine

Clemons, E. K., and Weber, B. W. "Restructuring Institutional Block Trading: An Overview of the OptiMark System." *Proceedings, HICSS-31, Vol. VI: Hawaiian International Conference on Systems Science*, 1998.

Copeland, D. G., and McKenney, J. L. "Airline Reservations Systems: Lessons from History." *Management Information Systems Quarterly*, 1988, *12*(3).

Crane, D. (ed.). *The Global Financial System: A Functional Perspective.* Boston: HBS Press, 1995.

Farrell, G. "Collision Course." *Context*, 1999 [month n/a].

Holland, J. H. *Hidden Order: How Adaptation Builds Complexity.* Reading, Mass.: Addison-Wesley, 1995.

Holland, J. H. *Emergence: From Chaos to Order.* Reading, Mass.: Addison-Wesley, 1998.

Morgan, E. V., and Thomas, W. A. *The London Stock Exchange: Its History and Functions.* New York: St. Martin's Press, 1971.

Mui, C. "It Takes a Village." *Context*, 1999 [month n/a].

Mui, C., and Downes, L. *Unleashing the Killer App: Digital Strategies for Market Dominance.* Boston: HBS Press, 1998.

Narayandas, D., and Rangan, V. K. *Dell Computer Corporation.* Boston: HBS Press, 1996.

Nolan, R. L., and Croson, D. C. *Creative Destruction: A Six-Stage Process for Transforming the Organization.* Boston: HBS Press, 1995.

Petruno, T. "Move Over, NYSE?: OptiMark System Creating a Buzz." *Los Angeles Times*, 1998 [date n/a].

Pine, B. J., II, and Gilmore, J. P. *The Experience Economy.* Boston: HBS Press, 1999.

Porter, M. *Competitive Advantage.* New York: Free Press, 1985.

Quinn, J. B. *Intelligent Enterprise: A Knowledge and Service Based Paradigm for Industry.* New York: Free Press, 1992.

Rayport, J., and Sviokla, J. "Managing in the Marketspace." *Harvard Business Review*, 1994 [month n/a].

Rayport, J., and Sviokla, J. "Exploiting the Virtual Value Chain." *Harvard Business Review*, 1995 [month n/a].

Rickard, J. T., and Lupien, W. "Optimal Market Structures Based upon Mutual Satisfaction." Paper presented at 30th Asilomar Conference on Signals, Systems, and Computers, 1996a.

Rickard, J. T., and Lupien, W. "Optimum Strategies for Opening Trading in Options." Paper presented at 30th Asilomar Conference on Signals, Systems, and Computers, 1996b.

Sviokla, J. "Virtual Markets." In S. Bradley and R. Nolan (eds.), *Sense and Respond.* Boston: HBS Press, 1998.

Sviokla, J., and Dailey, M. "OptiMark: Launching a Virtual Securities Market." In S. Bradley and R. Nolan (eds.). *Sense and Respond.* Boston: HBS Press, 1998.

Chapter Ten

Ford, R. "Beyond Borders: A Partial Response to Richard Briffault." *Stanford Law Review*, 1996, 48, 1113.

Froomkin, M. "The Internet as a Source of Regulatory Arbitrage." In B. Kahin and C. Nesson (eds.), *Borders and Cyberspace: Information Policy and the Global Information Infrastructure.* Cambridge, Mass.: MIT Press, 1997.

Fuller, L. L. *Legal Fictions.* [publisher n/a] 1967.

Holland, J. H. *Hidden Order: How Adaptation Builds Complexity.* Reading, Mass.:Addison-Wesley, 1995.

Johnson, D. R., and Post, D. G. "Law and Borders: The Rise of Law in Cyberspace." *Stanford Law Review*, 1996, 48, 1367.

Johnson, D. R., and Post, D. G. "And How Shall the Net Be Governed?: A Meditation on the Relative Virtues of Decentralized, Emergent Law." In B. Kahin and J. Keller (eds.). *Coordinating the Internet.* Boston: MIT Press, 1997.

Johnson, D. R., and Post, D. G. "The New Civic Virtue of the Internet." *The Emerging Internet.* Institute for Information Studies, 1998 [available at http://www.cli.org].

Katsh, M. E. *The Electronic Media and the Transformation of Law.* New York: Oxford University Press, 1989.

Katsh, M. E. *Law in a Digital World.* New York: Oxford University Press, 1995.

Kauffman, S. A. *The Origin of Order: Self-Organization and Selection in Evolution.* New York: Oxford University Press, 1993.

Kauffman, S. A. *At Home in the Universe: The Search for the Laws of Self-Organization and Complexity.* New York: Oxford University Press, 1995.

Kelly, K. *Out of Control: The New Biology of Machines, Social Systems, and the Economic World.* (Reprint ed.) San Francisco: Perseus Press, 1995.

Lessig, L. "The Zones of Cyberspace." *Stanford Law Review*, 1996, 48, 1403.

Lessig, L. "Constitution and Code." *Cumberland Law Review*, 1997, 27, 1.

Perritt, H. H., Jr. *Self-Governing Electronic Communities.* Unpublished manuscript, Stanford Law Review, 1995.

Perritt, H. H., Jr. "Jurisdiction in Cyberspace." *Law and the Information Superhighway.* New York: Wiley, 1996.

Post, D. G. "Anarchy, State and the Internet: An Essay on Law-Making in Cyberspace." Cyberspace Law Institute, 1996.

Post, D. G., and Johnson, D. R. "Borders, Spillovers and Complexity: Rule-Making Processes in Cyberspace (and Elsewhere)." Paper presented at the

Olin Law and Economics Symposium on International Economic Regulation, Georgetown University Law Center, April 5, 1997.

Romano, R. *The Genius of American Corporate Law*. Washington, D.C.: American Enterprise Press, 1993.

Vining, J. *Legal Identity: The Coming of Age of Public Law*. Chicago: University of Chicago Press, 1978.

Wriston, W. B. *The Twilight of Sovereignty: How the Information Revolution Is Transforming Our World*. [location n/a]: Replica Books, 1997.

Index